GW00363897

AIRLINES OF THE WORLD

AIRLINES OF THE WORLD

Christopher Chant

TIGER BOOKS INTERNATIONAL
LONDON

This edition published in 1997 by
Tiger Books International PLC
Twickenham

Printed in Singapore by Welpac Printing & Packaging Pte Ltd

ISBN1-85501-912-4

Introduction

Although the modern airline business began to develop in its definitive form during the 1930s, it was only after the end of World War II (1939-45) that it became truly 'big business' and increasingly a major force in the development of the world economy. From 1945 the airline business has grown spectacularly, and by the start of the 1970s there were only a very few countries that could not boast a national flag-carrying airline: such was the prestige attached to the possession of a national airline, moreover, that the creation of such a body became one of the first priorities of most countries that gained independence in the 1950s and 1960s.

The growth of passenger traffic, and to a lesser extent freight transport, during the late 1940s and early 1950s was steady, but accelerated rapidly to create the mass air transport market after the advent of the world's first true turbojet-powered airliners in the late 1950s. Starting in the long-haul market with types such as the Boeing Model 707 and Douglas (later McDonnell Douglas) DC-8 four-jet types, the mass air transport market soon added a medium-haul sector with the advent of the Boeing Model 727 three-engined airliner, and then a short-haul sector with the availability of twin-engined airliners such as the Aérospatiale Caravelle, BAC One-Eleven, Boeing Model 737 and Douglas (later McDonnell Douglas) DC-9. The market, already spurred by the increasing thirst of the world for air transport, was further encouraged by the improved operating economics made possible by the replacement of the turbojet by the turbofan, whose reduced specific fuel consumption offered the attractions of reduced fuel requirements for a given range, or greater range with the same fuel load.

The development of air transport was made possible not only by technology but also by the development of the regulatory framework in which the airlines operated. All aspects of the air transport business – as diverse as the routes which any airline is allowed to operate, the amount of leg-room to be provided to each passenger, seat prices, and the training regime for flight and cabin crews – are covered by national and international regulation by bodies whose long-term object is the benefit of civil aviation by the creation of an effective system allowing competition only where the safety of the passenger is not compromised.

In 1944, with the end of World War II in sight and the revival of civil air transport therefore imminent on a global basis, some 52 countries met to sign the Chicago Convention, which established the International Civil Aviation Organisation (ICAO). This is the United Nations' agency that formulates and recommends international technical and operational standards, usually in relation to safety. Typical of the work of ICAO, for example, is the implementation by many nations of the Chicago Convention's Annexe 16, which regulates take-off and landing noise, even though this has forced (and continues to compel) the retirement of elderly although still airworthy and commercially viable airliners.

The Chicago Convention defined the so-called 'freedoms of the air', which have been put into effect mainly by bilateral agreements between pairs of countries. The first of these freedoms is the privilege of overflying a territory without landing, and the second is the privilege of making a 'technical' landing to refuel or repair. Most air transport is undertaken on the basis of third- and fourth-freedom protocols, namely travel between two countries by the airlines of those countries. The fifth freedom allows an American operator, for example, to carry passengers from Frankfurt to Athens in the course of a flight between Washington and Rome via Frankfurt.

Most of the current bilateral agreements have, in essence, been based on the 1946 Bermuda Agreement between the UK and the USA that was terminated by the former in 1977. Only some 10 minutes after its expiry, intensive bargaining resulted in a new agreement by which, for example, the UK was granted the right to fly the direct route between London and San Francisco in exchange for American rights to undertake direct services from several US cities to London. The USA also agreed to limit the number of routes on which it permitted two US airlines to compete, and agreed to control the growth in the number of passenger seats available. It can therefore be deduced that the object of the revised agreement, and other bilateral agreements based on it, has been to create a more equable state of commercial opportunity between the nations involved without regard to the strength of their airline industries.

The International Air Transport Association (IATA) is the trade association of airlines offering scheduled services, while charter operators have their own association in the form of the International Air Charter Association (IACA). In general, it is the task of IATA to control fares, baggage allowances, type and extent of service, seat space, and even the commission paid to travel agents: for implementation, its recommendations must have the unanimous backing of the association's members, and become binding only after incorporation into the relevant bilateral treaties.

IATA also sets conditions of carriage for passengers and baggage, stemming from the Warsaw Convention of 1929. For most trips the convention limits an airline's liability for loss of or damage to checked-in baggage to some £5 per pound, or to some £200 for unchecked hand baggage, although higher figures apply on US flights.

Compensation for injury or death is also set by the Warsaw Convention at about £5,000 or £10,000 respectively on flights undertaken wholly outside the USA, with any flight including a stop in the United States involving a maximum liability of $75,000 including legal costs. These figures represent a 'strict' liability, in which the claimant does not have to prove negligence by the airline. Further agreements, such as the Hague Protocol and the Montreal Agreement, increase airlines' maximum liability of airlines, but in the late 1990s the whole framework of this type of airline liability was opened to the full spectrum of American-style litigation resulting in far higher awards.

In 1977 the IATA system came under serious attack when Laker Airways, not a member of IATA, started its Skytrain service between London and New York for a very low fare made possible by minimal facilities and only a few hours' advance booking. The service was licensed after years of opposition from the major airlines and after legal battles with the British government. 'Freddie' Laker's competitors responded with reduced stand-by fares for seats still unsold at the last minute as well as lower-cost booking fares for seats booked well in advance of the travel date. Airlines watched the experiment anxiously, for the failure of seat price controls could have resulted in a severe curtailment of passengers' choice of flights, and although the Laker operation later failed (in circumstances that are still a source of lucrative employment for lawyers) the idea of air travel at reduced rates and reduced levels of comfort has become firmly rooted.

American operators had other reasons for concern: fares within the USA were set by the Civil Aeronautics Board, and the airlines had been allowed to participate in the IATA pricing system only through a special exemption from American anti-trust legislation. However, the inauguration of Ronald Reagan's presidency in 1981 resulted in a considerable liberalisation of the American regulatory framework, opening the skies to a host of new operators (many of which did not survive) and causing a considerable decrease in fares.

The task of deciding and enforcing the air safety standards for aircraft and their crews is the responsibility of the civil aviation board of the country in which any airliner is registered, the two best known of these bodies being the Civil Aviation Authority in the UK and the Federal Aviation Authority in the USA. Before any new type of airliner may be certificated for commercial service, it must pass successfully through a series of manufacturer's trials to schedules laid down by the boards, and in addition the pilots of the relevant regularity authority must also undertake their own series of test flights to provide positive proof that the airliner flies safely in manoeuvres well beyond normal operating conditions.

When a new type of airliner has been awarded a certificate of airworthiness, each example of that airliner must be certified individually as complying with the type specification. Samples of newly delivered machines are tested by the board, and in service the aircraft must then be maintained by authorised procedures and personnel.

Further down the chain of influence on airline operations are a number of consumer organisations, such as the International Airline Passengers' Association and in the USA the Aviation Consumer Action Project, which voice the interests of the passenger; and the governments of several countries fund consumer groups, such as the Air Transport Users' Committee in the UK. The efforts of these organisations, in matters such as the improvement of immigration procedures and improvement of airport services, are generally supported by IATA, and the consumer bodies frequently intervene in matters such as the exertion of pressure on airlines to pay compensation to passengers 'bumped' from their flights as a result of overbooking by the airlines.

All aspects of airline safety are also aided by pressure from the professional associations of air crews and air traffic controllers: the International Federation of Airline Pilots' Associations (IFALPA), for instance, has played a major part in the adoption of many operating concepts and equipment items that are now standard. Typical of these features are better runway lighting and the mandatory installation of flight recorders.

Aer Lingus

Country of origin: Ireland

Generally accepted abbreviation: EI

Address: Head Office Block, Dublin Airport, Ireland

Type of operation: International, regional and domestic scheduled and charter passenger and cargo

Shareholding: Aer Lingus Group (wholly state-owned)

Subsidiaries: Aer Lingus Shannon & Aer Lingus Commuter (100% owned), Compania Hispania Irlandesa de Aviacion (Futura) (85%), Timas Ltd (74%), TEAM Aer Lingus Ltd (100%), Airmotive Ireland Holdings Ltd (100%), SRS Aviation (Ireland) Ltd (100%), Irish Helicopters Ltd (100%), Devtec Ltd (100%), Ferney Airport Services Ltd (UK) (100%), Copthorne Hotel Holdings Ltd (100%), International Airport Hotel Ltd (25%), Aer Lingus Espana Tourist Developments SA (70%), PARC Ltd (88%), and PARC CARE Ltd (100%)

Marketing alliances: General sales agency with British Airways

Notes: Under the Air Companies Act 1993, Aer Lingus holds the shares of two operating airlines, namely Aer Lingus flying intra-European air services and Aer Lingus Shannon (originally Aerlinte Eireann) flying transatlantic services. The group is also involved in a wide range of airline-associated and other activities, and its Fokker 50 and Saab 340 aircraft are flown by Aer Lingus Commuter

Personnel: 4,700

Fleet: 4 x Airbus A330-300
4 x BAe 146-300
6 x Boeing Model 737-400
9 x Boeing Model 737-500
6 x Fokker 50

Orders: 1 x Airbus A330-300

Main bases and hubs: Dublin, Cork, Shannon and Manchester

Domestic routes: Connaught, Cork, Dublin, Galway, Kerry County, Shannon and Sligo

International routes: Amsterdam, Birmingham, Boston, Bristol, Brussels, Copenhagen, Düsseldorf, East Midlands, Edinburgh, Frankfurt, Glasgow, Jersey, Leeds Bradford, London, Madrid, Manchester, Milan, Newcastle, New York, Paris, Rome, Salzburg and Zürich

Simulators: 1 x Boeing Model 737-200
1 x Boeing Model 737-300/400/500
1 x BAe One-Eleven 200/500

Maintenance services: TEAM Aer Lingus for airframes with 230 licensed airframe engineers, 230 licensed engine engineers, and 140 licensed avionics engineers

History: The account of the Irish state airline begins on 22 May 1936, when Aer Lingus Teoranta was registered as a private company to operate airline services, and this organisation operated its first service on 27 May of the same year with a flight from Dublin to Bristol using a de Havilland D.H.84 Dragon. Aer Rianta, which was created by the Irish government on 5 April 1937 to operate international air routes with the de Havilland D.H.89 Dragon Rapide, also came to constitute a part of the current airline. With the outbreak of World War II (1939-45), all Irish air services were suspended temporarily, although on 28 October 1939 the service between Dublin and Liverpool was reopened for continued operation throughout the war with a pair of D.H.89B aircraft and one Douglas DC-3.

On 9 November 1945 the airline resumed

its service from Dublin to Croydon with a DC-3, and on 17 June 1946 a service from Dublin to Paris was inaugurated. On 26 February 1947 Aerlinte Eireann Teoranta was formed as a subsidiary of Aer Rianta to operate transatlantic services, and for this purpose three Lockheed L-749A Constellations were delivered on 17 September 1947, but the service was then postponed indefinitely and the aircraft were sold to the British Overseas Airways Corporation (BOAC).

Aer Lingus later became the third airline in the world to order the radical turboprop-powered Vickers Viscount in November 1951, and on 7 March 1954 the first two Type 707 Viscounts were delivered to Dublin for a service debut on 11 April of the same year. Aer Lingus was the first airline in the world to operate the Fokker F.27 Friendship, its first two aircraft of this type being delivered on 19 November 1958 for a service debut on 15 December on the routes linking Dublin with Glasgow and Liverpool.

On 28 April 1958 Aerlinte Eireann Teoranta finally started its New York service using a Lockheed L-1049 Super Constellation leased from the American airline Seaboard and Western. Following the success of this service Aerlinte Eireann Teoranta ordered three examples of the four-turbojet Boeing Model 720-048. The first of these machines was delivered on 25 October 1960 and the airline's first turbojet service was operated on 14 December from Dublin to New York via Shannon. By the end of April 1961 the Boeings had taken over the transatlantic service from the Constellations, and in mid-1964 the Model 720-048 aircraft had been replaced by Boeing Model 707-348C airliners.

On 14 May 1965 Aer Lingus took delivery of its first BAC One-Eleven 208AL twin-jet airliner. This type entered service on the routes to Paris from Dublin and Cork on 6 June, and the type was then successively introduced on many of the airline's European services. The One-Eleven was then supplemented and finally supplanted by the Boeing Model 737, which is now the mainstay of the airline's fleet: the first Model 737-248 was delivered to Dublin on 28 March 1969. In January 1967 the airline ordered two examples of the Boeing Model 747-148 'jumbo jet', taking delivery of the first of these long-range, high-capacity transports on 15 December 1970. The Model 747s were at first operated on the airline's own transatlantic routes, but loads were generally insufficient for the viable operation of the two aircraft, which were therefore leased to other airlines for most of their lives.

Aer Lingus Teoranta and Aer Rianta were then integrated to fly an extensive international and regional network.

Aeroflot Russian International Airlines (ARIA)

Country of origin: Russia

Generally accepted abbreviation: SU

Address: 37a Leningradsky Prospekt, Building 9, Moscow 125167, Russia

Type of operation: International, regional and domestic scheduled and charter passenger and cargo

Shareholding: Combination of 51% shareholding by the government of the Russian Federation and 49% shareholding by Aeroflot employees

Marketing alliances: Cyprus Airways (joint service) and Lufthansa (co-operation on Moscow airport expansion)

Personnel: 15,000

Fleet:
10 x Airbus A310-300
1 x Antonov An-124-100
2 x Boeing Model 767-300ER
10 x Ilyushin Il-62M
18 x Ilyushin Il-76T/TD
18 x Ilyushin Il-86
6 x Ilyushin Il-96-300M/T
1 x McDonnell Douglas DC-10-30F (leased from McDonnell Douglas)
13 x Tupolev Tu-134
4 x Tupolev Tu-154B
25 x Tupolev Tu-154M

Orders:
10 x Boeing Model 737-400
17 x Ilyushin Il-96M
3 x Ilyushin Il-96T

Main base and hub: Moscow

Routes: 135 destinations in 100 countries are served by regular international services from Moscow to destinations in every continent, and domestic routes across the Russian Federation and CIS

International services to: Abu Dhabi, Accra, Addis Ababa, Amman, Amsterdam, Anchorage, Ankara, Antananarivo, Athens, Baghdad, Bamako, Bangkok, Barcelona, Beijing, Beirut, Belgrade, Berlin, Bombay, Bratislava, Brazzaville, Brussels, Bucharest, Budapest, Buenos Aires, Cairo, Cancum, Calcutta, Casablanca, Chicago, Cologne/Bonn, Colombo, Conakry, Copenhagen, Cotonou, Dacca, Dakar, Damascus, Delhi, Djibouti, Douala, Dubai, Dublin, Düsseldorf, Frankfurt, Genoa, Gothenburg, Hamburg, Hanoi, Harare, Helsinki, Hong Kong, Istanbul, Jakarta, Johannesburg, Kabul, Karachi, Kathmandu, Kuala Lumpur, Kuwait, Larnaca, Leipzig, Lima, Lisbon, Ljubljana, Lom, London, Los Angeles, Luanda, Lusaka, Luxembourg, Madrid, Mali, Malta, Marseille, Mexico City, Miami, Milan, Montreal, Munich, Nairobi, New York, Osaka, Oslo, Ouagadougou, Paris, Phnom Penh, Prague, Rio de Janeiro, Rome, Sal, Sana'a, San Francisco, Santiago, São Paulo, Seattle, Seoul, Shanghai, Shannon, Sharjah, Singapore, Skopje, Sofia, Stockholm, Sydney, Tehran, Tel Aviv, Tokyo, Tripoli, Tunis, Ulan Bator, Venice, Vienna, Warsaw, Washington, Zagreb, Zürich. Other international services are flown from Khabarovsk to San Francisco, Irkutsk to Niigata, Shenian and Ulan Bator, and Magadan to Anchorage; domestic services are flown from Moscow to Khabarovsk, Novosibirsk, St Petersburg, Yakutsk and Nurengri; and regional services are flown from Almaty, Baku, Kiev, Riga, Simferopol, Tallinn, Tbilisi, Vilnius and Yerevan

Simulators:
1 x Airbus A310
1 x Ilyushin Il-62
1 x Ilyushin Il-76
1 x Ilyushin Il-86
1 x Ilyushin Il-96
2 x Tupolev Tu-204
1 x Tupolev Tu-134
1 x Tupolev Tu-154

History: The origins of Aeroflot date back to 11 November 1921, when the airline Deruluft was formed by the USSR and Germany to operate services between the two countries. In March 1923 Dobrolet (Soviet Volunteer Air Fleet Company) began operations from Moscow to Odessa and Georgia, with other services to the central area of Asian Russia. Other airlines were formed during April 1925,

Continued on next page

Aeroflot continued from previous page

in the Ukraine as Ukvozduchput and in Georgia as Zakavia. These four airlines were the predecessors of Aeroflot, which was established in 1932 and was completed to its definitive form in 1964 by the addition of the Polar Aviation Division.

Up to the time of the collapse of the USSR in 1989 Aeroflot was the world's largest airline, with a huge network of scheduled domestic and international passenger and cargo services and with the ability to carry out charter flights on a worldwide basis. In addition to its airline activities, Aeroflot was also responsible for all the USSR's civil airports, navigation services, flying clubs and training as well as every aspect of aerial agriculture, forest fire patrol, aerial survey and air ambulance work.

By the standards of Western airlines, Aeroflot's re-equipment programme after World War II was very slow: the Ilyushin Il-12 did not enter service until 1948 and the Ilyushin Il-14 followed six years later, and both of these aircraft were decidedly inferior to the Western airliners of the period. However, on 15 September 1956 Aeroflot put into service its first turbojet-powered transport, the Tupolev Tu-104, on the route linking Moscow and Irkutsk, and at the time this was the only jet airliner service in the world.

In the period between 1959 and 1963 Aeroflot operated no less than five completely new types of aircraft, namely the Antonov An-10 and An-24, the Ilyushin Il-18, and the Tupolev Tu-114 and Tu-124. From the early 1960s the airline introduced the Tupolev Tu-154 and the Ilyushin Il-62, and these two types operated some 73% of Aeroflot's passenger flights until well into the 1980s. The airline took the credit for being the first airline in the world to operate passenger services with a supersonic transport, in the form of the Tupolev Tu-144, on 26 December 1975 when a service was inaugurated between Moscow and Alma-Ata.

Up to the time of the USSR's collapse, Aeroflot operated both an extensive domestic network (serving some 3,600 destinations) and an international network covering 86 countries in Africa, the Americas, Asia and Europe. Most of these flights originated from Moscow, and on the shorter domestic routes the aircraft used were mainly the Yakovlev Yak-40, Antonov An-24 and Tupolev Tu-134, while the ageing Antonov An-2 biplane was still used on some of the shortest routes. At that time the airline's equipment plans included substantial further purchases of types such as the Tupolev Tu-134 and Tu-154, Ilyushin Il-62, Il-76 and Il-86, Yakovlev Yak-42 and Antonov An-26, An-28 and An-32.

In its current form, ARIA is the international division of Aeroflot and is the successor to the original Aeroflot, all of whose domestic operations have been transferred to the host of airlines that have proliferated in the CIS since the demise of the USSR. As such, ARIA remains the only officially designated international airline in Russia and flies scheduled passenger and cargo flights to 135 cities in more than 100 countries, and has also introduced regular services to nine capitals within the CIS and to six cities within the Russian Federation. Nothing is more indicative of the airline's ambitions than the nature of its recent re-equipment, with the Ilyushin Il-96-300 and Boeing Model 767-300 introduced in 1994, and plans well advanced for the lease of further Western airliners pending full delivery of the Tupolev Tu-204. ARIA also plans to refurbish fourteen of its Il-86 airliners and to introduce a new powerplant on its Il-76 transports.

In 1994 ARIA carried 3.1 million passengers.

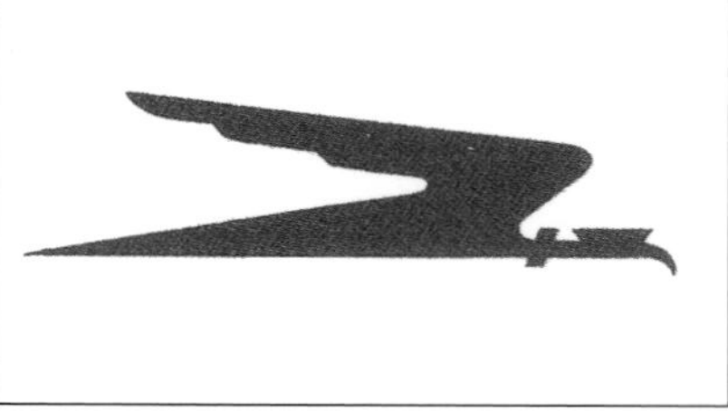

Aerolineas Argentinas

Country of origin: Argentina

Generally accepted abbreviation: AR

Address: Paseo Colon 185, Buenos Aires 1063, Argentina

Type of operation: Scheduled passenger and cargo services

Shareholding: Combination of Iberia (83%), employees (10%) and Argentine state (7%)

Marketing alliances: Marketing alliance and joint frequent-flyer plan with Iberia, codesharing and freight co-operation with Ladeco, block space agreement with Malaysia Airlines and codesharing agreement with VIASA

Notes: Aerolineas Argentinas is the national flag carrier of Argentina, and undertakes ground handling joint ventures with Pluna and VARIG

Personnel: 7,000

Fleet:
- 3 x Airbus A310-300
- 8 x Boeing Model 727-200
- 10 x Boeing Model 737-200 Advanced
- 6 x Boeing Model 747-200B
- 6 x McDonnell Douglas MD-88

Main base and hub: Buenos Aires

International services: Auckland, Bogotá, Caracas, Florianópolis, Frankfurt, Guayaquil, Lima, London, Los Angeles, Madrid, Mexico City, Miami, Montevideo, Montreal, New York, Panama, Paris, Pôrto Alegre, Punta del Este, Rio de Janeiro, Rome, Santiago, São Paulo, Toronto and Zürich

Simulators:
- 1 x Boeing Model 707-320
- 1 x Boeing Model 727-200
- 1 x Boeing Model 737-200
- 1 x Boeing Model 747-200

History: On 14 May 1949 the Argentine ministry of transport assumed control over the operations of all the country's airlines, with the exception of the air force-operated LADE, to create Aerolineas Argentinas. The four airlines that were incorporated were Aeroposta Argentina (formed in 1928), Aviacion del Litoral Fluvial Argentino (ALFA) (1938), Flota Aerea Mercante Argentina (FAMA) (1946), and Zonas Oeste y Norte de Aerolineas Argentinas (ZONDA) (1946).

The amalgamation of these airlines into a single entity was formalised on 1 January 1950 as Aerolineas Argentinas began operations under its own name. At this time the airline operated a highly mixed fleet of aircraft inherited from its predecessors, namely Short Sandringham flying boats from ALFA, Douglas DC-4 and DC-6 landplanes from FAMA plus various Avro York, Vickers Viking, Avro Lancastrian and Convair CV-240 landplanes from ZONDA, and, of course, the ubiquitous Douglas DC-3 from all the operators.

In March 1950 Aerolineas Argentinas began

regular services with Douglas DC-6 aircraft to New York, while the CV-240s and DC-3s were used mainly for domestic services, the last of the DC-3s being retired only in 1962. A measure of updated equipment began to reach the airline in March 1959, when Aerolineas Argentinas received its first turbojet-powered airliner in the form of the de Havilland Comet 4, and began its first international service with this type on 19 May with a service linking Buenos Aires and New York.

The airline's domestic and regional networks were upgraded into the jet age on 15 January 1962, when the first of four Sud-Aviation Caravelle VINs was delivered, and the operator's CV-240s were replaced by the turboprop-powered Hawker Siddeley HS 748 from 18 January. The British-built airliner began operation between Buenos Aires and Bahía Blanca on 2 April 1962.

On 23 November 1966 the airline took delivery of its first Boeing Model 707-387, and this and later deliveries soon replaced the Comet, of which the last two were sold in November 1971. For use on its domestic and regional services Aerolineas Argentinas ordered the Boeing Model 737-287, and before the delivery of the first of these machines on 27 February 1970 the airline leased a Boeing Model 737-204 from Britannia Airways between 24 January and 28 April 1970. The American twin-jet transports were complemented by a leased Hughes Airwest Boeing Model 727-2M7 delivered on 3 December 1977, and on 1 December 1978 Aerolineas Argentina's first Boeing Model 727-287 three-jet transport was delivered, and the airline was able to upgrade its domestic and regional services with the introduction of the Fokker F.28 Fellowship, of which the first was received on 13 January 1975.

On its long-haul routes to North America, Europe, South Africa and the Far East, Aerolineas Argentinas operates six examples of the Boeing Model 747-287B, the first of these having been delivered on 16 December 1976, and at one time also flew a Boeing Model 747SP-087.

Iberia increased its stake from 30% to 83% in March 1994, but will be relinquishing its stake as a condition of European Union agreement for a cash injection into Iberia.

Air Canada

Country of origin: Canada

Generally accepted abbreviation: AC

Address: Air Canada Centre, PO Box 14000, St Laurent, Quebec H4Y 1H4, Canada

Type of operation: International, regional and domestic scheduled and charter passenger services

Shareholding: 75% owned and controlled by Canadians with no one person or foreign group allowed to own more than 10% of the airline's voting shares

Subsidiaries: Air BC (100%), Air Ontario (100%), Air Alliance (100%), Air Nova (100%) and Northwest Territorial Airways (100%) as well as Galileo Canada and Air Canada Vacations

Marketing alliances: Major strategic alliances are in existence with United Airlines, Lufthansa, SAS and Korean Air, while lesser agreements exist with All Nippon Airways, Cathay Pacific Airways, Continental, Swissair, British Midland, Czech Airlines, Finnair, Iberia, LOT-Polish Airlines, Royal Jordanian Airlines and Air Jamaica

Notes: In 1995, the Open Skies agreement between Canada and the USA was signed in February, and this was followed by the announcement of a new Canadian international air transport policy applying to non-US points. The operator's services were enlarged in selected trans-border, international and domestic markets. In addition, Air Canada started services on 20 routes, mainly to the USA, converted 12 charter routes in the USA to scheduled services and added a total of 20 jet aircraft to its fleet. The airline provides aircraft and engine maintenance, and third-party services, such as ground handling, to airlines and other customers

Personnel: 20,000

Fleet: 34 x Airbus A320
2 x Airbus A319-100
14 x Airbus A340-300
3 x Boeing Model 747-100
3 x Boeing Model 747-200
3 x Boeing Model 747-400 Combi
23 x Boeing Model 767-200
4 x Boeing Model 767-300
19 x Canadair CL-65 Regional Jet
35 x McDonnell Douglas DC-9-30

Orders: 33 x Airbus A319
6 x Airbus A320
4 x Airbus A340-300
2 x Boeing Model 767-300
5 x Canadair Regional Jet

Options: 3 x Airbus A340-300
5 x Boeing Model 757-300
24 x Canadair Regional Jet

Main bases and hubs: Toronto, Montreal, Vancouver, Calgary and London

Domestic routes: 61 destinations in Canada

US services: Atlanta, Baltimore, Boston, Chicago, Cleveland, Columbus, Dallas-Fort Worth, Denver, Fort Lauderdale, Fort Myers, Hartford, Honolulu, Houston, Indianapolis, Kansas City, La Guardia and Newark, Las Vegas, Los Angeles, Maui, Miami, Minneapolis, Nashville, Orlando, Portland, Philidelphia, Raleigh-Durham, St Louis, San Francisco, Seattle, Spokene, Tampa, Washington DC, and West Palm Beach

US marketing alliances: Air Canada has codesharing partnerships with United Airlines for Chicago, Cincinnati, Denver, Kansas City, Minneapolis, Nashville, Phoenix and San Francisco, and with Continental Airlines for Newark

Caribbean services: Antigua, Bermuda, Bridgetown, Fort-de-France, Kingston, Montego Bay, Nassau, Pointe-à-Pitre, Port-au-Prince, Port-of-Spain, and St Lucia

Asian and Pacific services: Delhi, Hong Kong, Osaka, and Seoul

European services: Frankfurt, Glasgow, London, Manchester, Paris, Tel Aviv and Zürich

European marketing alliances: Belfast, Edinburgh, Glasgow, Leeds Bradford, Madrid, Teesside and Zürich

Middle Eastern marketing alliances: Amman with Royal Jordanian Airlines

Charter services: Aruba, Cancún, Myrtle Beach, Puerta Vallarta, San Juan and St Maarten

Simulators: 2 x Airbus A320-200
1 x Boeing Model 747-100
1 x Boeing Model 767-200
1 x McDonnell Douglas DC-9-30
1 x McDonnell Douglas DC-9-32

Maintenance services: Air Canada Technical Operations for airframes, engines and avionics with 420 licensed airframe engineers, 550 licensed engine engineers, and 200 licensed avionics engineers

History: Air Canada began life as Trans-Canada Air Lines Ltd (TCA), the flag carrier for the Dominion of Canada. At this time the operator's main shareholder was Canadian National Railways, an organisation wholly owned by the government of Canada. The airline flew its first scheduled service on 1 September 1937 using a Lockheed Model 10-A Electra on the route between Vancouver and Seattle. In the following March the operator added its first mail service, in this instance between Vancouver and Winnipeg, and on 1 April 1939 flew its first coast-to-coast service between Seattle and Montreal with intermediate halts at Vancouver, Toronto and Ottawa.

TCA began a transatlantic service on 22 July 1943 between Montreal and Prestwick with modified Avro Lancaster bombers, an altogether superior capability being offered by the Canadair DC-4M that flew its first service between Montreal and London on 15 April 1947. The availability of this new type helped the airline to enlarge its route network, and this soon extended south to destinations such as Florida and Mexico.

The airline's next milestone was the introduction of the Lockheed L-1049G Super Constellation, which operated its first service across the Atlantic on 14 May 1954, and on 1 April 1955 TCA became the first airline in the Americas to operate the turboprop-powered Vickers Viscount 724, which entered service on the route linking Montreal and Winnipeg. The first pure-jet airliner used by TCA was the Douglas DC-8-43, of which the first was delivered on 7 February 1960 for a service debut on 1 April of the same year on the Montreal to Vancouver service. Two months later the route between Montreal and London was added.

In 1964 TCA adopted the title of Air Canada together with a new livery. After various modifications, was redesigned in 1994 to the current scheme. On 11 February 1971 Air Canada took delivery of its first wide-bodied airliner in the form of a Boeing Model 747-133 and, together with the Lockheed L-1011 TriStars that were delivered from 14 January 1973 and the Douglas DC-8-63, this 'jumbo jet' type operated the airline's long-haul routes into the early-1980s, when the first of Air Canada's Airbus wide-body and Boeing 767 airliners were delivered.

Under the terms of the Air Canada Act of 1977 the airline became a direct wholly-owned subsidiary of the Canadian government, but has been completely privatised since July 1989. Through its domestic Connector Partners, another 54 communities and destinations in Canada and the USA are linked to the Air Canada network. Together with its regional airlines Air Canada now offers services to over 120 destinations, including over 90 cities in North America, 8 cities in Europe, 11 points in the Caribbean, and a number of destinations in Asia.

Air China

Country of origin: China

Generally accepted abbreviation: CA

Address: Beijing Capital Airport, Beijing 100621, China

Type of operation: International, regional and domestic scheduled passenger and cargo services

Shareholders: Wholly state-owned

Marketing alliances: Revenue-sharing with Asiana and Korean Air, co-operation with Austrian Airlines and Lufthansa, and joint maintenance with Ameco

Personnel: 8,300

Fleet:
2 x Antonov An-12
2 x Antonov An-24
3 x Airbus A340-300
4 x BAe 146-100
19 x Boeing Model 737-300
4 x Boeing Model 747SP
3 x Boeing Model 747-200 Combi
1 x Boeing Model 747-200F
8 x Boeing Model 747-400
6 x Boeing Model 767-200ER
4 x Boeing Model 767-300
3 x Boeing Model 767-300ER
2 x Lockheed L-100-30
6 x SAC Y-7

Orders: 3 x Airbus A340-300

Main base and hub: Beijing Capital Airport

Routes: Amsterdam, Anqing, Atlanta, Bangkok, Barcelona, Beihai, Berlin, Boston, Brussels, Budapest, Buenos Aires, Changchun, Changzhou, Chengdu, Chicago, Cologne, Dalian, Dallas/Fort Worth, Datong, Dubai, Düsseldorf, Frankfurt, Fukuoka, Fuzhou, Geneva, Gothenburg, Guangzhou, Guayaquil, Guilin, Haikou, Hailar, Hangzhou, Harbin, Helsinki, Hohhot, Hong Kong, Huanghua, Istanbul, Jakarta, Karachi, Kunming, Kuwait, London, Melbourne, Montevideo, Nanchang, Nanjing, Nanning, Nantong, New York, Ningbo, Osaka, Paris, Pinang, Pingdao, Quito, Rome, San Francisco, Seoul, Shanghai, Sharjah, Shenyang, Singapore, Stockholm, Sydney, Taiyuan, Tanjing, Tokyo, Tunxi, Ulan Bator, Vancouver, Vienna, Wuhan, Xiamen, Xi'an, Xiangfan, Yantai and Zürich

Simulators:
1 x Boeing Model 737-300
1 x Boeing Model 747-400
1 x Boeing Model 757
1 x Boeing Model 767

History: The airline now known as Air China was created in 1988 by renaming of the Beijing-based international division of the Civil Aviation Administration of China (CAAC), which was the Chinese equivalent of the Soviet Aeroflot organisation and was responsible for all civil aviation matters in China. In 1988 the various operating divisions of the CAAC were formed into separate airlines, each with its own name. Air China is the largest of the airlines currently operating in China, and has two subsidiary operations located in Inner Mongolia and Tianjin.

The first direct link with CAAC can be traced to 1939, when in the north-west of China the governments of China and the USSR established the Sino-Soviet Aviation Corporation to provide services between China and the USSR. The company became known as Hamiata as its main terminals were Hami in China and Alma-Ata in the USSR. The immediate predecessor of the current airline was the People's Aviation Corporation of China (SKOGA) which was established in 1952 by the USSR and China to take over and expand the transport services that had been undertaken by the CATC and CNAC, themselves created in March 1943 and July 1930, whose operations and aircraft had been transferred to Formosa in 1949 by the Kuomintang nationalist party as it was being defeated by the communists in the final stages of the Chinese Civil War. On its creation, SKOGA took over Hamiata, and Aeroflot helped to place the new Chinese organisation on a firmer technical footing by providing it with several examples of the Lisunov Li-2 aircraft,

which was the Soviet-made version of the Douglas DC-3.

SKOGA's first service connected Beijing (then Peking) with Hankow, Kunming and Canton, as well as Chia, Irkutsk and Alma-Ata so that the growing Chinese air network was linked with that of the USSR. In 1954 the Chinese government assumed full control of the airline and renamed it the Civil Aviation Administration of China, or Minhaiduy. For the first four years of its operations the CAAC relied on the Li-2, some of which may still be in service in remote areas, but more-modern equipment was introduced in the forms of the Ilyushin Il-14 with a powerplant of two piston engines and then, late in 1960, by the Ilyushin Il-18 with its powerplant of four turboprops.

In December 1961 the CAAC broke with its practice of operating only Soviet-built aircraft when it placed an order for six examples of the Vickers Viscount 843 four-turboprop airliner, of which the first was delivered on 6 July 1963 for a service debut in March 1964 on the route linking Peking and Shanghai.

In 1962 the airline revised its title to the Department of International Affairs of the General Administration of Civil Aviation of China, but the airline retained its abbreviated title of CAAC. To replace some of its ageing Soviet types, the CAAC bought four Hawker Siddeley HS 121 Trident 1E turbofan-powered airliners from Pakistan International Airlines in 1970, to be followed from 19 November 1971 by the first of four new Trident 2E airliners. The next type introduced on CAAC services was the Ilyushin Il-62, the first two aircraft of an order for five being delivered in late 1972 and operating the airline's first long-haul services in early 1973. On 23 August 1973 the CAAC received its first Boeing Model 707-3JB, and with this type the airline started a service from Peking to Tokyo in August 1974. The CAAC then introduced the Boeing Model 747, initially in the form of the Model 747SP-J6 of which the first of three was delivered on 29 February 1980. Since that time the airline has been equipped mainly with Boeing airliners, although Air China ordered three Airbus transports in the early 1990s.

Currently, Air China operates passenger and cargo services to many countries in the Asian, African, European and American continents as well as a modest network of domestic and regional services derived largely from the total of 171 domestic services that CAAC operated to link twenty-nine provinces of the country.

Air France

Country of origin: France

Generally accepted abbreviation: AF

Address: 45 Rue de Paris, Roissy Charles de Gaulle, Paris 95747, France

Type of operation: Scheduled passenger and cargo services

Shareholding: Groupe Air France

Subsidiaries: Air Afrique (16%), Aéropostale (20%), Air Austral (34%), Air Caledonie (2.7%), Air Inter (72.3%), Air Charter (80%), Air Comores (6.3%), Air Gabon (11.2%), Air Madagascar (3.5%), Air Mauritius (12.8%), Air Tahiti (7.5%), Air Tchad (33.7%), Austrian Airlines (1.5%), Cameroon Airlines (3.6%), Middle East Airlines (28%), Royal Air Maroc (4%), Sabena (33.3%), Tunis Air (5.6%), Jet Tours, Servair, Sodetair, Sodexi, Visit France, Jet Chandler International, Amadeus-France and Esterel

Marketing alliances: Codesharing with Air Canada and Japan Airlines, and co-operation agreements with Continental Airlines, Vietnam Airlines, Adria Airways, Aeroflot, Aeromexico, Aéropostale, Air Afrique, Air Austral, Air Gabon, Air Inter, Air Madagascar, Air Mauritius, Air Seychelles, Austrian Airlines, Balkan Bulgarian Airlines, Cameroon Airlines, Croatia Airlines, Czech Airlines, Japan Airlines, Korean Air, LOT-Polish Airlines, Lufthansa, Malev Hungarian Airlines, Middle East Airlines, Royal Air Maroc, Sabena, TAROM, Tunis Air, and Ukraine International Airlines

Personnel: 39,000

Fleet: 6 x Aérospatiale/BAC Concorde (5 in operation)

Continued on next page

Air France continued from previous page

13 x Airbus A300
9 x Airbus A310
65 x Airbus A320
5 x Airbus A321
11 x Airbus A340
43 x Boeing Model 737
32 x Boeing Model 747
5 x Boeing Model 767
5 x Fokker 100

Orders: 12 x Airbus A340-300
10 x Boeing Model 777-200 (IGW)

Main base and hub: Paris Charles de Gaulle

Services: 22 destinations in the Americas, 40 destinations in Africa and the Middle East, 18 destinations in Asia and the Pacific, 10 destinations in Guiana and the Indian Ocean, and 70 destinations in Europe

Simulators: 1 x Airbus A300-600
1 x Airbus A310-300
1 x Airbus A300-B2/B4
2 x Airbus A320-200
1 x Airbus A330
1 x Airbus A340
1 x Boeing Model 707-320
1 x Boeing Model 727-200 Advanced
1 x Boeing Model 737-200
1 x Boeing Model 737-300
1 x Boeing Model 737-500
1 x Boeing Model 747-100
1 x Boeing Model 747-200
2 x Boeing Model 747-400
1 x McDonnell Douglas DC-8-63/72/73
1 x McDonnell Douglas DC-10-30

Maintenance services: Air France Industries for airframes, engines and avionics with 2,865 licensed airframe engineers, 610 licensed engine engineers, and 510 licensed avionics engineers

History: France was an early entrant into the field of commercial airline operations as several pioneering companies were formed in 1919 after the end of World War I (1914-18). The most significant of these was the Lignes Aeriennes Farman (later the Compagnie Générale de Transport Aérien, or CGTA), which flew the nation's first international service on 8 February 1919 from Paris to London. Between 1919 and 1926 the CGTA expanded its route network to Belgium, Germany, the Netherlands and Scandinavia. During the same period the Compagnie Franco-Roumaine de Navigation Aérienne led the way to the south-east with a network of routes to the Balkans, Czechoslovakia and Poland, while the Lignes Aeriennes Latecoere (LAT) explored the route into western Africa as far south as Dakar, and within South America pending the development of a viable commercial air service across the South Atlantic (an objective that was achieved in 1930). Other air routes pioneered during this period of great French civil air transport expansion stretched across the Sahara, central Africa and as far east as Tananarive in Madagascar.

By 1923 the powerhouse of French airline operations was Air-Union, which came into existence by the amalgamation of the Compagnie des Messageries Aeriennes and the Compagnie des Grands Express Aériens. Other major players of the time were the Compagnie Internationale de Navigation Aérienne (CIDNA) that went east to Czechoslovakia and Turkey, and Air-Orient which was an Air-Union subsidiary that extended farther into the Middle East and Far East to reach Hong Kong and Saigon during 1938 after Air-Union had become Air France.

The key date for French civil aviation is 1933, when the CGTA, CIDNA, Air-Orient and Air-Union merged to form the Société Centrale pour l'Exploration de Lignes Aeriennes, the consolidated company operating as Air France and buying the assets of the Compagnie General Aéropostale (successor to LAT) on 30 August. At this time Air France possessed 259 aircraft and had inherited a very substantial route network, and immediately implemented plans for the disposal of all its single-engined types, elimination of duplicated routes, and increased service frequencies. Domestic services within France were allocated to an affiliate, Air Bleu, and this was completely revised in 1937 to improve France's internal mail service.

Just before the outbreak of World War II (1939-45), exploratory flights were made for the proposed transatlantic service to North America via the Azores and Bermuda, and at the time of France's defeat in June 1940 Air France's surviving aircraft were evacuated from France to North Africa, where they joined the Allied cause.

Limited services were resumed in 1945, and Air France's first transatlantic service was inaugurated in 1946 by Douglas DC-4 airliners of Air France Transatlantique. Air France was nationalised on 1 January 1946 as the Société Nationale Air France, and on 16 June 1948 the modern Air France was formed by the merger of the parent company with Air Bleu and Air France Transatlantique, and a period of consolidation and expansion followed, including the introduction of turbine power in 1953. Since that time, Air France's network has expanded into one of the largest in the world, with an intricate series of European routes complemented by long-haul services to most parts of the world excluding Australasia.

Air France now operates as part of Groupe Air France, whose other members include Air Charter and Air Inter Europe.

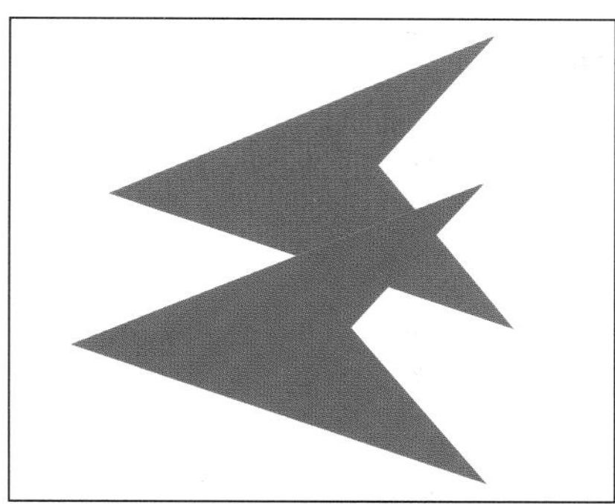

Air Inter

Country of origin: France

Generally accepted abbreviation: IT

Address: I Avenue du Maréchal Devaux, Paray-Vieille F-91551, France

Type of operation: International, regional and domestic scheduled and charter passenger and cargo services

Shareholding: 72.3% owned by Groupe Air France

Marketing alliances: Air France merging Air Inter with its European short-haul operations

Personnel: 11,150

Fleet: 8 x Airbus A300
9 x Airbus A319
35 x Airbus A320
5 x Airbus A321
4 x Airbus A330
5 x Fokker 100

Orders: 3 x Airbus A319-100
2 x Airbus A321
10 x Airbus A330-300

Options: 9 x Airbus A319

Main base and hub: Paris Orly

Route network: In France there are 61 permanent and 10 seasonal routes, and within Europe 18 permanent and 2 seasonal routes. The airline's main destinations are Agde, Ajaccio, Bastia, Béziers, Biarritz, Bordeaux, Brest, Calvi, Clermont-Ferrand, Dublin, Fréjus, Lille, Lorient, Lyon, Marseille, Montpellier, Mulhouse/Basel, Nantes, Nice, Paris, Perpignan, Quimper, Rennes, Strasbourg, Toulon/Hyères and Toulouse

Simulators: 2 x Airbus A300B2/B4
3 x Airbus A320-200
1 x Aérospatiale Caravelle III
1 x Dassault Mercure 100

Maintenance services: Air Inter specialises in airframe maintenance

History: Initially known as Lignes Aeriennes Interiors, Air Inter was created on 12 November 1954 to fly domestic services within France. It was only in 1958 that the airline actually began operations, starting with a service between Paris and Strasbourg on 17 March using leased aircraft. The route proved commercially unsuccessful and was ended only a few months later. Air Inter resumed operations in June 1960, again with leased aircraft but in this instance with a limited network of regular services. It was only in 1962 that Air Inter bought its first airliners, in the form of five Vickers Viscount 708 machines secured from Air France, but greater capability arrived in March 1967, when the airline's first Sud-Aviation Caravelle III twin-turbojet aircraft entered service.

The year 1967 was also notable in Air Inter's development for the signature of agreements with the French government for the establishment of a route network throughout metropolitan France, and with Air France and UTA for a dovetailing of the three operators' networks.

Air Inter became financially independent in 1972 with the ending of French government subsidies, and, on 4 June 1974, became the world's only operator of the Dassault Mercure 100 airliner, initially on the route linking Paris with Lyon. In 1977 Air Inter ceased charter operations after signing an agreement with Air France, for which it received a 20% stake in Air Charter International, established in 1966 as Air France's charter subsidiary.

Since 12 January 1990 Air Inter, Air France and UTA have been merged into Grouep Air France, and on 1 January 1996 Air Inter changed its name to Air France Europe although it still trades as Air Inter Europe until the planned full integration with Air France on 1 April 1997. The operator's aircraft currently carry Air France colours on the tail with 'Air Inter Europe' on the sides of the fuselage.

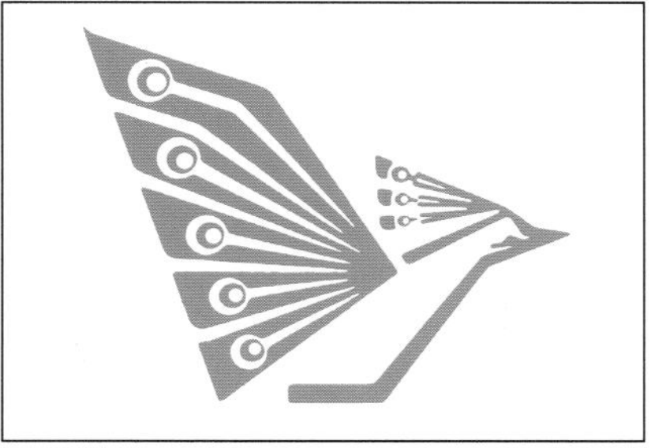

Air Lanka

Country of origin: Sri Lanka

Generally accepted abbreviation: UL

Address: 37 York Street, Colombo 1, Sri Lanka

Type of operation: International and regional scheduled passenger and cargo services

Shareholding: 100% owned by the Sri Lankan government

Marketing alliances: Codesharing with Gulf Air, Malaysia Airlines, and Middle East Airlines and revenue pooling agreements with Indian Airlines and Pakistan International Airlines

Personnel: 4,000

Fleet: 3 x Airbus A340-300
2 x Airbus A320-200
1 x Lockheed L-1011-100 TriStar
2 x Lockheed L-1011-200 TriStar
2 x Lockheed L-1011-500 TriStar

Main base and hub: Colombo

Route network: Abu Dhabi, Amsterdam, Bahrain, Bangkok, Bombay, Delhi, Dhahran, Dubai, Frankfurt, Fukuoka, Hong Kong, Jiddah, Karachi, Kuala Lumpur, Kuwait, London, Madras, Malé, Muscat, Paris, Riyadh, Rome, Singapore, Tiruchirapalli, Tokyo, Trivandrum, Vienna and Zürich

Simulators: None

Maintenance services: Air Lanka Engineering and Maintenance specialises in airframe maintenance and has 60 licensed airframe engineers, 60 licensed engine engineers, and 20 licensed avionics engineers

History: Air Lanka was created on 10 January 1979 to take over the services of the previous national flag carrier, Air Ceylon,

Continued on next page

Air Lanka continued from previous page

which had ceased trading on 31 March 1978. The new airline's first services were undertaken with two Boeing Model 707-312 four-turbofan airliners leased from Singapore Airlines. These aircraft reached Colombo on 15 August and 25 September 1979, and the airline started regional services in November of the same year with a leased Boeing Model 737-2L9.

The Model 707 airliners were replaced on the carrier's international services by Lockheed L-1011 TriStar three-turbofan airliners, which were Air Lanka's first wide-body transports: the first of these aircraft was leased from Air Canada from October 1980 and flew its first services on 2 November on the route linking Colombo and Paris, and the type was complemented on high-density routes by a Boeing Model 747-238B four-turbofan airliner leased from Qantas from June 1984.

Since that time the airline has standardised first on the TriStar and then on Airbus aircraft, starting with the A320 and now the A340 with the delivery of five new aircraft. Although still wholly owned by the government of Sri Lanka, the airline is to be privatised under a plan announced in January 1995.

Air New Zealand

Country of origin: New Zealand

Generally accepted abbreviation: NZ

Address: Quay Tower, Private Bag 92007, Auckland 1, New Zealand

Type of operation: International, regional and domestic scheduled passenger and cargo services

Shareholding: Air New Zealand Ltd including 41.9% by Brierley Investments and 19.4% by Qantas

Subsidiaries: Mount Cook Group Ltd (100%), Eagle Aviation Ltd (100%), Air Nelson Ltd (100%)

Marketing alliances: Codesharing with Mandarin Airlines, Qantas, Korean Air, Canadian Airlines, EVA and Japan Airlines, and other agreements with Delta Air Lines, Northwest Airlines, Midwest Airlines, LAN-Chile, SAS (hub co-ordination), Virgin Atlantic, Air Pacific, Lufthansa, USAir, and Polynesian Airlines

Notes: Air New Zealand is a domestic operator under the brand name of Air New Zealand National, and its domestic main services are supplemented by provincial services operated under the Air New Zealand Link banner by subsidiaries Mount Cook Airline, Eagle Air and Air Nelson. In August 1995 Air New Zealand signed an agreement with South African Airways to develop business opportunities in South Africa, New Zealand and Australia, and to study possible joint ventures at common gateways in Asia and Australia

Personnel: 7,915

Fleet:
- 12 x Boeing Model 737-200 Advanced
- 5 x Boeing Model 747-400
- 5 x Boeing Model 747-200 (including 1 leased to Air Pacific)
- 6 x Boeing Model 767-200ER
- 5 x Boeing Model 767-300ER

Orders:
- 6 x Boeing Model 737-300 (due for delivery in 1998)
- 1 x Boeing Model 747-400 (due for delivery in September 1998)

Main bases and hubs: Auckland, Los Angeles, Honolulu, Brisbane and Sydney

Route network: Asian destinations are Bangkok, Denpasar, Fukuoka, Hong Kong, Nagoya, Osaka, Seoul, Singapore, Taipei, and Tokyo; Australian destinations are Adelaide, Brisbane, Cairns, Hobart, Melbourne, Perth, and Sydney; European destinations are Frankfurt and London; North American destinations are Honolulu, Los Angeles, Toronto, and Vancouver; and Pacific Island destinations are Apia, Nadi, Norfolk Island, Nouméa, Nuku'alofa, and Papeete. There are also winter services to Queenstown from Brisbane and Sydney, and the airline's domestic services link Auckland, Christchurch, Dunedin, Hamilton, Queenstown, Rotorua, and Wellington

Simulators: 2 x Boeing Model 737-200
1 x Boeing Model 747-200B
1 x Boeing Model 747-400
1 x Boeing Model 767-200ER

Maintenance services: Air New Zealand Engineering Services specialises in airframes and engines with 315 licensed airframe engineers, 60 licensed engine engineers, and 65 licensed avionics engineers

History: Formed in April 1940, Tasman Empire Airways Ltd (TEAL) was originally owned by the governments of New Zealand (50%), Australia (30%) and Britain (20%). The airline operated its first service with a Short S.30 flying boat on 10 April 1940, this inaugural flight linking Waite Harbour, Auckland and Rose Bay, Sydney across the Tasman Sea. By the end of World War II, the airline was flying the service to Sydney four times per week with two S.30 machines that were replaced on 29 October 1947 by Short Sandringham flying boats, but as a result of engine problems the Sandringham aircraft were non-operational between 23 February and 17 June 1948. During this gap the service was operated by Douglas DC-4 four-engined airliners leased from Australian National Airways and Trans Australian Airways.

To replace the troublesome Sandringhams, TEAL bought four examples of the Short Solent 4 flying boat late in 1949, and the first of these was delivered on 29 September for a service debut on 14 November. Further expansion of the airline's capabilities occurred on 2 October 1950 with the operation of the first service from Wellington to Sydney, followed in June 1951 by the start of services from Christchurch to Melbourne and on 27 December by the 'Coral Route' from Auckland to Papeete in Tahiti via Suva and Aitutaki.

In May 1954 the British government relinquished its interest in TEAL to the Australian government, and the airline's first landplane, a Douglas DC-6, operated its first service between Auckland and Fiji on 14 May. Three more DC-6 aircraft were handed over to TEAL in May 1954 by the New Zealand government, which had assumed ownership of the aircraft from British Commonwealth Pacific Airlines after its sale to Qantas.

After a lengthy evaluation by TEAL and Qantas, it was announced in May 1958 that the Lockheed L-188 Electra four-turboprop airliner would replace the DC-6, and the first of three such aircraft was delivered on 15 October 1959 for its first operational service over the Tasman route on 1 December. By the end of the year all three Electra airliners were in service.

It had long been the ambition of the New Zealand government to complete its ownership of TEAL, and on 1 April 1961 this became a reality when it bought Australia's 50% interest in the airline.

With the expansion of services in the Far East and to the USA imminent at a time of burgeoning business and tourist traffic, the title Tasman Empire Airways Limited seemed a little incongruous and on 1 April 1965 the airline's name was changed to Air New Zealand. To cope with the expansion programme that was now necessary, the airline ordered three examples of the Douglas DC-8-52 four-turbojet airliner, the first of these being delivered on 19 July 1965 and the others following at short intervals. The DC-8 inaugurated the airline's first jet service on 3 October 1965 on the route linking Christchurch and Sydney, while on 14 December the airline started one of its most prestigious routes, namely Auckland to Los Angeles via Nandi and Honolulu. On 13 March 1966, the DC-8 operated the airline's first service to Hong Kong via Sydney, soon adding the service from Auckland to Singapore.

Following this considerable enlargement of its route network, Air New Zealand looked carefully to the future and appreciated that larger numbers of more capacious aircraft would be needed, and the type it selected was the Douglas (soon to be McDonnell Douglas) DC-10-30, a triple-turbofan transport of which three examples were ordered on 15 September 1970. The first of these wide-body airliners reached the airline on 27 January 1973 and the DC-10-30 flew its inaugural service between Auckland and Sydney on 7 February.

During 1976/77, the government of New Zealand discussed the feasibility and commercial advantage of merging the domestic airline, New Zealand National Airways Corporation (NZNAC), with Air New Zealand, and after agreement had been reached the two operators merged under the name Air New Zealand. At that time the fleet comprised 8 DC-10, 3 DC-8, 8 Boeing Model 737 and 18 Fokker F.27 Friendship aircraft, the first two and last two types being contributed by ANZ and NZNAC respectively. From September 1975 until October 1980 an aircrew interchange agreement with British Airways meant that Air New Zealand operated the Auckland to London (Heathrow) route via Los Angeles, where the New Zealand crew was replaced by a British crew.

In April 1980 the government of New Zealand granted permission for the airline to place an order for five Boeing Model 747-219B four-turbofan airliners, and the first of these machines was accepted on 22 May 1981. Air New Zealand currently operates a large international network with its Boeing Model 747 and Model 767 airliners, and an important regional and domestic network with Boeing Model 737 machines. Air New Zealand was privatised in 1988.

Alitalia

Country of origin: Italy

Generally accepted abbreviation: AZ

Address: Centro Direzionale, Viale Alessandro Marchetti 111, Rome I-00148, Italy

Type of operation: International, regional and domestic scheduled passenger and cargo services

Shareholding: Italian government (89.31%) in the form of the Instituto per la Ricostuzione Industriale

Subsidiaries: Air Europe (27.45%), Avianova (45%), Eurofly (45%), Malev (30%) and SISAM (60%)

Marketing alliances: Codesharing with British Midland, Continental Airlines, Gulf Air, Korean Air and Malev

Notes: Alitalia is the national flag carrier of Italy, in 1994 absorbed the domestic carrier ATI, and in July 1995 confirmed plans to sell its 56.2% ownership of Aeroporti di Roma (the company which operates Rome Airport) to Cofiri, which is also controlled by state-run holding company IRI. The new Alitalia restructuring plan includes a 1.5 trillion lire ($956.8 million) increase in capital subscribed mostly by the state holding company

Personnel: 18,675

Fleet:
2 x Airbus A300B2
14 x Airbus A300B4
11 x Airbus A321
7 x Boeing Model 747-200
5 x Boeing Model 747-200 Combi
1 x Boeing Model 747-200F
6 x Boeing Model 767-300
6 x McDonnell Douglas DC-9-32
8 x McDonnell Douglas MD-11
90 x McDonnell Douglas MD-82

Orders:
26 x Airbus A321
5 x McDonnell Douglas MD-82

Options: 20 x Airbus A321

Main bases and hubs: Milan and Rome

Route network: Domestic destinations include Alghero Sassari, Ancona, Bari, Bergamo, Bologna, Brindisi, Cagliari, Catania, Florence, Genoa, Lamezia Terme, Lampedusa, Milan, Naples, Olbia, Palermo, Pantelleria, Perugia, Pescara, Pisa, Reggio di Calabria, Rimini, Rome, Trapani, Treviso, Turin, Venice, and Verona; African destinations such as Accra, Algiers, Cairo, Casablanca, Dakar, Johannesburg, Lagos, Luxor, Nairobi, and Tunis; American destinations include Bogotá, Boston, Buenos Aires, Caracas, Chicago, Lima, Los Angeles, Mexico City, Miami, Montreal, New York, Rio de Janeiro, Santiago, Santo Domingo, São Paulo, and Toronto; Asian and Pacific destinations such as Bangkok, Beijing, Bombay, Delhi, Hong Kong, Manila, Melbourne, Seoul, Singapore, Sydney, and Tokyo; European destinations include Amsterdam, Ankara, Athens, Barcelona, Berlin, Brussels, Bucharest, Budapest, Cologne, Copenhagen, Dublin, Düsseldorf, Frankfurt, Geneva, Hamburg, Helsinki, Istanbul, Lisbon, London, Lyon, Madrid, Málaga, Malta, Marseille, Moscow, Munich, Nice, Nuremberg, Oporto, Oslo, Paris, Prague, Seville, Stockholm, Stuttgart, Tirana, Valencia, Vienna, Warsaw and Zürich; and Middle Eastern destinations such as Amman, Beirut, Dubai, Damascus, Jiddah, Kuwait, Tehran and Tel Aviv

Simulators:
1 x Airbus A321
1 x Boeing Model 727-200
1 x Boeing Model 747-200
2 x McDonnell Douglas DC-9-30
1 x McDonnell Douglas MD-11
3 x McDonnell Douglas MD-82
1 x Piper Cheyenne IIIA

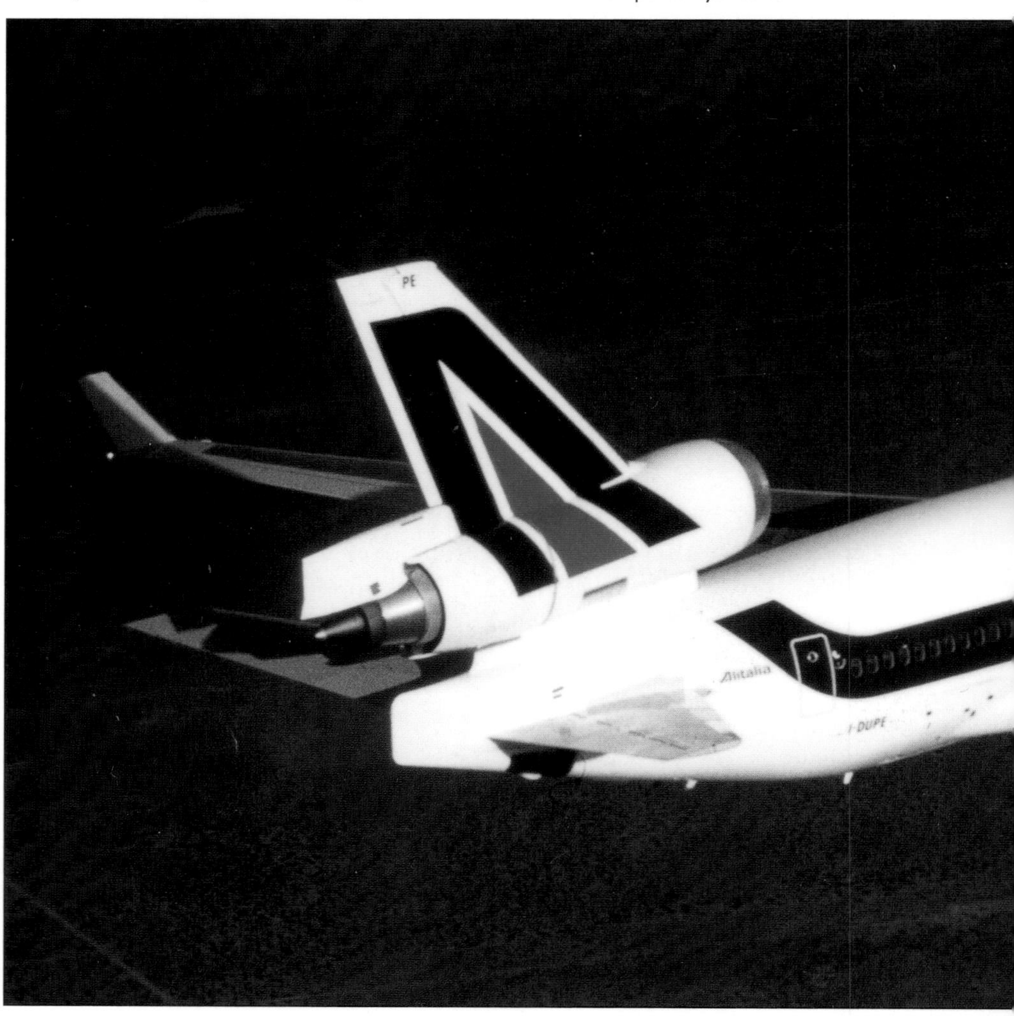

Maintenance services: Alitalia specialises in airframes

History: Aerolinee Italiane Internationale was established on 16 September 1946 by the Italian government (47.5%), British European Airways (BEA) (40%) and a number of private investors (12.5%); following its 1 September 1957 merger with Linee Aeree Italiane (LAI, created in 1946 by the Italian government and TWA), it was renamed Alitalia. The combined airlines operated as a single entity from 6 October 1957, and at this time BEA's interest was reduced to 9% before being completely sold during 1961.

The airline began domestic operations on 5 May 1947 between Turin and Catania via Rome using Fiat G.12 transport aircraft leased from the Italian air force and, like LAI, soon expanded into a major domestic, regional and inter-continental force. The first international flights were flown in 1947 to Cairo, Tripoli and Lisbon with the G.12 transports supplemented and then supplanted by Savoia-Marchetti SM.95 and Avro Lancastrian aircraft. In the early 1950s these original aircraft were gradually replaced by Douglas DC-4 and later by Douglas DC-6 four-engined transports of altogether superior capability.

Alitalia had to abandon the service linking Rome and London route because of lack of competitive equipment, but upon the delivery of its first Convair CV-340 on 24 April 1953 it was able to resume the route. Alitalia took delivery of its first Douglas DC-8-42 four-turbojet airliner on 28 April 1960, and on the following day confirmed its full entry into the turbine-powered era with the first of its Sud-Aviation Caravelle VIN twin-turbojet airliners. The smaller type entered operational service on the service between Rome and London on 23 May 1960, while the DC-8's first service took place on 1 June with a flight from Rome to New York.

The next landmark for Alitalia was its entry into the operation of wide-bodied airliners with the receipt of its first Boeing Model 747-143 on 13 May 1970, followed by that of its first McDonnell Douglas DC-10-30 on 6 February 1973. Alitalia has since developed into a considerably more capable airline operating a mixed fleet of Airbus, Boeing and McDonnell Douglas aircraft.

All Nippon Airways

Country of origin: Japan

Generally accepted abbreviation: NH

Address: Kasumigaseki Building 27F, 3-2-5 Kasumigaseki, Chiyodaku, Tokyo 100, Japan

Type of operation: International, regional and domestic scheduled and charter passenger and cargo services

Shareholding: Private-sector investors (100%)

Subsidiaries: All Nippon Airways has 160 affiliates including Air Nippon, Air Hokkaido, and ANA Enterprises

Marketing alliances: Austrian Airlines, Air Canada and Delta Air Lines; frequent-flyer programmes with British Airways, Cathay Pacific Airways, Malaysia Airlines, Pacific Airways, Singapore Airlines, Swissair and USAir

Notes: All Nippon Airways is Japan's largest passenger airline, with more than 50% of the domestic market, and ranks as the sixth largest airline in the world. The airline began scheduled international flights in 1986 and now operates to 31 cities in 18 countries

Personnel: 13,622

Fleet:
23 x Airbus A320-200
6 x Boeing Model 747LR
14 x Boeing Model 747SR
18 x Boeing Model 747-400
25 x Boeing Model 767-200
40 x Boeing Model 767-300
6 x Boeing Model 777-200

Continued on next page

All Nippon Airways continued from previous page

Orders: 10 x Airbus A321
(delivery from March 1998)
5 x Airbus A340
2 x Boeing Model 747-400
4 x Boeing Model 767-300
16 x Boeing Model 777-200
10 x Boeing Model 777-300

Main bases and hubs: Fukuoka, Hiroshima, Osaka Kansai International Airport, Narita, Nagoya and Tokyo

Route network: Domestic services to almost 50 destinations; Asian and Pacific services to destinations including Bangkok, Beijing, Dalian, Guam, Hong Kong, Kuala Lumpur, Seoul, Shanghai, Singapore, and Tsingtao; American services to destinations such as Los Angeles, New York and Washington DC; Australasian services to destinations including Brisbane and Sydney; and European services to destinations such as Frankfurt, London, Moscow, Paris, Rome and Vienna (in conjunction with Austrian Airlines)

Simulators: 1 x Airbus A320-200
3 x Beech Baron
1 x Boeing Model 737-200
1 x Boeing Model 737-500
1 x Boeing Model 747-200B
3 x Boeing Model 747-400
1 x Boeing Model 747SR
1 x Boeing Model 767-200
3 x Boeing Model 767-300
1 x Boeing Model 777-200
1 x Lockheed L-1011-1 TriStar
1 x NAMC YS-11A-200R
3 x Piper Cheyenne IIIA

Maintenance services: All Nippon Airways specialises in airframes and engines with 1,405 licensed airframe engineers, 50 licensed engine engineers, and 20 licensed avionics engineers

History: The operator now known as All Nippon Airways was established in December 1952 as the Japan Helicopter and Airplane Transport Company (JHATC) and began operations in December 1953 with a service between Tokyo and Osaka, using de Havilland Dove twin-engined light transports. Since that time the company has grown to become Japan's largest civil air operator with some 55% of the domestic market.

The JHATC changed its name to All Nippon Airways in December 1957, and in March of the following year merged with Kyokuto Airlines, a domestic operator that had started operations in March 1953 with a network of routes linking Osaka with points in southern Japan. In spite of strong competition from Japan Air Lines and the country's very significant railway network, All Nippon Airways grew rapidly and vigorously as the requirement for domestic travel flowered, and in November 1963 All Nippon Airways absorbed Fujita Airlines, following with Central Japan Airlines in 1965 and Nagasaki Airways during 1967.

Meanwhile, All Nippon Airways had moved into the jet age with the lease of a Boeing Model 727 three-turbofan transport from the manufacturer during 1964, and this machine entered service on the route between Tokyo and Sapporo in May of that year. A number of routes were later transferred to Nihon Kinkyori Airways (now Air Nippon), a third-level operator formed in March 1974 by Japan Air Lines, All Nippon Airways, Toa Domestic and other Japanese airlines, to operate government-subsidised feeder services to isolated island communities and remote mainland destinations.

All Nippon Airways inaugurated its first international scheduled operations with services to Los Angeles and Washington DC.

America West Airlines

Country of origin: USA

Generally accepted abbreviation: HP

Address: 4000 East Sky Harbor Boulevard, Sky Harbor International Airport, Phoenix, Arizona 85034, USA

Type of operation: Domestic and regional scheduled passenger services

Shareholding: Wholly owned subsidiary of America west Holdings corporation.

Marketing alliances: Codesharing with British Airways, Mesa Airlines, and Continental Airlines.

Notes: America West Airlines is a major carrier based in Phoenix, where it is the dominant airline, with its hub at Phoenix Sky Harbor International Airport. America West also possesses a hub at McCarran International Airport in Las Vegas, Nevada, and a mini-hub at Port Columbus International Airport, Ohio. America West operates one of the youngest aircraft fleets in the world, its fuel-efficient fleet of 101 aircraft comprising Airbus A320, Boeing Model 737 and Boeing Model 757 machines with an average age of only 9.4 years. The airline emerged from Chapter 11 protection against its creditors on 25 August 1994, and is now the ninth largest carrier in the USA with services to 90 or more destinations in 36 states, as well as Mexico and Canada

Personnel: 11,000

Fleet: 26 x Airbus A320
61 x Boeing Model 737
14 x Boeing Model 757-200

Main bases and hubs: Phoenix, Columbus, and Las Vegas

Route network: Domestic destinations such as Albuquerque, Anchorage, Atlanta, Austin, Baltimore, Boston, Brownsville, Bullhead City, Burbank, Charleston, Chicago (Midway), Chicago (O'Hare), Cleveland, Colorado Springs, Columbus, Corpus Christi, Dallas/Fort Worth, Denver, Des Moines, Detroit, Durango, El Paso, Farmington, Flagstaff, Fort Lauderdale, Fort Myers, Fresno, Gallup, Grand Junction, Greensboro/High Point, Harlingen, Honolulu, Houston, Indianapolis, Jacksonville, Kansas City, Kingman, Lake Havasu City, Las Vegas, Laughlin, Little Rock, Long Beach, Los Angeles, Louisville, McAllen, Miami, Milwaukee, Minneapolis/St Paul, Newark, New Orleans, New York (John F. Kennedy International), New York (LaGuardia), Norfolk/Virginia Beach, Oakland, Omaha, Ontario, Orange County, Orlando, Palm Springs, Pensacola, Philadelphia, Phoenix, Pittsburgh, Portland (Maine), Portland (Oregon), Prescott, Providence, Reno, Sacramento, St Louis, Salt Lake City, San Antonio, San Diego, San Francisco, San José, Seattle, Sierra Vista/Fort Huachuca, Tampa, Tucson, Washington DC (National), West Palm Beach, Wichita, and Yuma; and international destinations including Los Cabos, Manzanillo, Mazatlán, Mexico City, and Puerto Vallarta in Mexico and Vancouver in Canada. Many of these services are American West Express services operated for America West Airlines by the Mesa Air Group with a fleet comprising 8 Beech 1900 (5 1900C and 3 1900D) and 2 Fokker 70 aircraft supplemented as required by the aircraft of subsidiaries such as FloridaGulf, Liberty Express, Mountain West and WestAir

Simulators: 1 x Airbus A320
1 x Airbus A321
2 x Boeing Model 737-200
1 x Boeing Model 737-300/400
1 x Boeing Model 757-200ER

Maintenance services: America West Airlines

History: America West Airlines was created in September 1981 specifically to provide low-fare regional air services from its base at Phoenix, Arizona, and started scheduled operations on 1 August 1983 with 280 employees and three Boeing Model 737 twin-turbofan aircraft. The airline's network initially extended between Colorado Springs, Kansas City, Los Angeles, Phoenix and Wichita, but now operates on an extensive hub-and-spoke system centred on Phoenix Sky Harbor International Airport and serves many cities in the USA as well as a few destinations in Canada and Mexico.

In order to expand its operations in Arizona, the airline acquired de Havilland Canada Dash 8 aircraft to provide feeder services to Yuma and Flagstaff from the spring of 1987. Las Vegas and Columbus were then developed as other important centres for operations with 'Nite Flite' services connecting the city with numerous other destinations.

American Airlines

Country of origin: USA

Generally accepted abbreviation: AA

Address: PO Box 619616, Dallas/Fort Worth Airport, Texas 75261-9616, USA

Type of operation: International, regional and domestic scheduled passenger services

Shareholding: AMR Corporation

Subsidiaries: Canadian Airlines International (33%)

Marketing alliances: Codesharing with British Midland, BWIA International Airways, Canadian Airlines International, Gulf Air, LOT-Polish Airlines, Qantas and South African Airways

Notes: The US Department of Transport approved a one-year codeshare arrangement, which started on 1 June 1995, between Canadian Airlines International and American Airlines, permitting the US carrier, its American Eagle subsidiary and Canadian Airlines International to operate codeshare services between the USA and Canadian points and beyond. In addition, American Airlines is permitted to display its code on flights within Canada operated by Canadian Airlines International and its affiliate Canadian Regional, serving 87 Canadian cities. In August 1995 the Department of Transport selected American Airlines to provide a scheduled combination service in the market between Los Angeles and the Mexican city of Guadalajara, reversing its tentative initial decision to award the route to United Airlines

Personnel: 83,900

Fleet:
35 x Airbus A300-600R
81 x Boeing Model 727-200
90 x Boeing Model 757-200
8 x Boeing Model 767-200
22 x Boeing Model 767-200ER
41 x Boeing Model 767-300ER
75 x Fokker 100
16 x McDonnell Douglas DC-10-10
5 x McDonnell Douglas DC-10-30
17 x McDonnell Douglas MD-11
260 x McDonnell Douglas MD-80

Orders: 4 x Boeing Model 757-200

Options: 5 x McDonnell Douglas MD-11

Main bases and hubs: Chicago (O'Hare), Miami, Dallas/Fort Worth, and San Juan

Route network: Transatlantic routes to cities such as Birmingham, Brussels, Düsseldorf, Frankfurt, Glasgow (seasonal), London, Madrid, Manchester, Milan, Munich, Paris, Stockholm, and Zürich, with some 230 weekly departures to destinations including Boston, Chicago, Dallas/Fort Worth, Los Angeles, Miami, New York, and Raleigh/Durham; other destinations include points in the Caribbean, Canada, Japan, Mexico and Latin America; in 1993 American began a codeshare agreement with British Midland, which enables passengers to connect with Amsterdam, Belfast, Brussels, Edinburgh, Frankfurt, Glasgow, Leeds Bradford, Teesside, and Zürich from London (Heathrow); in February 1994 a codeshare between American Airlines and Gulf Air was established to allow for onward travel to Abu Dhabi, Bahrain, Doha and Muscat from London (Heathrow); and a codeshare with Qantas allows services from Los Angeles to Auckland and Melbourne; American Airlines has also applied for rights to fly services from Tokyo to Chicago, Los Angeles and New York

Simulators:
1 x Airbus A300-600R
1 x Airbus A310-100
2 x Boeing Model 727-100
4 x Boeing Model 727-200
2 x Boeing Model 757-200
2 x Boeing Model 767-200
2 x Fokker 100

2 x McDonnell Douglas DC-10-10/30 and MD-11
4 x McDonnell Douglas MD-80 and MD-82

Maintenance services: American Airlines Maintenance & Engineering Center specialises in airframes and engines with 2,800 licensed airframe engineers, 2,750 licensed engine engineers, and 175 licensed avionics engineers

History: American Airlines, currently ranked second in the USA in terms of the number of passengers carried and first in the world in terms of sales, was formed on 11 April 1934 to take over the interests of American Airways, itself established to unify the control of five earlier airlines within the Aviation Corporation (AVCO), which had been formed on 25 January 1930. These five companies were the result of mergers among airlines dating back as far as 1926, and the current airline represents the agglomeration of some 85 earlier operators.

The airline received its first mail contracts in 1934, covering the route between Fort Worth and Los Angeles. In July 1934 American Airlines advertised 51 miscellaneous types of aircraft for sale as it sought to rationalise and upgrade its inherited aircraft fleet, and on 9 September 1934 the airline introduced the all-metal cantilever monoplane Vultee V1-A on its Great Lakes to Texas services, supplementing its transcontinental Curtiss Condor sleeping service.

American Airlines was one of the sponsors of the most successful US airliner of the period leading up to World War II, namely the Douglas DC-3 that was developed from the DC-2. The operator had received its first DC-2 on 4 November 1934, and services with this type on the New York to Chicago route were initiated in December, but the DC-2s were not immediately put into service on the airline's transcontinental routes. American Airlines took delivery of its first DST (Douglas Sleeper Transport – a development of the DC-2 with a widened and lengthened fuselage) on 7 June 1936 and placed the type in service as a day transport on the route between New York and Chicago on 25 June; the airline received its first DC-3 (a dedicated day transport version of the DST) on 18 August, thus releasing the DST aircraft to start their coast-to-coast night service on 18 September.

By 1942 American Airlines was operating 74 Douglas DC-3s, but meanwhile the United States had entered World War II in December 1941 and the airline, like many other US carriers, began the movement of troops and essential equipment to destinations within the USA and to neighbouring countries. On 20 June 1942 American Airlines began regular services across the North Atlantic, following early in 1943 with flights to India. Towards the end of World War II, modified Consolidated Liberators were used on the first all-freight service from Los Angeles to New York, which started on 1 August 1944 and was supplemented by a DC-3 service from 15 October 1944.

On 1 June 1945, with the end of World War II only weeks away, the Civil Aeronautics Board allowed the planned amalgamation of American Export Airlines and American Airlines, thereby creating a very large operator. On 24 October American Export operated its first commercial transatlantic flight from New York to Hurn Airport, near Bournemouth on the southern coast of England. In 10 November 1945 American Export became American Overseas, and the full merger of the two airlines took effect on 5 December.

With the end of World War II, the Douglas four-engined transport – developed to meet a US Army requirement as the C-54 Skymaster became partially surplus to requirement just as production was at its height, and many such aircraft were released for civil service with the designation DC-4. American Airlines received 50 of this important type for service first on the route linking New York and Chicago (February 1946) and then on the transcontinental route between New York and Los Angeles (7 March 1946). The airliner remained in passenger service until December 1948, and American Airlines flew its last DC-4 freight service at the end of 1958. The DC-4 was replaced in passenger service by the Douglas DC-6, of which American Airlines received its first machine on 24 November 1946. American Airlines was the first operator to place the DC-6 in service, initially on its route between New York and Chicago. One year after the DC-6 entered service, American Airlines took delivery of its first Convair CV-240, which took its place alongside the DC-6 on 1 June 1948, and the airline eventually flew 75 examples of this twin-engined airliner.

In December 1951 American Airlines ordered 25 examples of the Douglas DC-7, a much improved development of the DC-6, and

Continued on next page

American Airlines continued from previous page

took delivery of the first of these machines on 10 October 1953 despite the fact that the new airliner had only temporary certification. On 29 November 1953 American Airlines placed the DC-7 in service in direct competition with TWA on the non-stop service between New York and Los Angeles with a flight time of 8 hours 15 minutes.

Until 1958 American Airlines operated only piston-engined aircraft in the forms of 85 DC-6, 58 DC-7 and 58 CV-240 transports. On 15 December 1955, the airline became the second operator, after National Airlines, to place an order for the Lockheed L-188 Electra, with its radical powerplant of four turboprop engines. The first of these aircraft was accepted on 27 November 1958, and entered service on 23 January 1959 for the New York to Chicago service: this aeroplane also had the unfortunate honour to be the first of the type to crash, an event that took place on 3 February 1959 in the course of a nocturnal approach to New York. The Electra was nevertheless the mainstay of American Airlines' short- and medium-haul fleet until the arrival of the Boeing Model 727, and the last L-188 remained in service until 1971.

On 25 January 1959 American Airlines began the first jet domestic service using its own aircraft, a Boeing Model 707-123, on the route between New York and Los Angeles. The first Model 707 was initially handed over on 25 October 1958, and after trials was redelivered on 16 March 1959. One other four-engine jet type to enter service with the airline at about that time was the ill-starred Convair CV-990, which began services on the New York to Chicago route on 18 March 1962.

During 1963 American Airlines and Eastern Airlines considered a merger, but the Civil Aeronautics Board rejected the idea. At about this time the airline decided that it should replace the turboprop-powered Electra with a faster and more economical turbofan-powered type, and ordered 25 examples of the Boeing Model 727-238 of which the first was delivered on 25 January 1964. Like many other American Airlines aircraft, the Model 727 first entered service on the New York to Chicago route, in this instance on 12 April 1964. To complement the Model 727s on shorter-range routes, in July 1963 American Airlines ordered the first 15 of an eventual 30 examples of a British twin-turbofan airliner, the BAC One-Eleven 401, and the first of these aircraft was accepted on 23 December 1965 for service from 6 March of the following year.

By the end of 1969 American Airlines had an all-jet fleet comprising 27 One-Eleven, 100 Model 707, 22 Model 720, and 98 Model 727 airliners.

American Airlines' first wide-body transport was a Boeing Model leased from Pan American, and this made its debut on 2 March 1970 between Los Angeles and New York, and it was June 1970 before American Airlines started to operate its own Model 747 'jumbo jet' aircraft. On 29 July 1971 the airline received its first Douglas (soon McDonnell Douglas) DC-10-10, and it was this machine that flew the airline's first flight between Los Angeles and Chicago on 5 August 1971.

On 30 November 1970 American Airlines bought Trans Caribbean Airways, whose routes it started to operate with its own aircraft on 2 March 1971. In the same month Western Airlines and American Airlines agreed to merge, but there was so much opposition that the plan was dropped. In August 1971 American Airlines started using the Model 707 on a new service across the Pacific from the US west coast to Sydney, Australia, but this service ended in 1974.

Throughout the remainder of the 1970s and into the mid-1980s, American Airlines concentrated on consolidation of its position as a pre-eminent American airline, and it was not until 4 November 1982 that it took delivery of a new type of airliner in the form of a Boeing Model 767-223, of which ten had entered service by December 1984 in the first stage of an expansion and re-equipment programme that has now given American Airlines a force of 71 such aircraft complemented by 90 examples of the Boeing Model 757-200. At the lower end of the range/payload spectrum, on 12 May 1983 American Airlines received the first of its initial order for 20 McDonnell Douglas MD-82 twin-turbofan airliners. This aeroplane entered revenue-earning service a mere two days later, and while the order for 20 aircraft was quite large by the standards of the day, in 1984 the airline contracted for a further 86 such aircraft (19 and 67 for delivery in 1984/85 and 1986/87 respectively) together with an option for a further 100 aircraft of the same type. American Airlines currently operates no fewer than 260 aircraft of the MD-80 series.

American Airlines is the world's largest earner, operates services to 164 cities within the USA and worldwide (and to 256 cities in conjunction with its subsidiary American Eagle). It will deliver 12 McDonnell Douglas MD-11 aircraft to Federal Express between January 1996 and October 1999 with the option to sell its remaining seven MD-11s between 2000 and 2002.

Ansett Australia

Country of origin: Australia

Generally accepted abbreviation: AN

Address: 501 Swanston Street, Melbourne, Victoria 3000, Australia

Type of operation: International, regional and domestic scheduled passenger and cargo services

Shareholding: The parent company is Ansett Australia Holdings and the main shareholders are the News Corporation and TNT

Subsidiaries: Ansett Australia, Ansett New Zealand, Ansett Air Freight, Australian Concessions, Ansett International, Traveland, Transport Industries Insurance, and Hayman Ansair

Marketing alliances: Air New Zealand, ANA, Singapore Airlines, United Airlines, Malaysia Airlines, EVA (codesharing), Cathay Pacific, Swissair, Austrian Airlines, and within Australia, Air Facilities, Augusta, Flightwest, Hazelton, Kendell, Lufthansa, Impulse, Sabair, Skywest, Tamair, and Virgin Atlantic

Notes: The airline began international services in 1993, and freight operations are handled by its cargo division, Ansett Air Freight. TNT announced in November 1995 that it had reached an outline agreement to sell its 50% interest in Ansett to Air New Zealand in two portions, but early in 1996 the agreement encountered problems with New Zealand's competition authorities

Personnel: 17,000

Fleet: 14 x Airbus A320-200
2 x BAe 146F
(operated by Ansett Air Freight)

7 x BAe 146-200
5 x BAe 146-300
1 x Boeing Model 727F (operated by Ansett Air Freight)
5 x Boeing Model 727-200LR (1 leased)
22 x Boeing Model 737-300 (4 leased)
3 x Boeing Model 747-300
8 x Boeing Model 767-200 (leased)
4 x Fokker F.28 Fellowship Series 1000
2 x Fokker F.28 Fellowship Series 3000
7 x Fokker F.28 Fellowship Series 4000
7 x Fokker 50

Main bases and hubs: Sydney and Perth

Route network: This includes a domestic portion covering numerous destinations in all the states of Australia, and a regional portion covering Denpasar, Hong Kong, Jakarta, Kuala Lumpur, Osaka, and the Cocos and Christmas Islands. Ansett Australia also holds rights for services to Seoul, Kuala Lumpur and Singapore, and has applied for a service to Taipei

Simulators: 1 x Airbus A320-200
1 x Boeing Model 727-200LR
1 x Boeing Model 737-300EFIS
1 x Boeing Model 767-200
1 x BAe 146-300

Maintenance services: Ansett Australia specialises in airframes and engines with 65 licensed airframe engineers

History: Reginald M. Ansett formed Ansett Airways in February 1936 with a Fokker Universal as its equipment, and the new airline began services between Melbourne and Hamilton on 17 February 1936. By 1939 the airline's route network had swelled to include those between Melbourne and Adelaide, Broken Hill and Sydney. Ansett operated no services in the course of World War II, but resumed operations on 5 February 1946 with three war-surplus Douglas C-47s acquired late in the preceding year. The revived Ansett started with routes linking Melbourne with Adelaide, Canberra and Hamilton, soon extended to Brisbane and Hobart.

Early in 1952 Ansett started a programme of expansion by the purchase of Barrier Reef Airways that operated a small network of seaplane services from Brisbane to Hayman Island, Sydney and Townsville, and by the acquisition in 1953 of the bankrupt Trans-Oceanic Airways' routes. In 1954 the three operations were consolidated into a single network, and with the delivery of its first Convair CV-240 on 23 April the airline was able to offer low-fare services between state capitals in competition with Trans-Australia Airlines and Australian National Airways. In March 1957 Ansett revealed a further expansion plan requiring the purchase of additional CV-240 and -340 aircraft as well as more-advanced turboprop-powered airliners in the form of four Vickers Viscount 832 and three Lockheed L-188 Electra aircraft.

On 4 October of the same year Ansett Transport Industries, the parent group of which Ansett Airways was a member, bought Australian National Airways to form Ansett-ANA, a title retained until late 1968, when the name Ansett Airlines was adopted. Further consolidation of this growing operator followed with the purchase on 5 February 1958 of Butler Air Transport, which was renamed Airlines of New South Wales on 15 December of the following year, and then of Guinea Airways that was renamed Airlines of South Australia.

The first of the Electra and Viscount aircraft were received on 27 February and 12 March 1959 respectively. The Electras remained operational as passenger transports (but later as freight transports) until 1984, when they were sold to Turbo Power International of the USA. Further turboprop equipment was also secured in 1959 in the form of the first of a rapidly growing fleet of Fokker F.27 Friendships, of which the first was accepted on 5 October. The type remains in service in both its basic and updated F.50 forms with the parent company and its four principal subsidiaries.

The airline received its first pure-jet aircraft on 9 September 1964, when it took delivery of a Boeing Model 727-77 three-turbofan airliner, and this type entered revenue-earning service on 2 November. From 13 April 1967 the Model 727 aircraft were complemented on shorter routes by the Douglas DC-9-31.

In January 1969 Ansett acquired Mac-Robertson Miller Airlines, which was renamed Airlines of Western Australia in July 1981. During the 1970s additional Model 727 aircraft, in the form of Model 727-277 machines, were taken in strength, and throughout most of the 1980s thirteen of these aircraft constituted the single largest element in Ansett's fleet. Ansett also decided to standardise on the Boeing Model 737 twin-turbofan type in place of the DC-9, and the first of twelve Model 737-277 airliners was delivered on 15 June 1981.

In 1979 Ansett Transport Industries, itself created in 1946 and the parent organisation for R.M. Ansett's transport interests, was taken over by the New Corporation and TNT Ltd. Further growth and consolidation followed, and in July 1981 Ansett created another subsidiary as Airlines of North Australia. Two years later, on 8 June 1983, the airline moved into the wide-body arena with the receipt of the first of its six Boeing Model 767-277 airliners. Further advanced equipment followed in the form of the Airbus A320-200, BAe 146 and Fokker F.28 Fellowship.

Since 1987 Ansett has been involved in a joint venture to set up Ansett New Zealand, bought Eastwest Airlines and Kendell Airlines and, before its recent disposal of these assets, owned part of America West and Ladeco. During 1994 Ansett absorbed its subsidiary airlines (Ansett West Australia, Ansett Express and Eastwest) to become Ansett Australia.

Austrian Airlines

Country of origin: Austria

Generally accepted abbreviation: OS

Address: PO Box 50, Fontanastrasse 1, Vienna A-1010, Austria

Type of operation: International, regional and domestic scheduled passenger and cargo services

Shareholding: Austrian government (51.9%), Swissair (10%), All Nippon Airways (9%), Air France (1.5%), and 27.6% publicly owned

Subsidiaries: Austrian Airtransport (80%), Austrian Services (100%), Touropa Austria, Transeurope, Austrian Holidays, Traviaustria, Interconvention, Austrian Aircraft Corporation, and Airest

Marketing alliances: Codesharing with Aeroflot, British Midland, CSA, Delta Air Lines, Iberia, KLM, LOT-Polish Airlines, Lufthansa, SAS, South African Airways, Swissair, TAROM, and Ukraine International; there are other agreements with Air China, Air France, All Nippon Airways, Finnair, and Malev

Personnel: 4,670

Fleet:
4 x Airbus A310-300
3 x Airbus A321-100
2 x Airbus A340-200
8 x Fokker 70
7 x McDonnell Douglas MD-81
6 x McDonnell Douglas MD-82
2 x McDonnell Douglas MD-83
2 x McDonnell Douglas MD-87ER
3 x McDonnell Douglas MD-87SR

Orders:
7 x Airbus A320-200
3 x Airbus A321-100
2 x Airbus A340-300

Options: 2 x Airbus A340

Main bases and hubs: Vienna, Graz, Klagenfurt, Linz, and Salzburg

Route network: African destinations such as

Cairo, Johannesburg, Nairobi and Tripoli; American destinations such as Chicago, New York and Washington; Asian and Pacific destinations such as Beijing and Tokyo; domestic destinations such as Graz, Innsbruck, Klagenfurt, Linz, Salzburg and Vienna; other European destinations such as Almaty, Amsterdam, Ankara, Athens, Belgrade, Berlin, Brussels, Bucharest, Budapest, Copenhagen, Düsseldorf, Frankfurt, Geneva, Gothenburg, Hamburg, Helsinki, Istanbul, Izmir, Kiev, Lisbon, Ljubljana, London, Madrid, Malta, Milan, Minsk, Moscow, Munich, Nice, Odessa, Oslo, Paris, Prague, Riga, Rome, St Petersburg, Sofia, Stockholm, Stuttgart, Thessaloniki, Timisoara, Tirana, Turin, Venice, Vilnius, Warsaw, Zagreb, and Zürich; Middle Eastern destinations such as Aleppo, Amman, Baghdad, Beirut, Cairo, Damascus, Dhahran, Larnaca, Riyadh, Tehran, and Tel Aviv; the airline also undertakes charter flights within Europe and Africa through its subsidiary Austrian Airtransport

Simulators: Details not available

Maintenance services: Austrian Airlines specialises in airframes and engines with 105 licensed airframe engineers, 50 licensed engine engineers, and 50 licensed avionics engineers

History: Otherwise known as Oesterreichische Luftverkehrs AG, Austrian Airlines was created on 30 September 1957 by the merger of Air Austria and Austrian Airways, neither of which had started operations at that time, and assumed the name of its predecessor of the period between the two world wars, itself absorbed into Deutsche Lufthansa on 1 January 1939 after the German annexation of Austria.

Austrian Airlines received its first airliner, a Vickers Viscount, on 23 February 1960, but up to this time ran its services with four Viscount 779 machines leased from Fred Olsen Air Transport. The new airline's first service was flown on 31 March 1958 on the route linking Vienna and London via Zürich, and in order to cope with the demands of its route network, which was growing rapidly during the early 1960s, the airline placed an order for the Sud-Aviation Caravelle VIR on 29 October 1962 and received the first of these machines on 18 February 1963.

On 30 April 1966 Austrian Airlines received the first of its two Hawker Siddeley HS 748 twin-turboprop airliners ordered for the operation of domestic services as well as routes into neighbouring countries. These aircraft were particularly useful for their short take-off and landing capability, allowing successful operation into airports in mountainous regions, and remained in service up to 6 September 1970.

In the later 1960s Austrian Airlines expanded its horizons to include long-range routes, and the operation of such services was initially made possible by the lease of a Boeing Model 707-329 from the Belgian operator Sabena on 1 April 1969. This aeroplane was used on the route linking Vienna and New York until 1971, when it was returned to Sabena. In 1971 the airline received a considerable boost to its short-range operations with the acceptance of its first Douglas DC-9-32 twin-turbofan transport on 10 June, and the receipt of further aircraft of the same type permitted Austrian Airlines to withdraw its fleet of Caravelles, the last of which made its ultimate revenue-earning flight on 26 July 1972.

On 24 September 1973 Austrian Airlines leased a McDonnell Douglas DC-8-73CF for use on cargo flights from Vienna to Hong Kong, a service that was flown between 29 September 1973 and 5 December 1974, when the aeroplane was returned to Overseas National Airways.

In August 1975 the airline received its first McDonnell Douglas DC-9-51, which entered service early the following month, and on 30 October 1977 Austrian Airlines became one of the launch customers for the MD-80, the lengthened and up-engined derivative of the DC-9, and received its first MD-81 on 3 October 1980. The advent of the DC-9-51 and MD-81 allowed the airline to dispose of its DC-9-32 fleet to Texas International Airlines.

The MD-81 has since been complemented by the MD-82, the MD-83 and two subvariants of the MD-87 as the mainstay of Austrian Airlines' medium-range operations, while responsibility for short-range service is entrusted to the Fokker 50, 70 and 100. The airline has also increased its capacity on high-density routes by the introduction of the Airbus A310 with other Airbus wide-body airliners in service or on order.

In 1964 Austrian Airlines established Austrian Airtransport as a subsidiary for the operation of charter and inclusive tour services using aircraft drawn from the parent company. Another subsidiary is Austrian Air Services, which flies local services with Swearingen SA 226 Metros, of which the first was delivered on 25 January 1980 for a service debut on 1 April. Austrian Airlines is currently ranked 40th in the world in terms of revenue, and 14th in Europe in terms of passenger and freight earnings.

Biman Bangladesh Airlines

Country of origin: Bangladesh

Generally accepted abbreviation: BG

Address: Biman Bhaban, 100 Motgheel Commercial Area, Dhaka 1000, Bangladesh

Type of operation: International, regional and domestic scheduled and charter passenger and cargo services

Shareholding: Bangladeshi government (100%)

Notes: The national flag carrier of Bangladesh, Biman Bangladesh Airlines flies services to 26 international destinations as well as operating a limited domestic route network

Personnel: 5,960

Fleet:
2 x Airbus A310-300
2 x BAe ATP
2 x Fokker F.28 Fellowship
5 x McDonnell Douglas DC-10-30

Orders: 2 x Airbus A310-300

Main base and hub: Dhaka

Route network: International services to Abu Dhabi, Bahrain, Bangkok, Bombay, Brussels, Calcutta, Delhi, Doha, Dubai, Frankfurt, Hong Kong, Jiddah, Karachi, Kathmandu, Kuala Lumpur, Kuwait, London, Muscat, New York, Paris, Riyadh, Rome, Sharjah, Singapore, Tokyo and Yangon; domestic services to Barisal, Chittagong, Cox's Bazar, Ishurdi, Jessore, Rajshahi, Saidpur, and Sylhet; additional services are planned to Amsterdam, Ho Chi Minh City and Jakarta

Continued on next page

Biman Bangladesh continued from previous page

History: Biman Bangladesh Airlines was created on 4 January 1972 as the national flag carrier of the new state of Bangladesh, previously known as East Pakistan. One month later the airline began to operate its first services with a Douglas DC-3 on routes from Dhaka to Chittagong, Sylhet and Jessore. The DC-3 was obsolete even as it entered service, and was soon replaced by a pair of Fokker F.27 Friendship Series 200 airliners that were delivered on 3 and 7 March 1972. During September the airline added two new F.27 Friendship Series 600 aircraft to its fleet, one of them donated by the Dutch government. For a short time in 1972 the airline also leased Douglas DC-6 aircraft.

Biman Bangladesh flew its first international service on 28 April 1972 on the route between Dhaka and Calcutta using an F.27 Friendship Series 200, and on 1 January 1973 started a weekly service from Dhaka to London (Heathrow) with a Boeing Model 707-321 four-turbofan airliner leased from Donaldson International. On 30 December of the same year, Biman Bangladesh took delivery of its first Model 707-351, and over the following eight years received additional Model 707 and F.27 aircraft to permit the expansion of the airline's route network to a number of other Asian destinations.

Domestic services were limited by the capacity of the F.27s, and to improve capability in the regional as well as domestic markets Biman Bangladesh bought two examples of the Fokker F.28 Fellowship, these aircraft being accepted in September and November 1981. By this time the airline was planning a considerable improvement in its long-range capacity, and moved into the market for wide-body aircraft with the purchase of two McDonnell Douglas DC-10-30 three-turbofan airliners. These aircraft were delivered in August 1983, and this type started a high-capacity service to London on 22 October.

Further expansion has been limited by the poverty of Bangladesh and thus of its airline, but the F.27 aircraft have been replaced by BAe ATP twin-turboprop transports and the DC-10 fleet has expanded to five, with further capability offered by the introduction of the Airbus A310-300.

British Airways

Country of origin: UK

Generally accepted abbreviation: BA

Address: Speedbird House, Heathrow Airport, Hounslow, Middlesex TW6 2JA, UK

Type of operation: International, regional and domestic scheduled and charter passenger and cargo services

Shareholding: Publicly quoted company

Subsidiaries: Air Liberté (67%), Air Mauritius (12.8%), Deutsche BA (49%), Qantas (25%), TAT European Airlines (49.9%)

Marketing alliances: Codesharing with Aeromexico, Qantas, TAT; other joint agreements with Aer Lingus, GB Airways, Deutsche BA, and Korean Air

Notes: In January 1993 British Airways formed an alliance with USAir which involved the purchase of $300 million of a new series of USAir convertible preferred stock, and the alliance permits British Airways to cover codesharing on USAir flights to 38 cities within the USA. This shareholding is now being relinquished. In 1992 British Airways secured a 49% holding in France's leading independent carrier, TAT European Airlines, and the airline also acquired 49% of Friedrichshafen-based regional carrier Delta Air Regionalflug. which was then renamed as Deutsche BA. British Airways owns Brymon European Airways, and in 1993 purchased 25% of Qantas, the Australian national flag carrier, for £290 million. British Airways is currently involved in seeking to establish a partnership with American Airlines. Franchise partners of British Airways currently include Brymon Airways, CityFlyer Express, Loganair, Manx Airlines and Maersk Air. In August 1995 British Airways reached a frequent-flyer agreement with Aeromexico.

Personnel: 55,296

Fleet:
- 7 x Aérospatiale/BAC Concorde
- 10 x Airbus A320
- 10 x BAe Jetstream ATP
- 39 x Boeing Model 737-200
- 33 x Boeing Model 737-400
- 15 x Boeing Model 747-100
- 16 x Boeing Model 747-200B
- 32 x Boeing Model 747-400
- 44 x Boeing Model 757-200
- 25 x Boeing Model 767-300ER
- 7 x Boeing Model 777-200
- 8 x McDonnell Douglas DC-10-30

Orders:
- 11 x Boeing Model 777
- 32 x Boeing Model 747-400
- 1 x Boeing Model 767-300
- 3 x Boeing Model 757-200

Main bases and hubs: Birmingham, Glasgow, London (Heathrow), London (Gatwick), and Manchester

Route network: This includes a domestic element comprising high-frequency 'Super Shuttle' services between London (Heathrow) and Belfast, Edinburgh, Glasgow and Manchester, a 'CityFlyer Express' service between London (Gatwick) and Newcastle, and services to destinations such as Aberdeen, Belfast, Birmingham, Bristol, Glasgow, Guernsey, Inverness, Jersey, Orkney Isles, Plymouth, Southampton and Stornoway; an African element to destinations such as Agadir, Cape Town, Casablanca, Dar es Salaam, Durban, Entebbe, Gaborone, Johannesburg, Lagos, Lilongwe, Lusaka, Marrakech, Mauritius, Nairobi, and the Seychelles; an Australasian and Pacific Rim element to destinations including Bangkok, Beijing, Bombay, Brisbane, Calcutta, Delhi, Dhaka, Hong Kong, Islamabad, Jakarta, Kuala Lumpur, Madras, Melbourne, Nagoya, Osaka Kansai, Perth, Seoul, Singapore, Sydney, Taipei, and Tokyo; a European element to destinations including Amsterdam, Annecy, Athens, Barcelona, Basel, Berlin, Bilbao, Bologna, Bordeaux, Bremen, Brussels, Budapest, Cologne, Copenhagen, Cork, Düsseldorf, Faro, Frankfurt, Geneva, Genoa, Gibraltar, Gothenburg, Hamburg, Hannover, Helsinki, Istanbul, Larnaca, Leipzig, Lisbon, Luxembourg, Lyon, Madrid, Málaga, Marseille, Milan, Montpellier, Moscow, Munich, Naples, Nice, Oporto, Oslo, Paris, Pisa, Prague, Rome, St Petersburg, Sofia, Stavanger, Stockholm,

Stuttgart, Thessaloniki, Toulouse, Turin, Valencia, Venice, Verona, Vienna, Warsaw, and Zürich; a Middle Eastern element to destinations such as Abu Dhabi, Amman, Baku, Bahrain, Beirut, Damascus, Dhahran, Dubai, Jiddah, Jordan, Kuwait, Muscat, Riyadh, Tehran, and Tel Aviv; a North American and Caribbean element to destinations such as Antigua, Atlanta, Baltimore, Barbados, Bermuda, Boston, Charlotte, Chicago, Dallas/Fort Worth, Grand Cayman, Grenada, Kingston, Los Angeles, Mexico City, Miami, Montego Bay, Montreal, Nassau, New York, Philadelphia, Pittsburgh, St Lucia, San Francisco, San Juan, Seattle, Tampa, Toronto, Vancouver, and Washington DC; and a South American element to destinations including Bogotá, Buenos Aires, Caracas, Rio de Janeiro, Santiago, and São Paulo

Simulators: 1 x Aérospatiale/BAe Concorde
3 x Boeing Model 737-236
1 x Boeing Model 737-436
1 x Boeing Model 747-136
1 x Boeing Model 747-236
1 x Boeing Model 747-236 Combi
3 x Boeing Model 747-436
1 x Boeing Model 757-236
1 x Boeing Model 757 and Model 767
1 x Boeing Model 767-336
1 x Boeing Model 777-236
1 x BAe One-Eleven 400
1 x BAe One-Eleven 500
1 x Lockheed L-1011
1 x Lockheed L-1011-500

Maintenance services: British Airways Engineering specialises in airframes with 1,920 licensed airframe engineers and 480 licensed avionics engineers

History: Currently ranked first in Europe and fifth in the world, British Airways can be traced back to 31 March 1924, when four pioneering British airlines (British Marine, Daimler Airways, Handley Page Air Transport and Instone Air Lines, the earliest of them established on 25 August 1919 and flying its first service on the same date) merged to create Imperial Airways for the development of air routes to the dominions and British possessions/mandates in the Middle East, India, the Far East, Australasia and Africa. It also operated a few European routes, the most important of them being between London and Paris.

In 1935 British Airways was established by the amalgamation of three small independent airlines and concentrated its commercial effort on the operation of air services within the continent of Europe. An Act of Parliament on 24 November 1939 served to merge Imperial Airways and British Airways, thus creating the

Continued on next page

British Airways continued from previous page

British Overseas Airways Corporation (BOAC), although it was not until 1 April 1940 that the two previous operators' combined fleet of 82 aircraft was formally taken over as the equipment of the new airline.

BOAC operated only limited services in World War II, but after the revival of more extensive services following the end of hostilities in Europe during May 1945, a separate division of BOAC was created in August 1946 to operate a growing network of routes throughout the UK and Europe, and this was designated British European Airways (BEA). In July and August 1950 BEA experimentally used a new turboprop airliner, the Vickers Viscount 630, on the routes linking London with Edinburgh and Paris, thus pioneering turbine propulsion for civil purposes, and in April 1953 the world's first true turboprop service was inaugurated on the route between London and Nicosia with the Viscount 701. Meanwhile BOAC had started the first true jet service in May 1952 with the de Havilland Comet 1, which was powered by four turbojets, on the route linking London and Johannesburg, and on 4 October 1958 BOAC operated the first jet service across the Atlantic to New York with the Comet 4, an enlarged and improved development of the Comet 1.

In March 1964 BEA began scheduled services with the de Havilland Trident 1C three-turbofan airliner, which was the first civil type with the ability to land in zero/zero conditions. Through the 1960s BEA and BOAC continued to enlarge their route networks and fleets, and the development of the mass air transport market during this period resulted in the establishment of BEA Airtours (later British Airtours) as BEA's separate charter and inclusive tour subsidiary. Starting with a fleet of Comet 4B airliners that were later replaced by Boeing Model 707-436 machines transferred from BOAC, the operator was finally equipped with Boeing Model 737-236 and Lockheed L-1011-200 TriStar 200 two- and three-turbofan airliners for the short- and long-haul routes respectively.

On 31 October 1970 BEA took over Cambrian Airways and BKS/Northeast Airlines for incorporation in its Regional Division.

On 22 April 1970 BOAC took delivery of its first Boeing Model 747-136 four-turbofan airliner, and flew its first North Atlantic services with this pioneering wide-body airliner one year later. By the provisions of the Civil Aviation Act of 1971, the British Airways Board was created on 1 September 1972 to rejoin the two divisions and British Air Services within a single organisation, but the BEA and BOAC names were retained until 1 April 1974.

One of the most important events in aviation history took place on 21 January 1976, when the first supersonic airliner developed in the Western world was introduced to revenue-earning service: this airliner was the Aérospatiale/BAC Concorde, and it first entered service on the route linking London and Bahrain.

British Airways was privatised in 1987 and in 1988 absorbed British Caledonian Airways. Throughout the 1980s the airline introduced large numbers of American narrow- and wide-body aircraft, most of them Boeing types, for its very large network of domestic, regional and inter-continental services.

British Midland

Country of origin: UK

Generally accepted abbreviation: BD

Address: Donington Hall, Castle Donington, Derby DE74 2SB, UK

Type of operation: International and regional scheduled passenger services

Shareholding: British Midland's parent company is the Airlines of Britain Holdings (ABH) group, and among the shareholders is SAS (40%)

Marketing alliances: Codesharing with Air Canada, Alitalia, American Airlines, Austrian Airlines, Iberia, Malaysia Airlines, SAS, TAP, United Airlines, Cathay Pacific, and Virgin Atlantic

Personnel: 3,900

Fleet: 6 x Boeing Model 737-300
6 x Boeing Model 737-400
13 x Boeing Model 737-500
3 x Fokker 70
5 x Fokker 100

Orders: 4 x Fokker 70

Main bases and hubs: Birmingham, London (Heathrow) and East Midlands

Route network: This includes services from London (Heathrow) to Amsterdam, Belfast, Bergen, Brussels, Dublin, Edinburgh, Frankfurt, Glasgow, Leeds Bradford, Nice, Palma, Paris, Prague, Teesside, and Zürich; from East Midlands to Amsterdam, Belfast, Glasgow, Jersey, Málaga, and Paris; from Jersey to Belfast, Edinburgh, Glasgow, Leeds Bradford, Liverpool, Luton, and Teesside; from Leeds Bradford to Glasgow; from Glasgow to Paris; from Edinburgh to Paris; and from Edinburgh/Glasgow to Copenhagen

Simulators: 1 x Boeing Model 737-300/400/500
1 x McDonnell Douglas DC-9-15/32

Maintenance services: British Midland specialises in airframes and engines with 65 licensed airframe engineers, 20 licensed engine engineers, and 25 licensed avionics engineers

History: The origins of British Midland can be found in the establishment by Air Schools, during October 1938, of a reserve flying school at Burnaston near Derby. During World War II the school trained pilots and navigators for the RAF, and expanded with the establishment of another training school near Wolverhampton. On 21 August 1947 the company started a small-scale charter service with a combination of British Taylorcraft Auster, Miles Gemini and Miles Messenger aircraft, and the success of this commercial transport effort persuaded Air Schools to expand this capability, and on 16 February 1949, Derby Aviation was registered as an airline. The new operator started scheduled passenger services on 18 July 1953 with a single de Havilland D.H.89A Rapide on

Continued on next page

British Midlk and continued from previous page

the route between Derby and Jersey via Wolverhampton.

In April 1955 Derby Aviation bought its first Douglas DC-3 for greater capacity and speed on the route to the Channel Islands, and this machine flew its first such service on 1 May of the same year. The success of this service is attested by the fact that, by the summer of 1958, Derby Aviation was operating three DC-3 airliners mainly for tour charters from Derby to Austria, France, Italy, Spain and Switzerland. The airline was also operating scheduled services from Derby to destinations such as Glasgow, the Isle of Man and Jersey as well as international destinations such as Antwerp and Ostend.

On 12 March 1959 the operator changed its name to Derby Airways as a reflection of its growing involvement in scheduled and charter operations. By 1960 the operator had a fleet of eight Douglas DC-3 transports and was carrying over 20,000 passengers a year on its scheduled services together with a considerably larger number on its charter flights.

On 30 July 1964 Derby Airways announced that it was changing its name to British Midland Airways (BMA), a change that took place on 1 October 1964, and the growing capability of this company meant that on 1 February 1965 the airline was able to introduce its first turboprop-powered type in the form of the Handley Page Dart Herald Mk 211. In April of the same year BMA moved to its current base, the newly opened East Midlands Airport at Castle Donington, and added new services to Palma and Gerona; a service to Newquay was added in 1966.

In January 1967 BMA took delivery of its first four-turboprop airliner, the Vickers Viscount 736, and this type entered service to complement the Canadair Argonaut aircraft that the airline had been operating on its scheduled flights since 1961. Autair International pulled out of scheduled operations in 1969, and BMA gained several of its routes including that linking London and Teesside: this service was originally flown by the Viscount but was later taken over by the airline's new BAC One-Eleven 523, of which the first was accepted on 17 February 1970.

On 15 April 1970 BMA moved into the long-range market with the purchase of a Boeing Model 707 that was placed in service on charter routes across the Atlantic, and to Africa and the Far East. In 1974 the airline dropped out of the inclusive charter market, however, and operated a total of eleven Model 707 transports in other roles including the lease of several aircraft to other operators.

On 29 February 1972 Channel Airways ceased operations, and BMA secured this operator's scheduled routes to the Channel Islands from Bournemouth and Southend. This required additional capacity, and the airline bought eleven Viscounts in 1972: up to 26 August 1976, when the first McDonnell Douglas DC-9 was accepted, the Viscount constituted the core of BMA's fleet. To complement the medium-range DC-9, BMA also operated the short-range Fokker F.27 Friendship twin-turboprop airliner, including three leased from Air UK and one from NLM, on its low-density routes in the UK and the international routes to Amsterdam, Brussels and Paris. Later equipment has included the Boeing Model 737 twin-turbofan type in three variants, as well as the Fokker 70 updated and lengthened development of the F.27 and also the Fokker 100 that is the modernised version of the F.28 Fellowship.

In 1968, it should be noted, BMA was bought by Minster Assets, an investment and banking group, but in 1978 the directors of the airline succeeded in a management buy-out. In 1982, BMA formed Manx Airlines to operate scheduled services from the Isle of Man. BMA, which had traded as British Midland since 1964, formally became British Midland in 1985 and two years later, in March 1987, the Airlines of Britain Holdings (ABH) group was established as a holding company for British Midland and its subsidiaries. Scandinavian Airlines System (SAS) took a 24.9% stake in ABH in 1988, increasing this to 35% in March 1992, and to 40% in 1994.

BWIA International Airways

Country of origin: Trinidad and Tobago

Generally accepted abbreviation: BW

Address: PO Box 604, Administration Building, Golden Grove Road, Piarco International Airport, Port of Spain, Trinidad and Tobago

Type of operation: International and regional scheduled passenger and cargo services

Shareholding: The Acker Group and Caribbean investors (33.5%) and the government of Trinidad and Tobago

Marketing alliances: Air Martinique, and codesharing with American Airlines and British Midland

Notes: BWIA International Airways is the national flag carrier of Trinidad and Tobago, and in May 1995 signed a joint marketing agreement with Air Martinique, and services to Martinique are to be routed through St Lucia for passenger transfer to Air Martinique onward flights

Personnel: 2,500

Fleet: 2 x Airbus A321-100
4 x Lockheed L-1011-500 TriStar
5 x McDonnell Douglas MD-83

Orders: 6 x Airbus A321-100
3 x Airbus A340-300
5 x EMBRAER EMB-145 (possible)

Main base and hub: Port of Spain (Piarco International Airport)

Route network: A Caribbean element with destinations such as Antigua, Barbados, Georgetown, Grenada, Kingston, St Lucia and St Maarten; a European element with destinations including Frankfurt, London and Zürich; and a North American element with destinations such as Miami, New York and Toronto

Simulators: None

Maintenance services: None

History: On 27 November 1939 Lowell

Yerex, a New Zealander who had earlier established the Honduran airline Transportes Aereos Centro-Americanos, formed British West Indian Airways. The new airline flew its first service with a Lockheed L-18 Lodestar between Port of Spain and Barbados on 26 November 1940. On 11 May 1943 the airline became a limited company and, on behalf of the British government, the British Overseas Airways Corporation (BOAC) took an interest in the airline. This took place within the context of World War II, and during this period British West Indian Airways purchased additional Lockheed twin-engined aircraft for an expansion of its route network to the Leeward and Windward Islands during 1943, between Kingston and both St Kitts and Port of Spain during 1944, and between Port of Spain and Georgetown during 1944.

Early in 1947 the government of Trinidad bought Yerex's 28% interest in the airline, and at the same time British South American Airways acquired a 47% shareholding, on 1 October purchasing the balance of the shares via its subsidiary British International Airlines, by which name British West Indian Airways was known up to 24 June 1948. On 30 July 1949 British South American Airways was amalgamated with BOAC, which now assumed control of the West Indian operator. During this period the airline's equipment comprised three types of twin-engined transport, namely the Lockheed Lodestar, Douglas DC-3 and Vickers Viking Mk IA: the first of an eventual eight of this last type was received on 20 July 1948, and the type remained in service up to 1950.

In October 1949 British West Indian Airways took over British Caribbean Airways, which brought with it services between Nassau in the Bahamas and the cities of Miami and Palm Beach in Florida. Further expansion followed in 1952 when British South American Airways transferred to British West Indian Airways the international services of Bahamas Airways, which it had bought in August 1948, leaving Bahamas Airways as a domestic operator. In June 1953 British West Indian Airways contracted for four examples of the world's first turbine-engined airliner, the Vickers Viscount, in the form of the Viscount 702 variant, and took delivery of the first of these machines on 28 July 1955 for a service debut on the route between Trinidad and San Juan in Puerto Rico on 2 December 1955.

British West Indian Airways was the first Caribbean operator of a turboprop-powered type in the form of the Viscount, and on 29 April 1960 started a transatlantic service, between Trinidad and London via Barbados and New York, with another turboprop-powered type, a Bristol Britannia 312 leased from BOAC. In November 1961 the government of Trinidad and Tobago secured a 90% holding in the company, and bought the remaining 10% in 1967.

The airline sold its last Viscounts in 1965, when the operator launched its first service with a pure-jet type, namely the Boeing Model 727-78 of which the first was received on 21 December 1964. On 15 December of the following year British West Indian Airways started to operate another jet type in the form of a leased Boeing Model 720-048, and this was followed by Boeing Model 707 airliners during December 1968. British West Indian Airways eventually flew 13 examples of the Model 707, of which one made the operator's inaugural jet service to London in April 1974.

From 1976 the Model 727 was replaced by the McDonnell Douglas DC-9-51, the first of which was leased from Finnair and was received on 24 July 1976. The Model 707 was finally replaced by the Lockheed L-1011-500 TriStar, the first of which was received on 28 January 1980 and still flies the airline's long-haul flights.

On 1 January 1980 Trinidad and Tobago (BWIA International) Airways was formed by the merger of BWIA with the other government-owned airline, Trinidad & Tobago Air Services. This merger allowed the combined airlines to fly scheduled passenger and cargo services from Piarco Airport to eleven points in the Caribbean as well as other services to Miami, New York, Toronto and London.

In March 1994 the Acker Group and a team of Caribbean investors bought 33.5% of British West Indian Airways.

Aérospatiale/BAe Concorde

In January 1996 the Concorde completed 20 years of operational service with Air France and British Airways, the only airlines to have bought this supersonic airliner, one of two such transports to have entered full service and now the only one still in service after the early end of the Tupolev Tu-144's airline career.

The Concorde can trace its history to 1955, the year in which several British aircraft manufacturers collaborated with government agencies in undertaking preliminary design work leading to the creation in the following year of a Supersonic Transport Aircraft Committee (STAC) to study the feasibility of a Super-Sonic Transport (SST). The STAC considered a number of projected designs including the Bristol Type 198, a designation that comprised several different aircraft configurations. The layout that received greatest approbation was a slender delta-winged configuration with eight engines and estimated performance that included transatlantic range at a speed of Mach 2. By means of a continuous refinement, the Type 198 was transformed into the

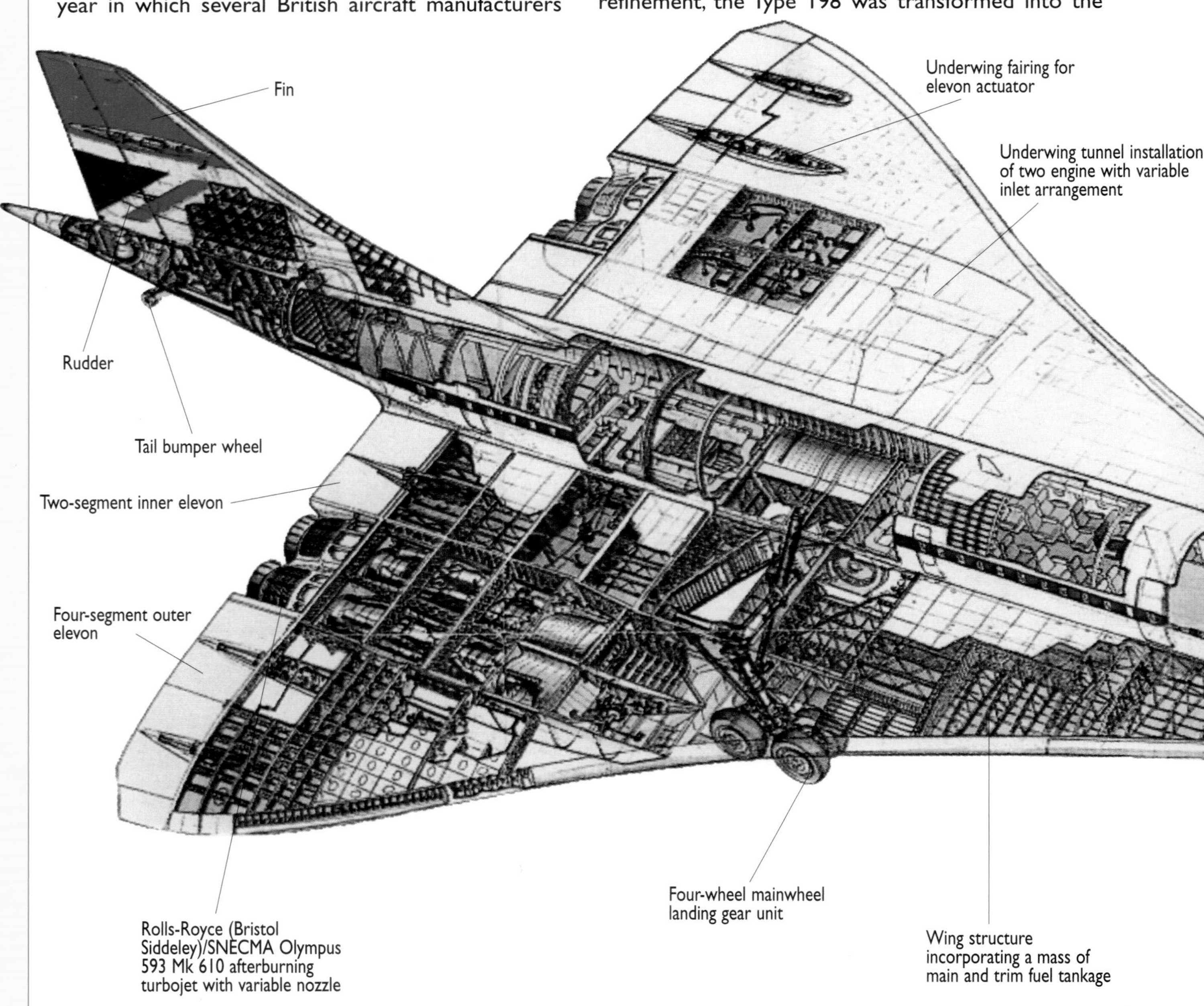

somewhat smaller Type 223 with a four-engined powerplant and provision for 110 passengers carried on the route linking London and New York.

As the British were proceeding in this fashion, the French were undertaking a similar national effort directed at basically the same type of aeroplane. By 1961 this process had led to the concept of the Sud-Aviation Super Caravelle which, it soon emerged, bore a striking similarity to the Type 223 as a result of the convergence of thinking by the British and French design teams.

Throughout these two separate design efforts, the British and French governments had become all too aware of the high cost that would be entailed in the final design, development, manufacture and marketing of the supersonic airliners at a purely national level. Both governments therefore decided that a common approach offered commercial as well as conceptual advantages, and the two separate national projects were amalgamated into one collaborative programme. The required inter-governmental agreement was signed on 29 November 1962, and listed the principal airframe elements as the British Aircraft Corporation and Aérospatiale, into which Bristol and Sud respectively had been absorbed, and the main powerplant elements as Rolls-Royce and SNECMA:

Aérospatiale/BAe Concorde

Type: Supersonic airliner

Accommodation: Flightcrew of up to four and, in a cabin 129ft 0in (39.32m) long, 8ft 7.5in (2.63m) wide and 6ft 5in (1.96m) high, up to 144 passengers in a four-abreast seating plan at 32in (0.81m) pitch or 128 passengers in a four-abreast arrangement at 34in (0.86m) pitch; British Airways has the cabin of its aircraft arranged for 100 passengers

Powerplant: Four Rolls-Royce (Bristol Siddeley)/SNECMA Olympus 593 Mk 610 turbojets each rated at 38,050lb st (169.25kN) with afterburning, and supplied with fuel from an internal capacity of 26,350Imp gal (119,787 litres)

Weights: Empty operating 173,500lb (78,700kg); typical payload 25,000lb (11,340kg); maximum take-off 408,000lb (185,069kg)

Performance: Maximum cruising speed 1,354mph (2,179km/h) or Mach 2.05 at 51,300ft (15,635m); initial climb rate 5,000ft (1,525m) per minute; service ceiling about 60,000ft (18,290m); range 3,870 miles (6,228km) at Mach 2.02 with maximum payload

Dimensions: Span 83ft 10in (25.56m); length 203ft 9in (62.10m); height 37ft 5in (11.40m); wing area 3,856.0sq ft (358.25sq m)

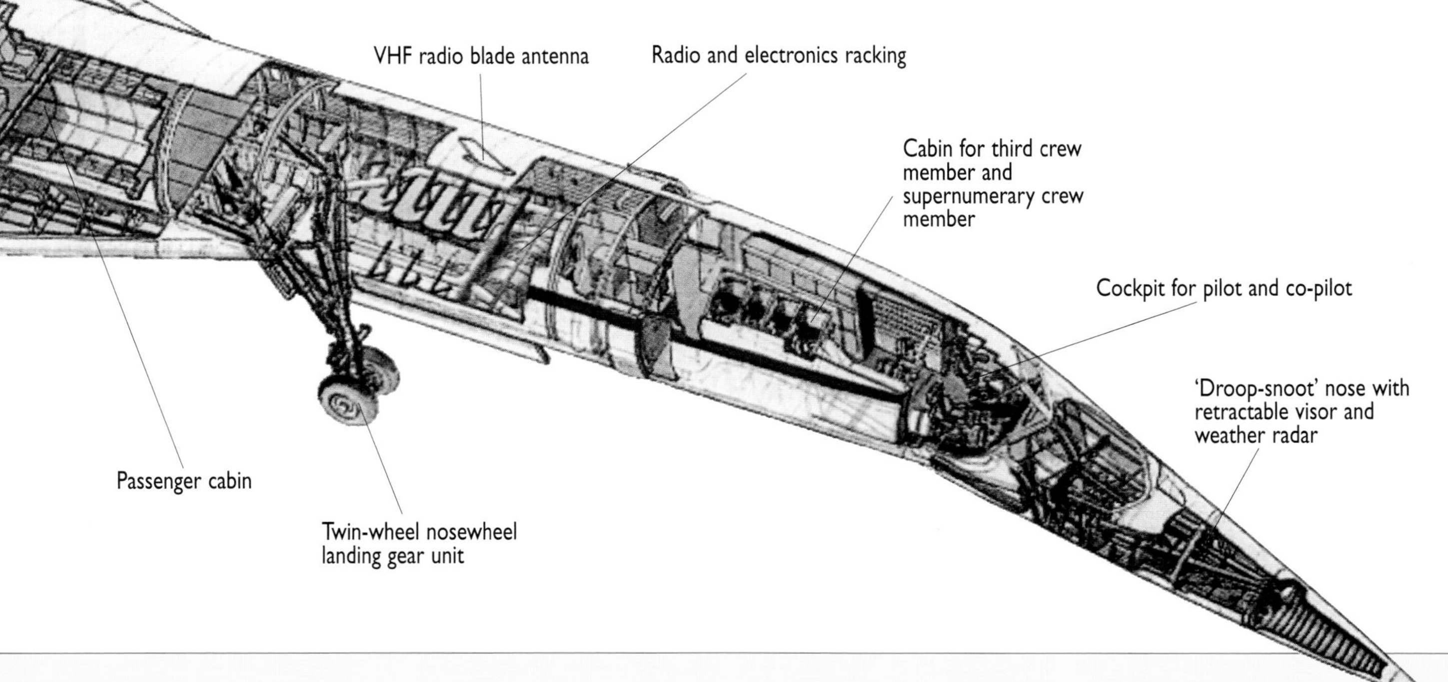

One of the most distinctive features of the Concorde is its large delta wing, which has fixed leading edges of ogival shape and a virtually straight trailing edge carrying powerful elevons (inboard and outboard of the twin engine installations) that are moved collectively for pitch control and differentially for lateral control.

the Type 223 had been planned round the Bristol Siddeley Olympus afterburning turbojet, and Bristol Siddeley had now been taken over by Rolls-Royce.

The collaborative airliner, which was later named Concorde, was undertaken in a number of related and interdependent steps including the construction and thorough testing and evaluation of two prototypes known as Concordes 001 and 002, the incorporation of any changes in two pre-production aircraft originally known as Concordes 01 and 02 and then as Concordes 101 and 102, and only then the launch of production with Concorde 201. Production of an initial batch of 16 aircraft was authorised by the two governments, and production of major airframe and engine components was divided between companies in the UK and France without duplication. Separate final assembly lines were set up at Filton and Toulouse for the assembly of alternate aircraft in the UK and France.

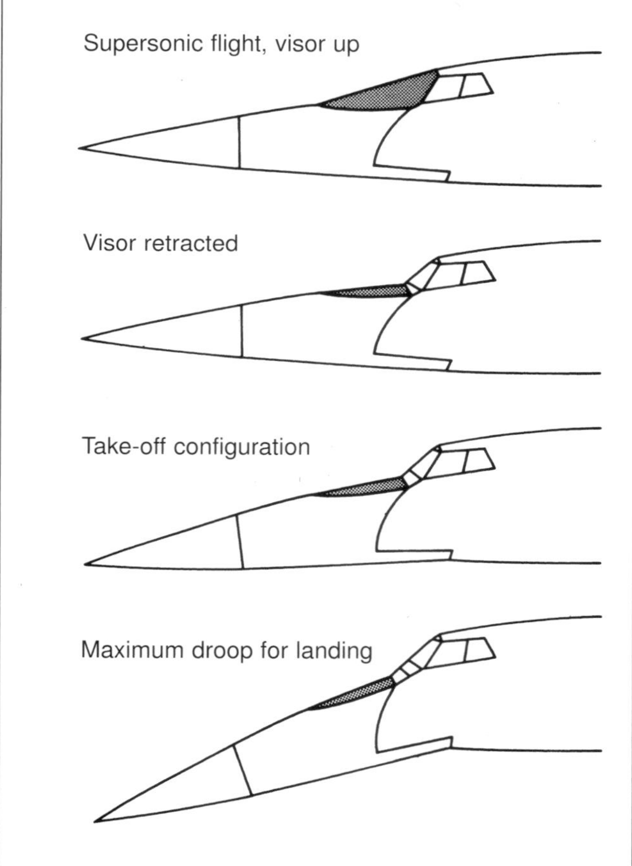

The 'droop-snoot' nose can be raised with a visor for improved contours in supersonic flight or to a fully drooped position with the visor lowered to provide an adequate field of vision as the aeroplane lands at a high angle.

Concorde 001 first lifted off from Toulouse on 2 March 1969, first reached Mach 1 on 1 October 1969, and first attained Mach 2 on 4 November 1970 (in the course of its 102nd flight). Concorde 002 was the first to fly in the UK, lifting off from Filton on 9 April 1969.

The two prototypes were slightly smaller than the standard established for the production aircraft, which had longer front and rear fuselages, revised nose visors, changes to the wing geometry, and an uprated powerplant. These new features were progressively introduced on Concorde 101 that was first flown from Toulouse on 17 December 1971, and on Concorde 102 first flown from Filton on 10 January 1973. The definitive production standard was incorporated in the first production aircraft, which were the Concordes 201 and 202 first flown at Toulouse and Filton on 6 December 1973 and 13 February 1974 respectively. Concordes 203 to 216 were completed alternately by the two assembly lines, the last two aircraft making their initial flights on 26 December 1978 and 20 April 1979 respectively.

The Concorde received full certification for passenger-carrying operations in France on 13 October 1975, and in the UK on 5 December 1975, and the type made its first revenue-earning flights simultaneously on 21 January 1976 with Air France and British Airways, which respectively operated services between Paris and Rio de Janeiro via Dakar, and between London and Bahrain. Services to Washington followed on 24 May 1976 and to New York in December 1977. British Airways flew a service from London to Singapore via Bahrain jointly with Singapore Airlines in 1979/80, and in the same period Braniff leased aircraft time from Air France and British Airways to extend the Washington service to Dallas/Fort Worth. British Airways extended its service from Washington to Miami in 1985, and for a time Air France operated services via Washington to Caracas and to Mexico. Many other destinations around the world have also been reached in an extensive charter programme run primarily by British Airways.

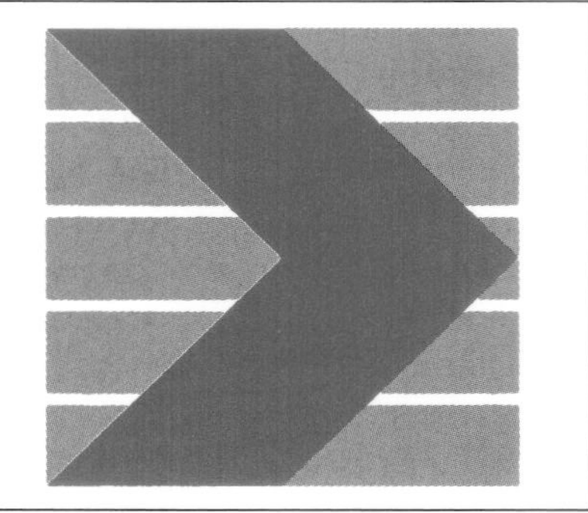

Canadian Airlines International

Country of origin: Canada

Generally accepted abbreviation: CP

Address: #2800-700 2nd Street SW, Calgary, Alberta T2P 2W2, Canada

Type of operation: International, regional and domestic scheduled and charter passenger and cargo services

Shareholding: Canadian Airlines International is part of the Canadian Airlines Corporation (formerly PWA Corporation), and American Airlines has a 33% shareholding

Subsidiaries: Air Atlantic (45%), Time Air (100%), Ontario Express (100%), Canadian Regional (100%), Canadian Holidays (100%), Canadian Holidays (USA) (100%), Air-way Aviation (33%), Greatours (100%), T3 Aircraft Support Services (14%), Transpacific Tours (100%), and Canadian Airlines Fuel Corporation (100%)

Marketing alliances: Air New Zealand, Alitalia, American Airlines, Japan Airlines, Lufthansa, Malaysia Airlines, Mandarin Airlines, Philippine Airlines, Qantas and VARIG

Notes: In 1994 Canadian Airlines International delivered more than 7.7 million passengers to more than 150 destinations in 18 countries on five continents. As a result of a codeshare agreement starting on 1 June 1995 with American Airlines, but approved by the US Department of Transportation for only one year, Canadian's service to cities in the USA increased from 10 to more than 60 daily flights. Canadian North is a separate division that operates a route network expanding from southern bases across the Northwest Territories, northern Manitoba and northern Quebec, and has signed a commercial agreement with Aklak Air, an air carrier owned and operated by Inuits in the Northwest Territories

Personnel: 15,200

Fleet: 12 x Airbus A320-200
43 x Boeing Model 737-200
4 x Boeing Model 747-400
11 x Boeing Model 767-300ER
10 x McDonnell Douglas DC-10-30

Orders: 2 x Airbus A320-200

Main bases and hubs: Calgary, Toronto and Vancouver

Route network: 110 destinations in Canada and 15 in the USA, while the major destinations in the Asian and Pacific regions include Auckland, Bangkok, Beijing, Hong Kong, Honolulu, Kuala Lumpur, Melbourne, Nadi, Nagoya, Shanghai, Sydney, Taipei, and Tokyo; in the European region Frankfurt, London, Milan, Munich, Paris, and Rome; in the North American region Banff, Boston, Calgary, Edmonton, Los Angeles, Montreal, San Francisco, Seattle, Toronto, Vancouver, Washington DC, and Winnipeg; and in the South and Central American regions Buenos Aires, Mexico City, Monterrey, Rio de Janeiro, Santiago and São Paulo. The codesharing agreement with American Airlines covers Atlanta, Boston, Chicago, Dallas/Fort Worth, Denver, Fort Lauderdale, Fort Myers, Honolulu, Houston, Las Vegas, Los Angeles, Miami, Minneapolis/St Paul, New Orleans, New York, Orange County, Orlando, Philadelphia, Phoenix, St Louis, St Petersburg, San Diego, San Francisco, Sarasota, Seattle, Tampa, Washington, and West Palm Beach. Canadian Airlines International also plans services to Delhi, Ho Chi Minh City and Manila

Simulators: 3 x Boeing Model 737-200 Advanced
1 x Boeing Model 767-300ER

Maintenance services: Canadian Airlines International Maintenance & Engineering specialises in airframes and engines with 1,135 licensed airframe engineers

History: Canadian Airlines International, which ranks 28th in the world and 10th in North America, began operations on 1 January 1988 after being created in March 1987 by an amalgamation of Canadian Pacific Airlines, Eastern Provincial Airways, Nordair and Pacific Western Airlines. Between 1991 and 1994 Canadian Airlines International streamlined and consolidated its operations and fleet, reached a voluntary financial restructuring of more than $700 million of debt, and negotiated an agreement with the AMR Corporation including a $246 million equity investment by AMR.

The largest single element in the merger that created Canadian Airlines International was Canadian Pacific Airlines, whose origins can be traced back to 1928, when Major General Sir James O'Brien amalgamated the Canadian Fairchild Company, Laurentide Air Services and other Canadian transportation elements to create Inter-Provincial Airways. On the west coast of Canada and at much the same time, James Richardson had merged Commercial and Pacific Airways to form Western Canada Airways. In 1930 Inter-Provincial Airways and Western Canada Airways merged as Canadian Airways, the immediate predecessor of Canadian Pacific Airlines, or CP Air as it was known later in its life. In 1933 the Canadian Pacific Railways organisation took a major shareholding in the airline, which operated a fleet of some 60 aircraft including 14 Junkers W 33 and W 34 machines.

The consolidation of 30 January 1942 between Canadian Airways and nine smaller operators (Arrow Airways, Dominion Skyways, Ginger Coote Airways, Mackenzie Air Service, Prairie Airways, Quebec Airways, Starratt Airways, Wings Ltd and Yukon Southern Air Transport) produced Canadian Pacific Airlines. During World War II, however, there was considerable dispute about the nature of the route network to be operated by the new airline, for it was the policy of the Canadian government not to permit direct competition by two Canadian operators on the same routes. This attitude inevitably favoured the state-owned Trans-Canada Air Lines, and as a result, Canadian Pacific Airlines ended World War II with a large fleet of aircraft whose only modern types were nine examples of the Lockheed Lodestar.

The old aircraft were soon supplemented by 17 Douglas C-47 military transports adapted for the civil role, but Canadian Pacific Airlines received little joy in air route allocations until 1948, when Canada's entitlement of routes to the Far East and Australia came under discussion: at this time Trans-Canada Air Lines lacked adequate equipment and personnel to take up the country's options, which therefore went to Canadian Pacific Airlines.

For its expanded service network the airline needed new and better equipment, and settled

initially on four examples of the Canadair C-4 that was the Canadian licence-built version of the Douglas DC-4, and the first of these aircraft was delivered in May 1949 for the launch of the service from Canada to Australia, via the Hawaiian Islands and Fiji, on 13 July of the same year, with a service to Hong Kong following from 19 September. In the following year Canadian Pacific Airlines took delivery of a number of DC-4 aircraft surplus to the requirements of Pan American World Airways, and these machines remained in service until 1953, when the airline took delivery of its first Douglas DC-6B.

As the airline's international route network was developing, so too was its domestic network as Canadian Pacific Airlines bought five Convair CV-240 twin-engined airliners from Continental Airlines, the first of these aircraft being received on 22 December 1952 and flying its first service on the route linking Vancouver and Sandspit on 2 February 1953. On 16 October 1953 the airline flew its first service to a South American destination (from Vancouver to Peru via Mexico) with the DC-6B.

During this period the Americans and Canadians were co-operating on the construction of the DEW (Distant Early Warning) line of radar stations between Baffin Island in the east and the border of the Yukon and Alaska in the west, and to provide a capability for the delivery of materials to the DEW Line's inhospitable sites, Canadian Pacific Airlines bought eight Curtiss C-46F transports from Flying Tigers. The first of these machines was received on 28 January 1955 and the type remained in service with Canadian Pacific Airlines until the early 1960s.

During this period many of the airline's domestic services were reallocated to other operators, most notably Pacific Western and Transair, which also acquired some of the C-46F transports as these became surplus to Canadian Pacific Airlines' requirements. On 3 June 1955 the airline operated its first trans-polar service from Vancouver to Amsterdam via Edmonton and Sondre Stromfjord with a DC-6B: Canadian Pacific Airlines had selected Amsterdam as its primary European destination as Trans-Canada Air Lines operated into London.

In 1958 Canadian Pacific Airlines received its first turboprop-powered type in the form of the Bristol Britannia 314, of which the first was delivered on 9 April. The Britannia had been ordered for use on the trans-polar route to Amsterdam, and flew its first service to the Netherlands on 1 June, with additional services to Tokyo and Hong Kong following on 23 August. After two unsuccessful efforts to operate the de Havilland Comet turbojet-powered airliner in the early 1950s, Canadian Pacific Airlines finally received its first turbojet-powered aircraft, a Douglas DC-8-43 on 22 February 1961. The DC-8 replaced the Britannia on the trans-polar route to the Netherlands on 31 May 1961, and eventually replaced the DC-6B and Britannia on the whole of the airline's international network.

In the second half of 1968 the airline adopted the name CP Air. On 21 October the airline took delivery of its first Boeing Model 737-217, and with the introduction of this new type on its domestic network the airline was able to retire its last piston-engined aircraft, the DC-3 and DC-6B aircraft, on 27 April 1969. About one year later another Boeing type arrived in the form of the Model 727-17 three-turbofan airliner, of which the first was received on 11 March 1970. This new aircraft joined the Model 737 on the airline's domestic network.

The last two types to join the airline's fleet were the Boeing Model 747-217B and McDonnell Douglas DC-10-30 in 1973 and 1979 respectively. These two wide-body transports then undertook all of the airline's international services.

Cathay Pacific Airways

Country of origin: Hong Kong

Generally accepted abbreviation: CX

Address: Swire House, 9 Connaught Road, Central Hong Kong, Hong Kong

Type of operation: International and regional scheduled passenger and cargo services

Shareholding: Swire Pacific (43.91%), China Trust (10%), CAAC (5%), China Travel Service (5%)

Subsidiaries: Dragonair (43%) and Air Hong Kong (75%)

Marketing alliances: Codesharing with British Midland and Vietnam Airlines, and other agreements with Air Hong Kong, Air Mauritius, Dragonair, Japanese Airlines, Korean Air, Lufthansa, and Singapore International Airlines

Notes: Cathay Pacific Airways is the national flag carrier of Hong Kong, and is currently in the process of gaining a larger Chinese influence as Hong Kong approaches the time of its reversion to Chinese rule. In October 1995 the airline announced a codesharing agreement with British Midland on services to Glasgow, by which the service from Hong Kong to London is tied into a British Midland service from London to Glasgow. An agreement with China Airlines, completed in December 1995, was extended until February 1996 to allow two operators to fly between Hong Kong and Taiwan. Cathay Pacific Airways currently operates an extensive network of services from Hong Kong to 44 destinations in 27 countries

Personnel: 13,855

Fleet:
5 x Airbus A340-300
11 x Airbus A330-300
7 x Boeing Model 747-200B
4 x Boeing Model 747-200F
6 x Boeing Model 747-300
19 x Boeing Model 747-400
2 x Boeing Model 747-400F
4 x Boeing Model 777-200

Orders:
1 x Airbus A330-300
5 x Airbus A340-300
7 x Boeing Model 777-300

Options:
9 x Airbus A330-300/A340-300
6 x Boeing Model 747-400 (delivery up to 2000)
10 x Boeing Model 777-300

Main base and hub: Hong Kong

Route network: An African element to destinations such as Johannesburg and Mauritius; an American element to destinations including Los Angeles, New York, Toronto and Vancouver; an Australasian and Pacific Rim element to destinations such as Adelaide, Auckland, Bangkok, Beijing, Bombay, Brisbane, Cairns, Cebu, Colombo, Denpasar, Fukuoka, Hanoi, Ho Chi Minh City, Jakarta, Kaohsiung, Kuala Lumpur, Manila, Melbourne, Nagoya, Osaka, Perth, Pinang, Sapporo, Seoul, Singapore, Surabaya, Sydney, Taipei, and Tokyo; a European element to destinations including Amsterdam, Frankfurt, London, Manchester, Paris, Rome, Stockholm, and Zürich; a Middle

Eastern element to destinations such as Bahrain and Dubai; and a specialised cargo element to destinations including Bahrain, Bombay, Chicago, Dubai, Frankfurt, London, Los Angeles, Melbourne, New York, Paris, Seoul, Sydney, Taipei, Tokyo, Toronto, and Vancouver

Simulators: 1 x Airbus A340
1 x Boeing Model 747-200
3 x Boeing Model 747-400
1 x Boeing Model 777
1 x Lockheed L-1011-1 TriStar

Maintenance services: See below

History: Currently ranked 19th in the world and fifth in Asia, Cathay Pacific Airways was established on 24 September 1946 to implement a freight service between Shanghai and Sydney. The airline received its first equipment, one Douglas DC-3 two-engined transport, in late September, and two machines of the same type followed on 3 October. In 1948 the John Swire organisation took a majority shareholding in the operator, and since that time various Swire groups have held an interest in Cathay Pacific.

On 7 September 1949 the company took delivery of its first Douglas C-54 Skymaster four-engined transport, allowing it to expand its route network during the following five years to Calcutta, Saigon and Borneo. Cathay Pacific received its first pressurised aeroplane, a Douglas DC-6, on 1 December 1954, and this was followed by delivery of a DC-6B on 9 June 1958. Further commercial success and expansion followed, and Cathay Pacific was able to take delivery of its first turbine-powered aircraft, one Lockheed L-188 Electra four-turboprop transport, on 1 April 1959, and exactly a fortnight later Cathay Pacific became the first airline in Asia to place this type into service. In 1959 Cathay Pacific merged with Hong Kong Airways, an associate of BOAC flying Vickers Viscount airliners between Far Eastern destinations.

Technical competitiveness has always been important to Cathay Pacific, so in 1961 the airline ordered a single example of the Convair CV-880 four-jet transport, and this machine arrived on 20 February 1962 for a debut in revenue-earning service on the route linking Hong Kong and Tokyo via Manila on 8 April. During the 1960s Cathay Pacific bought another eight examples of the CV-880, the last of them reaching the operator on 26 June 1970. Late in 1970, however, it was clear that Cathay Pacific's swelling level of success required greater payload capability, and the airline opted for the Boeing Model 707. Two such aircraft were bought from Northwest Orient Airlines, the first entering service on 3 August 1971. Cathay Pacific eventually acquired 12 Model 707 transports from Northwest Orient, the last arriving in August 1974, and the availability of this type allowed the retirement of the CV-880, which flew its last Cathay Pacific service on 15 September 1972.

Between 1971 and 1974 Cathay Pacific continued to expand, and this persuaded the airline to investigate the advantage of operating wide-body aircraft. During March 1974, therefore, Cathay Pacific placed an order for two examples of the Lockheed L-1011-1 TriStar three-turbofan aircraft: the airline took delivery of the first of these machines on 8 August 1975 and placed it in service on 16 September.

By the second half of the 1980s Cathay Pacific was planning a westward expansion of its route network to points as far distant as London, and accordingly placed an order for the Boeing Model 747-267B with a powerplant of four Rolls-Royce RB211 turbofans. The airline took delivery of the first of these machines on 20 July 1979, and operated its first service to London with this type on 17 July 1980. Eventually the airline operated a fleet of 38 such 'jumbo jets' on passenger and freight operations to a growing number of long-haul destinations. Further capability has been provided by the adoption of the Boeing Model 777 airliner and the A330 and A340 airliners produced in Europe by Airbus.

The Swire Group is also associated with the Hong Kong Aircraft Engineering Company, which was formed in November 1950 to carry out maintenance of Cathay Pacific's aircraft as well as those of numerous other airlines. Other companies within the Swire Group carry out ground handling and catering services at Hong Kong's Kai Tak Airport.

China Airlines

Country of origin: Taiwan

Generally accepted abbreviation: CI

Address: 131 Nanhing East Road, Section 3, Taipei 104, Taiwan

Type of operation: International, regional and domestic scheduled passenger and cargo services

Shareholding: China Aviation Development Foundation

Subsidiaries: Far Eastern Air Trans (19%) and Mandarin Airlines (100%)

Marketing alliances: Codesharing with Continental Airlines, Garuda and Vietnam Airlines, and purchase and exchange of space with Cargolux, Japan Asia Airways and Martinair

Personnel: 8,050

Fleet: 6 x Airbus A300B4
6 x Airbus A300-600R
3 x Boeing Model 737-200
3 x Boeing Model 747-200
6 x Boeing Model 747-200F
6 x Boeing Model 747-400
4 x Boeing Model 747SP
2 x Boeing Model 747-400
4 x McDonnell Douglas MD-11

Orders: 6 x Boeing Model 737-800
8 x Boeing Model 747-400

Options: 9 x Boeing Model 737-800
4 x Boeing Model 747-400
4 x Boeing Model 777-200

Main base and hub: Taipei

Route network: An African element to destinations such as Johannesburg; an Asian and Pacific element to destinations including Bangkok, Denpasar, Fukuoka, Ho Chi Minh City, Hong Kong, Honolulu, Jakarta, Kaohsiung,

Continued on next page

China Airlines continued from previous page

Kuala Lumpur, Manila, Nagoya, Okinawa, Phuket, Seoul, Singapore, and Tokyo; a European element to destinations such as Amsterdam, Frankfurt and Luxembourg; a Middle Eastern element to destinations such as Dubai; and a North American element to destinations including Anchorage, Chicago, Dallas, Los Angeles, New York and San Francisco

Simulators: 1 x Airbus A300B4
1 x Boeing Model 747-200
1 x Boeing Model 747-400
1 x McDonnell Douglas MD-11

Maintenance services: China Airlines General & Maintenance Office specialises in airframes and engines with 460 licensed airframe engineers, 100 licensed engine engineers, and 30 licensed avionics engineers

History: Currently ranked 33rd in the world and 10th in Asia, China Airlines is the national flag carrier of the Republic of China (Taiwan), and was established on 16 December 1959 by a number of retired Taiwanese air force personnel. The airline's first equipment was a pair of Consolidated PBY-5A Catalina amphibian flying boats, and these were initially operated on domestic charter services. The airline moved forward to scheduled domestic services in October 1962 with a mixed fleet of Douglas DC-3 and DC-4 aircraft as well as a number of Curtiss C-46 Commando transports. In 1965 China Airlines became the national flag carrier of Taiwan.

Late in 1969 China Airlines moved into the world of turbine-powered aircraft with the receipt of the first of two NAMC YS-11 twin-turboprop airliners, but before this the airline had launched its first international service on 2 December 1966 with a Lockheed L-1049H Super Constellation on the route linking Taipei and Saigon. The L-1049H operated this service up to March 1976, when it was replaced by the airline's first Boeing Model 727-109 three-turbofan airliner. The L-1049H remained in service up to 1980, being used only for charter work within South-East Asia.

To allow expansion of its route network and payload capability, China Airlines placed an order for two examples of the Boeing Model 707-309C four-turbofan transport, and the first of these was received on 7 November 1969. In February 1970 the availability of this long-haul type allowed the inauguration of a new route to San Francisco via Tokyo, and intermediate halts at Los Angeles and Honolulu were later added.

From 1971 to 1977 China Airlines operated four examples of the Sud-Aviation Caravelle for domestic and charter work, but in 1976 these were replaced by three examples of the Boeing Model 737-281 twin-turbofan airliner, of which the first was received on 9 April 1976. China Airlines was also improving its long-haul capability with the acceptance of the first Boeing Model 747 four-turbofan wide-body aircraft in the form of the Model 747-132 and Model 747SP, of which the first examples were delivered on 16 May 1975 and 6 April 1977 respectively. To help expand its position in the regional market, China Airlines has operated the Airbus A300 since 22 June 1982, while for the long-haul routes that do not require the capacity of the Model 747, two Boeing Model 767-209 twin-turbofan airliners were ordered: the first of these entered service between Taipei and Hong Kong on 30 December 1982. On this date China Airlines became the first airline in Asia to operate the type and the first airline in the world to operate both the A300 and the Model 767.

China Airlines currently operates a fleet of Airbus, Boeing and McDonnell Douglas aircraft, and the most important change in recent years has been the adoption of the Model 737-800 version of the Model 737 twin-turbofan series in moderately large numbers for an improvement on the airline's short-haul capabilities. Shares of China Airlines were first listed on the Taiwan stock exchange in 1993.

Continental Airlines

Country of origin: USA

Generally accepted abbreviation: CO

Address: PO Box 4607, 2929 Allen Parkway, Houston, Texas 77019, USA

Type of operation: International, regional and domestic scheduled passenger services

Shareholding: Continental Airlines is a publicly quoted company in which Air Canada has a 19.6% shareholding

Subsidiaries: America West Airlines (17.7%)

Marketing alliances: Codesharing with Air Canada (together with other joint ventures), Alitalia, America West Airlines, Czech Airlines, and joint marketing with SAS

Notes: In August 1995 the application to amend its codesharing agreement with Alitalia encountered stiff opposition as the change would allow Continental Airlines to fly transatlantic services using Alitalia's designator codes

Personnel: 43,000

Fleet:
33 x Boeing Model 727-200
13 x Boeing Model 737-100
18 x Boeing Model 737-200
65 x Boeing Model 737-300
37 x Boeing Model 737-600
17 x Boeing Model 757-200
28 x McDonnell Douglas DC-9-32
1 x McDonnell Douglas DC-10-10
16 x McDonnell Douglas DC-10-30
6 x McDonnell Douglas MD-81
56 x McDonnell Douglas MD-82
6 x McDonnell Douglas MD-83

Orders:
8 x Boeing Model 757-200
12 x Boeing Model 767-300
5 x Boeing Model 777

Options:
46 x Boeing Model 737-500
25 x Boeing Model 757-200

Main bases and hubs: Cleveland, Denver, Guam, Honolulu, Houston and Newark

Route network: A domestic element to 90 destinations in the USA and an international element to 56 destinations in countries and regions such as Australia, Canada, Central America, Ecuador, France, Germany, Indonesia, Japan, Mexico, Micronesia, New Zealand, the Philippines, Spain, and the UK. Continental Airlines also operates an extensive network of domestic feeder services in the guise of Continental Express

Simulators:
1 x Boeing Model 727-200
1 x Boeing Model 727-224
1 x Boeing Model 737-200
1 x Boeing Model 737-300
1 x Boeing Model 737-500
1 x Boeing Model 757-200

Continued on next page

Continental Airlines continued from previous page

1 x McDonnell Douglas DC-9-30
1 x McDonnell Douglas DC-10-10/30
1 x McDonnell Douglas MD-82

History: Currently rated fifth in the world and fifth in the USA, Continental Airlines can trace its history to 6 April 1926, when Varney Speed Lines (South West Division) started life with contracts to carry air mail for the US Post Office. Varney Air Lines was taken over by United Airlines on 30 June 1930, but in July 1934 this operation again became a separate entity as Varney Air Transport began passenger and air mail services on the route linking El Paso with Albuquerque and Pueblo, using three examples of the Lockheed Vega high-wing transport. In 1936 Varney Air Transport bought the route between Pueblo and Denver from Wyoming Air Service and, with this expansion of its route network, moved base from El Paso to Denver, where it changed its name to Continental Airlines on 1 July 1937.

During World War II Continental Airlines was one of the many operators that carried out military transport and training duties for the US Army Air Forces, but it reverted to civil operations in 1945, and in 1948 was sufficiently well re-established to buy the latest short-haul equipment in the form of the Convair CV-240. At the end of 1954 Continental Airlines bought Pioneer Airlines and its extensive route network in Texas and New Mexico. On 1 May 1957 Continental Airlines started a service on the route linking Chicago and Los Angeles via Kansas City and Denver: flown with Douglas DC-7B four-engined airliners, this operation marked Continental Airlines' emergence as a main-line trunk carrier within the United States. The airline started to use the Vickers Viscount 812 four-turboprop airliner on the Chicago to Los Angeles service on 26 May 1958, thereby moving into the field of turbine-powered civil aircraft, and went one step further on 8 June 1959 when it started to operate the Boeing Model 707-124 turbojet-powered airliner.

In 1963 Continental Airlines again moved its main base, this time to Los Angeles, and by 1969 had further enlarged its route network to the west by the inclusion of destinations such as the Hawaiian Islands, which were served from Chicago in an operation inaugurated on 9 September 1969. On 18 May 1970 Continental Airlines received its first Boeing Model 747 wide-body four-turbofan transport, and the availability of this high-capacity type did much to speed the growth of the airline even though the Model 747 was later supplemented by the introduction of a large number of the three-turbofan McDonnell Douglas DC-10 series. Continental Airlines started an expansion to the east during 1974 with services to destinations such as Miami, followed later by Newark and Washington DC.

During October 1981 the Texas Air Corporation, parent of Texas International Airlines, bought a controlling interest in Continental Airlines: Texas International Airlines, known until 1969 as Trans-Texas Airways and originally created in 1940 as Aviation Enterprises, had begun scheduled services in October 1947. The operations of Continental Airlines and Texas International Airlines were consolidated and combined from 31 October 1982 to create a single carrier under the name Continental. This was not a good time for airlines, however, as the price of fuel was increasing rapidly and passenger demand was declining as operators were forced to raise their fares; as a result, Continental was compelled to file for Chapter 11 protection against its creditors in the course of September 1983. Continental's domestic network was reduced from 78 to 25 destinations and its personnel strength declined from 12,000 to 4,200. Following approval by the US bankruptcy court of its plan for reorganisation, submitted in September 1985, Continental emerged from Chapter 11 protection during 1986 to operate a network serving 57 domestic destinations from primary hubs at Denver and Houston, and 28 international destinations in Australasia, Canada, Europe, the Far East and Mexico. In the same year Continental was integrating the services of New York Air and the People Express Group into its own operation after the purchases of these airlines during February.

Frank Lorenzo, Continental's owner, sold his share in the airline to SAS in August 1990, and Continental once again filed for Chapter 11 protection during December 1990. The airline emerged from a 29-month Chapter 11 re-organisation in May 1993 after Air Canada and Texas-based Air Partners had received approval of the bankruptcy court to invest $450 million. Shortly before this, in March 1993, Continental was a major operator of the Boeing Models 727, 737 and 757 as well as the McDonnell Douglas MD-80 series, but had cancelled firm orders and options for 20 Airbus A330 and A340 aircraft. Shortly after emerging from Chapter 11 protection, however, the airline placed orders for a total of 92 Boeing aircraft with options on 98 more. In August 1993 Continental signed a strategic alliance with Air France.

CSA Czech Airlines

Country of origin: Czech Republic

Generally accepted abbreviation: OK

Address: Airport Praha, Ruzyne 16008, Czech Republic

Type of operation: International, regional and domestic scheduled and charter passenger and cargo services

Shareholding: The Fund of National Property, Konsolidacni Bank and EBRD

Subsidiaries: Slovak Air Services, CSA Airtours, and Amadeus Marketing CSA Ltd

Marketing alliances: Codesharing with Luxair, joint services with Air France, Iberia and Turkish Airlines, and block space agreements with KLM, LOT-Polish Airlines and Lufthansa

Personnel: 3,870

Fleet:
2 x Airbus A310-300
2 x ATR 42-300
4 x ATR 72-200
2 x Boeing Model 737-400
5 x Boeing Model 737-500
3 x Tupolev Tu-134A
4 x Tupolev Tu-154M

Orders: 5 x Boeing Model 737-500

Main base and hub: Prague

Route network: This includes most European capitals as well as cities in the Near, Middle and Far East, North and West Africa, and North and Central America, and including Abu Dhabi, Athens, Bahrain, Bangkok, Beirut, Bucharest, Cairo, Damascus, Dubai, Geneva,

Istanbul, Kiev, Kuwait, Larnaca, London, Lwów, Manchester, Montreal, Ostrava, Riga, Sharjah, Singapore, Sofia, Tatry/Poprad, Toronto, and Zürich, and, as a result of codesharing with Continental Airlines, Baltimore, Chicago, Cleveland, Newark and Washington DC

Maintenance services: CSA Czech Airlines Technical Division specialises in airframes with 380 licensed airframe engineers, 85 licensed engine engineers, and 140 licensed avionics engineers

History: The operator now known as Czech Airlines came into its current existence on 26 March 1995 as a redesignation of Ceskoslovenské Statni Aerolinie (CSA), which was established as the Czechoslovak national flag carrier on 28 July 1923. CSA flew its first service on 28 October 1923 between Prague and Uzhorod using the Aero A.14, but later equipment included the de Havilland D.H.50 and Farman Goliath purchased from the UK and France respectively. In 1930 CSA started its first international service, in this instance to Zagreb in Yugoslavia, and the international route network was slowly expanded to destinations in Austria, Romania and the USSR. During the 1930s CSA purchased the Savoia-Marchetti S.M.73 from Italy, and four Airspeed Envoy and one Saro Cloud from the UK.

From 15 March 1939 the operations of the CSA and Ceskoslovenské Letecká Společnost (CLS) were nationalised and private airlines were integrated into those of Deutsche Lufthansa after Germany's annexation of Czechoslovakia, but CSA reverted to state-owned status after the end of World War II, resuming operations on 1 March 1946 with Douglas C-47 and Junkers Ju 52/3m services to a number of European capitals. By the end of 1947 CSA was planning larger-scale operations including transatlantic services with the Douglas DC-4. These plans were completely revised after the communist assumption of power in Czechoslovakia during 1948.

This meant the effective end of purchases from Western sources in these early days of the Cold War, and CSA therefore had to turn to Soviet sources of supply. Early in 1949 CSA bought the first two of an eventual eight Ilyushin Il-12 twin-engined transports that proved to be very limited in capability, and it was only in the mid-1950s that the airline was able to begin any real expansion by the purchase of the Ilyushin Il-14 twin-engined airliner, which was built under licence in Czechoslovakia. A major milestone in the airline's development took place in 1957, when CSA became the first foreign company to operate the twin-jet Tupolev Tu-104A, which entered service at first on CSA's services to Brussels, Moscow and Paris, and succeeded the Il-14 on the service linking Prague and London in April 1960.

Early in the same year CSA was finally able to begin the process of retiring its wholly obsolete Il-12 piston-engined aircraft in favour of the larger and more capable Ilyushin Il-18 four-turboprop type. Services to Bombay, Dakar and Djakarta were inaugurated, and discussion was started with the Canadian authorities about the possibility of a service to Montreal via Amsterdam. Thus by 1960 CSA was approaching the stage of becoming the communist world's first airline with a worldwide network.

On 3 February 1962 CSA launched a service to Havana in Cuba with a leased Bristol Britannia 318, and in May 1968 additional capability came with the airline's lease from Aeroflot of an Ilyushin Il-62 four-turbofan airliner, a type which CSA later bought. On 4 May 1970 CSA started its first service between Prague and New York via Amsterdam and Montreal, with the Il-62.

By the late 1970s CSA was operating an extensive network of routes between Prague and most European capitals as well as destinations in the Middle and Far East, West Africa, and North and Central America, using the Il-62 for longer-haul services and the Il-18 and Tupolev Tu-134 for shorter-haul services. The airline also flew a domestic network with types such as the Let L-410 Turbolet and the Yakovlev Yak-40.

With the collapse of the Soviet bloc in the late 1980s, CSA was finally able to start the process of discarding its Soviet-supplied aircraft, which were unreliable and costly to operate, and acquiring more-modern aircraft of Western origins as and when financing became available.

Air Traffic Control

One of the keys to successful air transport is safety for aircraft as they manoeuvre on the ground at the airport and as they traverse the airways linking the world's airports. The nerve centre of the airport in this respect is the control tower from which, at the world's busiest airports, controllers may co-ordinate up to 2,000 aircraft movements a day.

The tower is generally the dominating feature of any airport as it must be sufficiently tall to provide the controllers at its top with an unobstructed view across the whole aircraft-operating area of the airport. Control towers at larger airports have two control rooms. At the top is the visual control room, from which controllers exercise the responsibility for aircraft as they taxi, take-off, and prepare to land. In this control room assistants work on the aircraft departures and arrivals log from which landing charges are prepared, and operate the computer that prints out the estimated time of arrival of each flight and scheduled times of departure. A ground movement planning controller books 'slots' (available times) along the airways for departures.

Located further down the tower is the windowless approach control room in which approach controllers at radar scopes guide inbound traffic onto the relevant runways. This operation is made as smooth as possible to cause minimum delay to the airlines' schedules and the lives of the passengers, but should a delay occur through damage to or blocking of a runway, a shift in the wind direction, or unexpected overloading of the system, aircraft are directed into holding 'stacks', in which they fly a prescribed orbit around a radio beacon until they receive landing clearance. The aircraft in two or more stacks are integrated by the approach control team before they are handed over to the radar director, who then weaves the streams extending back from the runway threshold out along the approach path. A safe separation distance of 3 to 4 miles (4.8 to 6.4km) between incoming aircraft provides a landing interval of about one minute. Aircraft overflying the congested airport zone are controlled by a separate radar director.

The radar screens are ringed with concentric circles, called range marks, representing distances of 2, 5 and 10 (3.2, 8 and 16.1km) from the antenna. Using a compass rose laid over the radar scope, controllers can make an accurate determination of aircraft positions, and dotted and solid lines encircle radio navigation reference points. The radar echoes on the scope pinpoint each aeroplane: in modern displays with alphanumeric symbology, each 'target' is labelled with its flight number, altitude and route as a means of ensuring identification that is both rapid and sure.

The type of concentration required to track large numbers of aircraft as they fly at high speed in a small area is particularly intense, and controllers therefore work for only a two-hour period in any one shift, with a break of at least 30 minutes between periods.

Modern airliners are not affected by crosswinds to the same extent as their propeller-driven predecessors, but the planning process for a new airport still ensures that the runways are aligned along the line of the prevailing winds. Paved runways were originally laid out in a triangular pattern so that at least one of them was aligned relatively close to the wind from any direction, but the modern system has one or two runways aligned with the prevailing winds. With the triangular arrangement of intersecting runways, still seen at a number of longer-established major airports, it was possible for aircraft to take off from one and land on another, although only alternately, although the concept of parallel runways allows both to be operated simultaneously, even at busy times. A subsidiary runway may be built at an angle for use by small aircraft.

As a modern airliner may weigh some 400 tons as it lands at about 125mph (201km/h), it possesses considerable momentum and is difficult to stop. Consequently, the surface of the runway has to be strong and carefully graded for drainage, and scored with grooves to prevent an airliner's landing wheels from skidding on a film of water: grooves are made 2in (5cm) apart either by a cutting wheel or during construction when the surface is still soft, and require refurbishment about every six years. In conditions of rain, ice and snow, friction meters measure the runway's braking action and the information is relayed to pilots.

The flight plan, already filed by the airliner's crew before it boards its aeroplane, comes into effect at the moment the crew contacts air traffic control by calling for permission to start up the engines. Congestion along the route can result in delay until there is space for the flight on the airways, so it is important that an airliner becomes airborne at the time prescribed for its 'slot', as failure to meet this target means inevitable delay until a new 'slot' can be allocated.

Changing frequency from that used for permission to start the engines, the co-pilot radios the ground movement controller for clearance to taxi. From a 'nose-in' stand he asks for 'push-back' clearance, but before issuing permission for a nose- or tail-first departure of the airliner from the ramp, the

controller has to consider the effect that either manoeuvre will have on an airport crowded with aircraft already in motion or about to start moving. A simple clearance may mean that another flight will have to be re-routed to a stand or runway, and an erroneous decision can result in chaos.

On the taxiway, which is watched by the ground movement controller with binoculars or ground radar screen, the captain is given airways clearance. At most airfields this is in the form of a Standard Instrument Departure (SID) and a 'squawk': the SID is a route instruction informing the crew which levels (altitudes) and airways it must use to start the flight, while the 'squawk' is a four-figure number code which the crew sets on a transponder, which is a radio unit that transmits an incoming signal in a different form. The 'squawk' is displayed as an identification number beside the flight's echo on the air traffic controller's radar screen.

At the holding point on the taxiway just short of the designated runway, control of the airliner is transferred to an air traffic controller, whose task it is to guide the aircraft into the air.

The sky around any airport is filled with aircraft flying at different speeds and in different directions, and crossing over and under each other at different heights: the task of keeping them all separated is the primary responsibility of the air traffic (or tower) controller.

Generally there is a minimum separation time of one minute between two aircraft of the same type taking off in different directions, while if they are taking off in the same direction the time gap is two minutes, and a light aircraft lifting off behind a wide-body airliner may be held back by 10 minutes to avoid the turbulent air left in the airliner's wake.

As soon as an airliner has taken off and is committed to the climb on its SID, the air traffic controller will transfer responsibility for the machine to the first radar sector (departure) controller for further climb clearance toward cruising level. Aircraft usually follow airways, which are divided into three main altitude bands. The highest altitudes, between 45,000ft (13,715m) and the upper limit of usable airspace, are the zones for supersonic airliners and high-flying 'bizjets'; below them, subsonic airliners occupy the lower airways; and the levels below that zone are usually flown by slower propeller-driven aircraft. Many sectors are restricted to military use, and this often requires civil airways to be compressed into gaps between them.

A method of avoiding congestion is required in the busy sections of lower-altitude airways above the VOR (VHF Omnidirectional Range) navigation beacons where airways intersect, and this is provided by area controllers. These controllers are located in specialised air traffic control centres away from airports, and are responsible for huge volumes of airspace. Area controllers keep track of dozens of aircraft at a time on large-diameter radar scopes, and advise pilots of the altitudes and headings to fly as a means of keeping clear of congested regions.

Delta Air Lines

Country of origin: USA

Generally accepted abbreviation: DL

Address: Atlanta International Airport, Hartsfield, Atlanta, Georgia 30320, USA

Type of operation: International, regional and domestic scheduled passenger and cargo services

Shareholding: Sanford C. Bernstein, the Capital Group, and the Fidelity Management Trust

Subsidiaries: Singapore Airlines (2.7%) and Swissair (4.5%)

Marketing alliances: Codesharing with Aeroflot, Aeromexico, All Nippon Airways, Austrian Airlines, Korean Air, Malev Hungarian Airlines, Sabena, Singapore Airlines, Swissair, TAP-Air Portugal, VARIG, Vietnam Airlines, and Virgin Atlantic

Notes: Delta Air Lines operates more than 2,600 flights per day to 197 cities in 26 countries around the world, and also operates a wide-ranging feeder system within the USA in the form of Delta Connection

Personnel: 59,100

Fleet:
129 x Boeing Model 727-200
54 x Boeing Model 737-200
13 x Boeing Model 737-300
89 x Boeing Model 757
15 x Boeing Model 767-200
26 x Boeing Model 767-300
17 x Boeing Model 767-300ER
55 x Lockheed L-1011 TriStar
13 x McDonnell Douglas MD-11
120 x McDonnell Douglas MD-88

Orders:
4 x Boeing Model 757
16 x Boeing Model 767ER
3 x McDonnell Douglas MD-11
18 x McDonnell Douglas MD-90

Options:
78 x Boeing Model 737
36 x Boeing Model 757
14 x Boeing Model 767ER
22 x McDonnell Douglas MD-11
86 x McDonnell Douglas MD-90

Main bases and hubs: Atlanta, Cincinnati, Dallas/Fort Worth, Frankfurt, Los Angeles, New York, Orlando and Salt Lake City

Route network: A domestic element comprising 192 destinations in the USA; an American element to destinations including Acapulco, Calgary, Edmonton, Guadalajara, Hamilton, Ixtapa/Zihuatanejo, Juarez, Mazatlán, Mexico City, Montreal, Nassau, Puerto Vallarta, St Croix, St Thomas, San Juan, Toronto, and Vancouver; an Asian and Middle Eastern element to destinations such as Bombay, Nagoya, Seoul and Tokyo; and a European element to destinations including Amsterdam, Athens, Barcelona, Berlin, Brussels, Bucharest, Budapest, Copenhagen, Dublin, Frankfurt, Helsinki, Istanbul, Lisbon, London, Madrid, Manchester, Munich, Paris, Prague, Rome, St Petersburg, Shannon, Stuttgart, Vienna, Warsaw, and Zürich

Simulators:
1 x Airbus A310-300
6 x Boeing Model 727-200
2 x Boeing Model 737-200
1 x Boeing Model 737-300EFIS
3 x Boeing Model 757-200
1 x Boeing Model 767-200
1 x Boeing Model 767-300ER
1 x Lockheed L-1011-1 TriStar
2 x Lockheed L-1011-250 TriStar
1 x Lockheed L-1011-500 TriStar
1 x McDonnell Douglas DC-9-30
1 x McDonnell Douglas MD-11
5 x McDonnell Douglas MD-88

Maintenance services: Delta Air Lines specialises in airframes and engines with 4,500 licensed airframe engineers, 4,500 licensed engine engineers, and 2,400 licensed avionics engineers

History: In 1925 C.E. Woolman created Delta Air Services as the world's first commercial crop-dusting company. On 16 June 1929 the company began passenger operations between Atlanta and Birmingham (Alabama), and shortly after this extended the service to Salas (Texas) via Jackson (Mississippi). However, passenger services were suspended on 16 September 1930 when Delta did not obtain any of the new air mail contracts that would have provided a measure of the subsidy required during the depression. The successful applicant for the air mail contract was American Airlines, which added some of Delta's routes into its own network.

The airline introduced its current name, Delta Air Lines, during 1934, and in the same year received its first air mail contract for the route linking Charleston (South Carolina) and Fort Worth (Texas), using Travel Air aircraft. In November 1940 Delta Air Lines received its first Douglas DC-3, and by 1942 was flying five DC-3 and four Lockheed L-10A Electra aircraft for services on a network that included Cincinnati, Savannah and New Orleans.

In December 1941 Delta Air Lines trans-

ferred two-thirds of its fleet to aid in the American war effort after the United States entered the war. During February 1942 the airline created a modification centre at its Atlanta base, where 1,000 aircraft were processed. Emergency work on 45 Boeing B-29 Superfortress bombers was also undertaken in 1945.

Returning largely to civil operations as the end of World War II approached, Delta Air Lines was granted the prime service between Chicago and Miami during July 1945, and operated this service on a four-times-per-day basis from 1 December 1945 with DC-3 aircraft that flew a route with many intermediate stops for the loading and offloading of passengers. The airline inaugurated a non-stop service in November 1946 using Douglas DC-4 four-engined aircraft, the first of which the airline received on 14 December 1945. Three years later, on 5 November 1948, Delta Air Lines accepted the first of an initial three Douglas DC-6 aircraft, and these aircraft replaced the DC-4 on the Miami route during December. The DC-6 was replaced by the superior and fully pressurised Douglas DC-7 on 1 April 1954.

On its shorter-haul services Delta Air Lines used 20 Convair CV-340 aircraft, of which the first was delivered on 18 December 1952.

Chicago and Southern Air Lines merged with Delta Air Lines on 1 May 1953, and this amalgamation brought many new routes (including international services) and aircraft, the latter including eight undelivered CV-40 and six Lockheed L-649A Constellation aircraft. Eventually, Delta Air Lines operated 38 of the Convair aircraft, all of which were later upgraded to CV-440 standard. Another expansion took place on 1 February 1956 when the airline started services to New York and Washington using four Lockheed L-049 Constellations bought from Pan American World Airways.

By the autumn of 1958 the airline's fleet totalled 77, including 28 CV-440, 21 DC-7 and 12 DC-3 aircraft. On 18 September 1959 Delta Air Lines operated its first jet service, from New York to Atlanta, with a Douglas DC-8-11, of which the first had been received on 21 July 1959. Eight months later, on 15 May 1960, Delta Air Lines flew its first service with another four-engined jet airliner, the Convair CV-880.

Soon after this it became clear that a modern replacement was needed for the CV-440, and in April 1963 Delta Air Lines contracted for the delivery of an initial 14 examples of the Douglas DC-9-14 twin-jet type. The first of these was delivered on 9 June 1966, and Delta Air Lines was the first airline to operate the DC-9 on a revenue-earning basis when the type entered service on 8 December of that year.

By 1969 the airline had become an all-jet operator, its fleet comprising 129 aircraft in the form of 68 Douglas DC-9, 45 DC-8 and 16 CV-880 aircraft. Further development of the airline's route network and equipment followed, a notable landmark being the arrival of its first wide-body airliner, a Boeing Model 747-132, on 26 September 1970: this flew its first commercial flight on 25 October 1970. On 10 October 1972 Delta Air Lines leased its first McDonnell Douglas DC-10-10 three-turbofan airliner from United Airlines.

On 1 August 1972 Northeast Airlines and Delta Air Lines merged, the former contributing a number of Fairchild FH-227 twin-turboprop and Boeing Model 727 three-turbofan transports to the combined airlines' fleet, together with many east coast destinations and services to the Bahamas and Bermuda. Delta Air Lines now provided services to 99 cities.

The DC-10 did not last long in service with Delta Air Lines, for the type was replaced by the Lockheed L-1011 TriStar, of which the airline received an initial example on 3 October 1973 for service from 16 November. Thus, in a period of only three years, Delta operated all three of the USA's first wide-body airliners.

On 1 May 1978 Delta Air Lines launched a new service to London from New Orleans and Atlanta with two examples of the L-1011-200 TriStar leased from TWA. Through the 1980s further expansion and re-equipment followed as Delta Air Lines absorbed Western Airlines in April 1987 and standardised on a combination of the Boeing Model 737 and McDonnell Douglas MD-80/90 series for its short-haul and/or low-density routes, the Boeing Model 727 for medium-haul routes, and a combination of the Boeing Models 757 and 767, the L-1011 TriStar and the McDonnell Douglas MD-11 for long-haul routes depending on density.

Delta Air Lines is currently rated third and fourth in the USA and the world respectively.

Airport Layout

The airports that serve the world's major cities are really towns in their own right as they are intended to provide all the services needed not only by travellers and airport staff, but also by the traveller's 'meeters and greeters' and the increasingly large number of people who visit airports to absorb the atmosphere and see the sights of modern air transport. Airports are also major points for the traveller's change between air services and surface transport in virtually every form. Moreover, as a result of their proximity to major urban centres, airports are also closely connected in environmental terms with nearby built-up areas and local countryside.

As air transport has evolved, the small grass airfields of the early days have grown out of all recognition, acquired concrete runways and terminal buildings and, unfortunately, become polluters in terms of noise, and have thus caused disaffection in the communities that have grown around them or into which they have themselves extended. This is a symptom typical of the development and exploitation of modern technology, in which benefits and problems seem to proliferate hand-in-hand.

This problem peaked in the 1980s and now appears to be less acute as the development of larger yet comparatively quieter aircraft has offered distinct advantages: greater size has trimmed the growth in the number of take-offs and landings, while quieter operation has led to a reduction in overall noise levels under flightpaths.

While the airport is faced with the difficulties of co-existence in its area whilst serving the interests of air travellers, airlines and its workers, the team that runs the operations at each airport must be involved primarily with the provision of safe, convenient and regular flights. As a result, the airport necessarily has to be sited in a location that provides approach and take-off paths clear of obstacles and other hazards; other requirements are runways of adequate length and strength, lighting that conforms fully with the relevant regulations, radar and radio aids suitable for the types of operation envisaged, and taxiways of the right width leading to ample parking areas close to the terminal buildings.

For many years, larger and heavier airliners demanded the creation of runways that were both longer and stronger, but the emergence of new propulsion and lift-enhancement technologies has begun to trim these lengths once more. Although aircraft up to a weight of 500 tons are now envisaged, the current standard runway of 12,000ft (3,665m) is thought to be adequate even under hot conditions when available engine power is reduced: the one exception to this tendency is the airport located at high altitude, where the safe take-off and landing distances are lengthened due to the lower air density.

In providing for the comfort and convenience of the increasing number of people who use airports, the authorities seek to offer the best possible access

by road, rail, and helicopter. The most demanding vehicle at the air/surface interface is the car, which places great demands on the provision of adequate parking space located as close as possible to terminal buildings that are well signposted and located as short a walking distance as possible between arrival/departure point and aircraft. Few airports can realistically claim to have satisfied all these complex requirements to an adequate degree, but all continue to push toward this elusive goal in a process of modernisation and expansion.

The task of the airport planner and operator has been complicated to a considerable degree by the fact that while passenger traffic has grown considerably, this growth has been comparatively outstripped by the increased volume of air freight. Airports are therefore faced with the need to provide good cargo-handling facilities and adequate warehouse space for customs clearance and other related activities.

It should never be forgotten that an airport is a business concern, and should function efficiently and economically. In the USA most major airports are owned or operated by city authorities, while most of the major airports in the UK are the responsibility of the British Airports Authority. Airports are extremely costly to operate, and one that handles less than about three million passengers per year has difficulty in generating income to overtake expenditure. The airport authorities generate revenue from airlines in the form of landing and parking fees, and from numerous concessions such as the renting of premises for offices, duty free and other shops, bars and restaurants.

Large airports have a major working population, ranging from air traffic controllers, customs and immigration officials to traffic clerks, loaders, apron personnel, caterers, administrative staff and flightcrews. Including personnel involved in aircraft maintenance, the workforce may total 50,000 or more; together with the workforce's families, an airport-dependent community can constitute more than 250,000 people.

Many of the airport staff live close to the airport in the type of community that has generally developed around an airport's perimeter as employment demand by the airport and its associated trades has grown. It is for this reason, therefore, that large, modern airports have become virtually embedded in built-up areas as towns have grown up around them.

Along the flightpaths to and from the runways, a major problem affecting nearby communities has always been noise, and this has often been aggravated by the pollution caused by increased traffic on local roads. Modern aircraft are comparatively quieter than the earlier jets, however, and this fact has gone some way to improving the environmental impact of airports. What cannot be denied is the importance of major airports to the economy of all advanced nations: trade, travel and overall prosperity of the modern world depend increasingly on the services offered by airports.

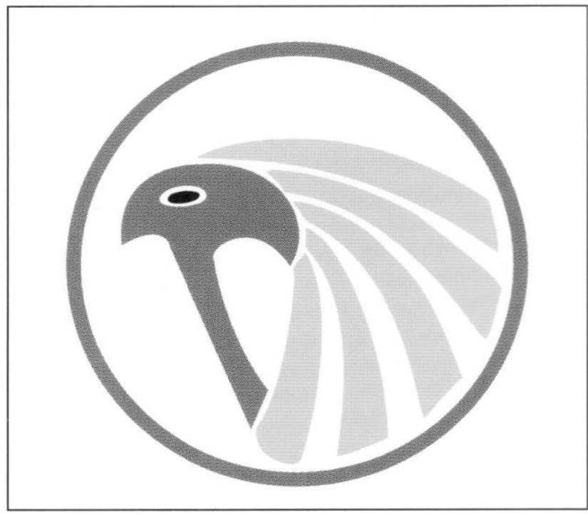

Egyptair

Country of origin: Egypt

Generally accepted abbreviation: MS

Address: Cairo International Airport, Cairo, Egypt

Type of operation: International, regional and domestic scheduled and charter passenger and cargo services

Shareholding: Government-owned

Marketing alliances: Joint services with Aeromexico, Air Sicilia, American Airlines, AOM French Airlines, Bangkok Airways, China Airlines, Cubana, Garuda, Japan Airlines, Korean Air, Philippine Airlines, Singapore Airlines, TWA, United Airlines and VARIG

Notes: Egyptair plans to use its new Airbus A340 aircraft on non-stop routes such as those from Cairo to Japan, the west coast of the USA, and Australia, and its new Boeing Model 777 aircraft on the routes from Cairo to London and New York

Personnel: 5,000

Fleet: 9 x Airbus A300-600R
3 x Airbus A300B4
7 x Airbus A320
3 x Airbus A340-200
1 x Airbus A340-300
3 x Boeing Model 737-200
5 x Boeing Model 737-500
2 x Boeing Model 747-300 Combi
3 x Boeing Model 767-200ER
2 x Boeing Model 767-300ER

Orders: 4 x Airbus A321-100
3 x Airbus A340-200
3 x Boeing Model 777-200

Options: 2 x Airbus A340-200
2 x Boeing Model 777

Main base and hub: Cairo

Route network: A domestic element to destinations such as Abu Simbel, Alexandria, Aswan, Cairo, Hurghada, Luxor, Mersa Matruh, New Valley, St Catherine, Sharm el Shaykh, and Taba; an African element to destinations including Abidjan, Accra, Addis Ababa, Asmara, Benghazi, Cape Town, Dar es Salaam, Entebbe, Harare, Johannesburg, Kano, Khartoum, Lagos, Nairobi, and Tunis; an American element to destinations such as Los Angeles and New York; a European element to destinations including Athens, Barcelona, Brussels, Budapest, Copenhagen, Düsseldorf, Frankfurt, Geneva, Istanbul, Kiev, Larnaca, London, Madrid, Milan, Moscow, Munich, Paris, Rome, Stockholm, Vienna, and Zürich; and a Middle and Far Eastern element to destinations such as Abu Dhabi, Aden, Amman, Bahrain, Bangkok, Beirut, Bombay, Damascus, Dhahran, Doha, Dubai, El Ain, Jiddah, Karachi, Kuwait, Manila, Muscat, Osaka, Ras al-Khaimah, Sana'a, Sharjah, Singapore, Sydney, and Tokyo

Simulators: 1 x Boeing Model 707-320

Maintenance services: Egyptair Technical Division specialises in airframes and engines with 150 licensed airframe engineers, 18 licensed engine engineers, and 70 licensed avionics engineers

History: It is possible to trace the origins of Egyptair to May 1932, when Misr Airwork was established as a joint undertaking by the Misr Bank of Egypt and Airwork Ltd of the UK. The airline flew its first services in July of the same year, the first route operating between Cairo and Mersa Matruh via Alexandria with de Havilland D.H.84 Dragon aircraft, and by the end of the year Aswan, Asyut and Luxor had become destinations. The airline started international services, to Lydda and Haifa in Palestine, during 1934 and added Baghdad in 1936. On charter services the airline initially flew the de Havilland D.H.83 Fox Moth. By 1937 traffic had expanded and Misr Airwork was now operating five examples of the de Havilland D.H.89 Rapide and two examples of the de Havilland D.H.86 Express as well as two examples of the D.H.84 Dragon, and by 1939 the operator's international network from Cairo connected Baghdad, Cyprus, Haifa, Istanbul, Jiddah, Khartoum and Tehran.

During World War II Misr Airwork was taken over by the Egyptian government, which retained the civil operator's basic route network and increased capacity by a considerable degree on some routes. A new service to Beirut via Palestine was inaugurated during this period.

After the end of World War II, passenger traffic increased steadily and, lacking the aircraft to cope with this demand, Misr Airwork suspended operations from 6 April 1946 until a resumption was made possible by the arrival of more-modern equipment in the form of Beech Model 18 twin-engined light transports and Vickers Viking twin-engined medium transports: the first two Vikings were delivered on 1 November 1948. In 1949 Airwork sold its interest in the airline and the company was renamed Misrair.

During the 1950s the airline introduced the Douglas DC-3 as its standard type, but in March 1954 decided to advance into the turbine-powered age with an order for three examples of the Vickers Viscount 739: the first of these arrived on 23 November 1955 and Misrair flew its first Viscount service on 16 March 1956.

Five years later Misrair moved into the era of pure-jet propulsion with the receipt of its first de Havilland Comet 4C on 10 June 1960 for a service debut on 16 July.

On 23 December 1960 Misrair amalgamated with Syrian Airways to form United Arab Airlines. It was planned that other Arab airlines of the Middle East should subsequently become part of this alliance, but the instability of regional politics prevented this from occurring. The Syrian element withdrew from United Arab Airlines in 1961, so the operator became wholly Egyptian once more. Another

aircraft type received in that year was the Douglas DC-6B, of which three were delivered.

During 1964 United Arab Airlines expanded with the re-establishment of Misrair as its domestic and regional element. By this time Egypt had become closely connected with the USSR, and this fact was reflected in the adoption of a Soviet type, the Antonov An-24 twin-turboprop airliner, of which seven were received to complement seven DC-6B heavier transports. During the 1960s and early 1970s the airline had several Soviet types in its fleet, namely the Ilyushin Il-18D between 1968 and 1975, the Ilyushin Il-62 leased in 1971, and the Tupolev Tu-154 between 1973 and 1975. United Arab Airlines received its first Boeing Model 707-366C on 18 September 1968, and on 10 October 1971 changed its name to EgyptAir, which was changed to Egyptair on 10 October 1974.

With the bitter end to the Egyptian and Soviet relationship in the mid-1970s, followed by the return of Egyptair's Soviet aircraft, the airline had to acquire new aircraft and opted for the Boeing Model 737 to meet its short-haul requirements and the Airbus A300 for its medium-haul routes. Egyptair had to wait for the delivery of its own aircraft, and in the interim operated Model 737 aircraft leased from Aer Lingus and Transavia from October 1975, and A300 aircraft leased from TEA of Belgium from April 1977.

Egyptair currently operates Airbus and Boeing aircraft to the exclusion of all other types but two examples of the Fokker F.27 Friendship twin-turboprop transport, and has considerably expanded its domestic, regional and international capabilities.

El Al

Country of origin: Israel

Generally accepted abbreviation: LY

Address: PO Box 41, Ben Gurion International Airport, Tel Aviv 70100, Israel

Type of operation: International, regional scheduled and charter passenger and cargo services

Shareholding: Government-owned

Subsidiaries: Starline (48%)

Marketing alliances: None

Notes: Between 1982 and February 1995 El Al operated under the auspices of an official receiver, but has now emerged from this in preparation for privatisation

Personnel: 3,410

Fleet:
- 2 x Boeing Model 737-200
- 1 x Boeing Model 747-100F
- 4 x Boeing Model 747-200B
- 3 x Boeing Model 747-200B Combi
- 1 x Boeing Model 747-200F
- 3 x Boeing Model 747-400B
- 6 x Boeing Model 757-200
- 2 x Boeing Model 767-200
- 2 x Boeing Model 767-200ER

Main base and hub: Tel Aviv

Route network: An African element with destinations such as Cairo, Johannesburg and Nairobi; an Asian element with destinations such as Bangkok, Beijing, Bombay, Delhi and Hong Kong; a European element with destinations including Amsterdam, Antalya, Athens, Barcelona, Berlin, Brussels, Bucharest, Budapest, Cologne, Copenhagen, Frankfurt, Geneva, Istanbul, Lisbon, London, Madrid, Manchester, Marseille, Moscow, Munich, Paris, Rome, Vienna, Warsaw, Zagreb, and Zürich; and a North American element with destinations such as Baltimore, Boston, Chicago, Los Angeles, Miami, Montreal, New York, and Toronto

Simulators: Details not available

Maintenance services: Details not available

Continued on next page

El Al continued from previous page

History: Currently ranked 42nd in the world, El Al was created on 11 November 1948 with equipment comprising one Douglas DC-4 and two Curtiss C-46 Commando transports transferred from this Israeli airline's predecessor, the Israeli Air Transport Command (LATA). Israel's national flag carrier, El Al was formed initially to replace the domestic carrier Aviron and also to operate flights that were difficult for the Israeli air force to carry out. The new operator's first service, undertaken on 31 July 1949, was a flight linking Tel Aviv and Paris.

El Al bought three examples of the Lockheed L-049 Constellation four-engined airliner in June 1950. These machines reached Israel during May 1951 and entered service from 16 May between Israel and New York, via Athens or Rome and London. In addition to its services to European destinations and New York, El Al established a route to South Africa on 1 October 1953, and for a short time in 1955/56 this service to Johannesburg was operated by leased Douglas DC-6B aircraft.

Further modernisation to the airline's fleet took place in December 1960, when El Al leased one Boeing Model 707-441 (PP-VJB) from the Brazilian operator VARIG for its transatlantic service, which was soon entrusted to the Israeli operator's own Model 707 aircraft, of which the first was received on 22 April 1961. By the end of 1961 El Al had retired all its Constellation aircraft, leaving it with Britannia and Model 707 aircraft. El Al kept the Britannia in service up to the mid-1960s, after which the operator has flown only Boeing aircraft.

On 26 May 1971 El Al took delivery of its first wide-body transport in the form of a Boeing Model 747-258B, and since this time the Model 747 has been the mainstay of El Al's commercial operation for high-density passenger, freight and combined passenger/-freight services. These 'jumbo jets' have been complemented more recently by the Boeing Models 757 and 767, of which the first example was delivered on 12 July 1983, for additional capability on medium-density routes. On its European and Middle Eastern routes, El Al flies the Boeing Model 737: the airline initially leased two Model 737-2M8 aircraft from Trans European Airlines from 1 November 1980, but then received the first of its own two Model 737-258 aircraft in 1982.

In 1977 El Al created El Al Charter Services as a charter subsidiary, and the parent company leases aircraft and crews to this subsidiary, whose name was changed to Sun d'Or on 27 September 1981.

Emirates Airlines

Country of origin: United Arab Emirates

Generally accepted abbreviation: EK

Address: Airline Centre, Flame Roundabout, PO Box 686, Dubai, United Arab Emirates

Type of operation: International, regional and domestic scheduled passenger services

Shareholding: Wholly owned by the government of Dubai

Subsidiaries: Emirates Sky Cargo Freight Forwarding

Marketing alliances: Codesharing with KLM and United Airlines

Notes: In June 1995 Emirates Airlines started a weekly Boeing Model 747 freight service between Dubai and Singapore using an aircraft leased from US-based Atlas Air. This service is supplementary to the operator's six weekday passenger flights to the same destination. In December 1995 the government of Australia granted Emirates Airlines permission to operate three weekday services between Dubai and Australia

Personnel: 2,000

Fleet: 6 x Airbus A300-600R
10 x Airbus A310-300
3 x Boeing Model 777-200A

Orders: 4 x Boeing Model 777B (delivery in 1997)
16 x Airbus A330-200

Main base and hub: Dubai

Route network: Destinations include Abu Dhabi, Amman, Athens, Bangkok, Beirut, Bombay, Cairo, Colombo, Comores Islands, Damascus, Delhi, Dhahran, Dhaka, Doha, Dubai, Frankfurt, Hong Kong, Istanbul, Jakarta, Jeddah, Johannesburg, Karachi, Kuala Lumpur, Kuwait, Larnaca, London, Malé, Manchester, Manila, Melbourne, Muscat, Nairobi, Nice, Paris, Riyadh, Rome, Sanaa, Shiraz, Singapore, Tehran, and Zürich

Simulators: 1 x Airbus A300-600R
1 x Airbus A310-300
1 x Boeing Model 777

Maintenance services: Details not available

History: Emirates Airlines was established in 1985 as the national flag carrier of the United Arab Emirates, and started services with two Boeing Model 727-200 three-turbofan aircraft (sold to Qatar Airways early in 1995) for its domestic and regional services, and Airbus aircraft for its longer-haul routes, which are being substantially enlarged in capacity by the delivery of seven Boeing Model 777 airliners.

EVA Airways

Country of origin: Taiwan

Generally accepted abbreviation: BR

Address: EVA Air Building, 376 Hsin-nan Road, Sec. 1, Luchu, Taoyuan Hsien, Taiwan

Type of operation: International, regional and domestic scheduled and charter passenger and cargo services

Shareholding: EVA Airways is wholly owned by the Evergreen Corporation of Taiwan

Subsidiaries: Great China Airlines (25%) and Makung Airlines (32%)

Marketing alliances: Garuda, All Nippon Airways and Ansett Australia

Notes: EVA signed letters of intent for the purchase of Boeing Model 777 aircraft during June 1995, and in October of the same year started its first European freight operation with a service linking Taipei and Amsterdam, where the airline also opened new offices. EVA Airways is planning to purchase an extra 19% of Makung Airlines

Personnel: 5,000

Fleet: 2 x Boeing Model 747-400 Combi
10 x Boeing Model 747-400
4 x Boeing Model 767-200
5 x Boeing Model 767-300
6 x McDonnell Douglas MD-11

Orders: 10 x McDonnell Douglas MD-90

Main base and hub: Taipei

Route network: An American element with destinations such as Anchorage, Los Angeles, New York, San Francisco and Seattle; an Asian and Pacific element with destinations including Bali, Bangkok, Brisbane, Fukuoka, Ho Chi Minh City, Jakarta, Kaohsiung, Kuala Lumpur, Maldives, Manila, Melbourne, Pinang, Singapore, Sydney, Tainan, and Taipei; a European element with destinations such as Amsterdam, London, Paris and Vienna; and a Middle Eastern element with destinations such as Dubai

Simulators: 1 x Boeing Model 747-400
1 x Boeing Model 747-300ER
1 x Boeing Model 767-300ER
1 x McDonnell Douglas MD-11

Maintenance services: EVA Airways specialises in airframes and engines with 155 licensed airframe engineers, 155 licensed engine engineers, and 25 licensed avionics engineers

History: EVA Airways was established in March 1989 as Taiwan's first privately owned international air operator, and began operations in 1991. Since that time the airline has grown rapidly and extensively, and is now ranked 45th in the world with a route network reaching 26 key points in Asia, Australasia, Europe and the USA, with further expansion planned.

Finnair

Country of origin: Finland

Generally accepted abbreviation: AY

Address: Tietotie 11a, Helsinki Vantaa Airport, Finland

Type of operation: International, regional and domestic scheduled and charter passenger and cargo services

Shareholding: Finnish government (60.7%)

Subsidiaries: Travel agencies, tour operators, hotel operations, catering and travel information

Marketing alliances: Air Canada, Air China, Austrian Airlines, Braathens, Delta Air Lines, Lufthansa, Maersk Air, and Transwede

Personnel: 7,500

Fleet: 6 x ATR 42
12 x McDonnell Douglas DC-9-50
4 x McDonnell Douglas MD-11
18 x McDonnell Douglas MD-82 and MD-83
3 x McDonnell Douglas MD-87

Orders: 4 x Boeing Model 757-200

Main bases and hubs: Helsinki, London (Gatwick) and Stockholm

Route network: A domestic element with destinations such as Ivalo, Kittilä, Kokkola, Kuusamo, Oulu, Pietarsaari, and Vaasa; a European element with more than 30 destinations; a Middle Eastern, Asian and Pacific element with destinations including Bahrain, Bangkok, Beijing, Dubai, Osaka, Singapore, and Tokyo; and a North American element with destinations such as Miami, New York, and Toronto

Simulators: 1 x ATR 42
1 x ATR 72
1 x McDonnell Douglas DC-9-10/30/50
1 x McDonnell Douglas DC-10-30
1 x McDonnell Douglas MD-11
1 x McDonnell Douglas MD-82/83/87
1 x Beech King Air 300

Maintenance services: Finnair specialises in airframes and engines with 200 licensed airframe engineers, 150 licensed engine engineers, and 85 licensed avionics engineers

History: Currently ranked 35th in the world and 11th in Europe, Finnair is one of the longest-established airlines in the world, for its origins can be traced to 1 November 1923, when Bruno Lucander created Aero O/Y with

Continued on next page

Finnair continued from previous page

financial help from local interests. The new airline flew its first service between Helsinki across the Gulf of Finland to Reval in Estonia using a Junkers F 13 floatplane, and its most significant international link was established on the route linking Helsinki with Stockholm on 2 June 1924 in conjunction with the Swedish airline ABA. In 1925 the route on the eastern side of the Baltic Sea was extended southward to Konigsberg in East Prussia, and on 29 June 1932 Aero O/Y took delivery of its first Junkers 52/3m three-motor transport, which supplanted the Junkers G 24W floatplane on the Konigsberg service.

A major change became evident on 15 June 1937 when Aero O/Y accepted its first landplane in the form of a de Havilland D.H.89 Dragon Rapide, and this soon entered service between Riga and Liepaja. By the time of the Russo-Finnish 'Winter War' of 1939/40, Aero O/Y's fleet comprised two Ju 52/3m and two D.H.89 aircraft. The 'Winter War' resulted in the cancellation of only eight of Aero O/Y's scheduled 389 flights, six of these being attributable to weather conditions rather than Soviet action, but during the 'Continuation War' of 1941-44, when Finland was allied with Germany, all services were cancelled.

Aero O/Y resumed operations in August 1945 with domestic services from Hyvinkää to Vaasa, Kerni and Jyväskylä, and in 1946 the government of Finland acquired a 70% shareholding in the airline. Aero O/Y accepted the first of six Douglas DC-3 twin-engined transports on 6 June 1947, and resumed services to Stockholm on 1 November: the airline had earlier operated two examples of the Douglas DC-2 from 28 April 1941. The availability of the DC-3 fleet permitted an expansion of the airline's international network, and on 15 April 1951 Düsseldorf and Hamburg were added to the destinations served by the airline, which was now operating under the name Finnair although this change was not formally adopted until July 1968.

Finnair acquired its first truly modern aircraft on 27 January 1953, when it took delivery of its initial Convair CV-240, and with this type Finnair was able to start a service linking Helsinki with London, via Hamburg and Amsterdam, on 1 September 1954. Finnair also became the first non-Soviet bloc airline to serve Moscow with the start of a CV-240 service on 18 February 1956.

Finnair missed out the intermediate step of turboprop-powered airliners, and instead proceeded straight to the pure-jet type with a January 1958 order for three examples of the Sud-Aviation Caravelle IA: the first of the aircraft was accepted on 18 February 1960 and the type operated its first revenue-earning services on 1 April on the routes from Helsinki to Stockholm and Frankfurt. Finnair received the first of its larger turbofan-powered Super Caravelle 10B aircraft on 22 July 1964, and this type remained in service until 30 April 1983, when a final service was flown from Helsinki to Monastir in Yugoslavia.

With the Super Caravelle established as the workhorse of Finnair's international network, the CV-240 replaced the DC-3 on the airline's domestic network. In general, however, Finnair was notably cautious in its expansion after World War II, and it was not until November 1966 that the airline placed its first order for long-haul aircraft in the form of two Douglas DC-8-62CF four-turbofan transports with which to expand the international network to North America. Finnair accepted delivery of its first DC-8 on 27 January 1969, and this soon entered service between Helsinki and New York via two intermediate stops. Finnair was satisfied with the DC-8, and accordingly ordered the Douglas DC-9-10 for its short-haul routes, accepting the first of these aircraft on 24 January 1971. Since that time Finnair has operated two other variants of the basic DC-9 series, as well as three variants of the lengthened and modernised MD-80 series: the Finnish operator received its first examples of the DC-9-40, DC-9-50 and MD-82 in March 1981, January 1976 and March 1983 respectively.

Finnair received its first wide-body airliner, a McDonnell Douglas DC-10-30, on 27 January 1975, and in its original DC-10 and updated MD-11 forms this three-turbofan transport replaced the DC-8-62CF on the North American and most intercontinental routes. In April 1980 Finnair bought the first two of an eventual three Fokker F.27 Friendship twin-turboprop transports from Icelandair for the operation of low-density services to destinations such as Umeå, Vaasa and Turku in the remoter parts of Finland.

The F.27 aircraft did not remain in service for long, and while it still operates mainly McDonnell Douglas aircraft, Finnair is now also an operator of Airbus aircraft in the form of two A300B4 transports.

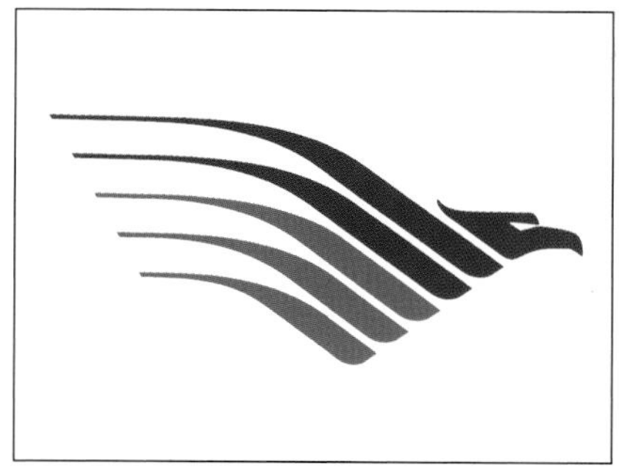

Garuda Indonesia Airways

Country of origin: Indonesia

Generally accepted abbreviation: GA

Address: Merdeka Selatan 13, Jakarta 10110, Indonesia

Type of operation: International, regional and domestic scheduled passenger and cargo services

Shareholding: Government-owned

Subsidiaries: Merpati Nusantara Airlines

Marketing alliances: Codesharing with KLM, China Airlines and Iberia, joint flight with Aeroflot, and pooling with EVA Airways and Japan Airlines

Notes: In July 1995 Garuda Indonesia Airways launched a joint freight service with KLM between Amsterdam and Jakarta, via Bombay and Kuala Lumpur, using a Boeing Model 747 leased from Atlas Air

Personnel: 13,270

Fleet:
10 x Airbus A300-600R
9 x Airbus A300B4
4 x Airbus A330-300
12 x Boeing Model 737-300
7 x Boeing Model 737-400
6 x Boeing Model 747-200
5 x Boeing Model 747-400
5 x McDonnell Douglas DC-10
7 x McDonnell Douglas MD-11

Orders:
5 x Airbus A330
5 x Boeing Model 747-400
3 x McDonnell Douglas MD-11ER

Main bases and hubs: Denpasar and Jakarta

Route network: A domestic element with more than 30 destinations including Denpasar, Jogjakarta, Medan, Padang and Surabaya; an American element with destinations including Los Angeles; an Asian and Pacific element with destinations such as Adelaide, Auckland, Bangkok, Bombay, Brisbane, Cairns, Darwin,

Continued on next page

Garuda continued from previous page

Fukuoka, Guangzhou, Ho Chi Minh City, Hong Kong, Honolulu, Kuala Lumpur, Melbourne, Nagoya, Perth, Port Hedland, Seoul, Singapore, Sydney, Taipei, Tokyo, and Townsville; a European element with destinations including Amsterdam, Berlin, Brussels, London, Madrid, Paris, Rome, Vienna, and Zürich; and a Middle Eastern element with destinations such as Abu Dhabi, Jiddah and Riyadh

Simulators: 1 x Airbus A300B4
1 x Boeing Model 737-300
1 x Boeing Model 747-200
1 x Fokker F.28 Fellowship Series 1000/4000
1 x McDonnell Douglas DC-9-30
1 x McDonnell Douglas DC-10-30
1 x McDonnell Douglas MD-11

Maintenance services: Garuda Indonesia Maintenance specialises in airframes and engines with 535 licensed airframe engineers, 240 licensed engine engineers, and 85 licensed avionics engineers

History: In 1928 KLM (Royal Dutch Airlines) established the Koninklijke Nederlandsch Indische Luchtvaart Maatschappij (KNILM) for the operation of air services to the Netherlands East Indies from 1 November of that year. During the 1930s various types of Fokker aircraft were used, and KLM also supplied KNILM with more-advanced Douglas DC-2 and Lockheed Model 14 twin-engined aircraft. By 1934 KNILM was operating a network covering seven towns in the Netherlands East Indies and was also flying a service to Singapore; four years later the airline was serving a domestic network of 12 destinations as well as the international destinations of Saigon and Darwin.

When the Japanese invaded the Netherlands East Indies in the first months of 1942, all KNILM's services were halted and all possible aircraft were evacuated to Australia and, if feasible, to the United States where the airline re-established itself in New York. Services in the Netherlands East Indies were resumed after the end of World War II in 1945, and on 1 August 1947 KLM absorbed KNILM, which became the KLM Island Division with a fleet of 20 Douglas DC-3 landplanes and eight Consolidated PBY-5A Catalina amphibious flying boats.

Since the end of World War II a nationalist effort had been fighting to make the Netherlands East Indies into the independent republic of Indonesia, and in August 1950 the republic was proclaimed after the Netherlands had granted full sovereignty in November 1949. On 21 December 1949 Garuda Indonesian Airways came into being as a joint venture between the governments of Indonesia and the Netherlands, and on 31 March 1950 the new operator was officially registered as the successor to KNILM.

Garuda received its first new transport on 28 September 1950 when it took delivery of the first of an eventual 19 Convair CV-240 aircraft for use on major routes, for which feeder operations were undertaken by an eventual 14 examples of the de Havilland D.H.114 Heron, of which the first was delivered in October 1953.

A major change occurred on 12 July 1954 when the Indonesian government nationalised Garuda, and in September 1956 KLM's technical support agreement was terminated. Fleet modernisation was now vital, and on 15 March 1957 Garuda ordered three examples of the Lockheed L-188 Electra four-turboprop airliner: the first of these arrived on 14 January 1961 with the others following a mere 10 days later. Garuda also wanted to expand its route network as well as provide additional capacity, and as a result it ordered three examples of the jet-powered Convair CV-990. The airline took delivery of the first of these fast jetliners on 3 September 1963, and the type was placed in service on Far Eastern routes to destinations such as Manila and Tokyo, with a link to Amsterdam following in March 1965. During 1968 Garuda replaced the CV-990 aircraft on the Amsterdam service with the Douglas DC-8-55, of which the first had been received on 19 July 1966. Garuda also leased a number of extra DC-8 aircraft from KLM.

Further re-equipment followed from 1969, when the airline's regional capability was enhanced by the introduction of Fokker F.27 Friendship Mk 600 twin-turboprop and Douglas DC-9-32 twin-jet aircraft to complement and then supplant the Convair CV-340 and CV-440 aircraft. Garuda received its first F.27 and DC-9 aircraft in August and October 1969 respectively. The F.27 was soon replaced by the Fokker F.28 Fellowship twin-turbofan type. The first of these aircraft was delivered on 19 August 1971, and Garuda became the world's largest operator of this type with 45 received in Series 1000, 3000 and 4000 forms.

As its longer-haul services were growing rapidly, the advent of the wide-body airliner was very important for Garuda, which entered the market for this type in the early 1970s with an order for the McDonnell Douglas DC-10-30 three-turbofan type as successor to the DC-8. Before receiving its own aircraft, Garuda leased one similar machine from KLM between October 1973 and March 1975.

On 1 January 1963 Garuda had absorbed the domestic operation of De Kroonduif in New Guinea, but one year later transferred this network to PN Merpati Nusantara. In October 1978 Garuda took over PN Merpati Nusantara, which operated domestic services with a fleet of F.27 Friendship, de Havilland Canada DHC-6 Twin Otter, CASA-Nurtanio NC-212 Aviocar and Vickers Viscount aircraft. Although wholly owned by Garuda, this airline continued to operate semi-independently as Merpati Nusantara Airlines until September 1989, when it was absorbed fully into Garuda: many of the older aircraft are still operated, although more-modern equipment includes 7 BAe 748 and Jetstream ATP, 3 Boeing Model 737-200, up to 40 CASA-IPTN CN-235, 20 F.28 and 6 Fokker 100 aircraft.

Further consolidation of Garuda's international capability followed the adoption of the Boeing Model 747, of which the airline received its first example on 2 July 1980. Given the growth in tourism and local wealth, Garuda found that its DC-9 fleet lacked adequate capacity and therefore ordered another wide-body type, the Airbus A300B4-220, the first of an eventual nine being accepted on 11 January 1982. The DC-9 was later supplanted by the Model 737, and further capability was added by the introduction of another Airbus type, the A300-600 that is to be complemented by the A330.

Garuda in the national flag carrier of Indonesia, and is currently ranked 34th in the world and ninth in Asia.

Gulf Air

Countries of origin: Bahrain, Oman, Qatar and United Arab Emirates

Generally accepted abbreviation: GF

Address: PO Box 138, Manama, Bahrain

Type of operation: International and regional scheduled and charter passenger and freight services

Shareholding: Gulf Air is wholly owned by the governments of Bahrain, Qatar, the Sultanate of Oman and the United Arab Emirates

Subsidiaries: Gulf Helicopters (100%) and Jet Airways (20%)

Marketing alliances: Codesharing with American Airlines

Personnel: 5,500

Fleet: 14 x Airbus A320
2 x Airbus A340
18 x Boeing Model 767

Orders: 6 x Airbus A330

Main bases and hubs: Abu Dhabi, Bahrain, Doha and Muscat

Route network: An African element to destinations such as Casablanca, Dar es Salaam, Entebbe, Johannesburg, Khartoum, Kilimanjaro, Nairobi, and Zanzibar; an American element with destinations such as Houston and New York; a European element with destinations including Amsterdam, Athens, Brussels, Frankfurt, Geneva, Istanbul, Larnaca, London, Manchester, Paris, Rome, and Zürich; and a Middle Eastern and Asian element with destinations such as Amman, Bangkok, Beirut, Bombay, Colombo, Damascus, Delhi, Dhahran, Dhaka, Fujairah, Hong Kong, Jakarta, Jiddah, Karachi, Kuala Lumpur, Kuwait, Madras, Manila, Melbourne, Ras al-Khaimah, Riyadh, Sana'a, Sharjah, Shiraz, Singapore, Sydney, Tehran, and Trivandrum

Simulators: 1 x Airbus A320-200
1 x Airbus A340-300
1 x Boeing Model 767-300ER
1 x Lockheed L-1011-200 TriStar

Maintenance services: Gulf Aircraft Maintenance Company (GAMCO)

History: Currently ranked 43rd in the world, Gulf Air is the flag carrier of the Persian Gulf states of Bahrain, Oman, Qatar and the United Arab Emirates. The airline can trace its origins to 24 March 1950, when F. Bosworth, a Briton, started local services with one Avro Type 652A Anson. This operator was the Gulf Aviation Co. Ltd., and its services linked Bahrain, Doha, Dhahran and Sharjah. During its first year the airline boosted its fleet to a strength of four aircraft by the addition of two Austers and a de Havilland D.H.86, but considerably enhanced its capability on 13 June 1951 with the delivery of an initial de Havilland D.H.104 Dove 1.

Continued on next page

Gulf Air continued from previous page

During October 1951 the airline became a subsidiary of BOAC, and the greater capital now available allowed the purchase of four examples of the de Havilland D.H.114 Heron 1B, of which the first was received on 11 July 1956, and four examples of the Douglas DC-3 shortly afterwards.

During this period there was considerable demand for additional capacity as the world's oil companies moved in strength into the Persian Gulf, and on 6 January 1967 the airline took its first turboprop-powered airliner, a Fokker F.27 Friendship Mk 600. The airline was able to satisfy its short-haul requirements with this and the Shorts Skyvan, of which the first two were delivered in November 1970, while longer-haul services were provided initially by a Hawker Siddeley Trident 1E leased from Kuwait Airways but later by the BAC One-Eleven 432FD, of which the first was delivered in November 1969.

In April 1970, the airline started to operate to London from Abu Dhabi, Bahrain, Doha and Dubai using a Vickers VC10 of BOAC. Late in 1973 the airline was renamed Gulf Air, and Bahrain, Oman, Qatar and the United Arab Emirates became equal shareholders in the newly named company on 1 April 1974. Also formed in 1974 was Doha-based Gulf Helicopters, with Gulf Air as its only shareholder. On 24 May 1981 the Gulf Air Light Aircraft Division merged with Oman International Services to create Oman Aviation Services using aircraft drawn from the pool provided by two companies' fleets. The major effect of this merger on Gulf Air was to leave it with only two types of aircraft: the Boeing Model 737-2P6 (the first of which was received on 28 June 1977) for regional services to neighbouring countries in the Middle East, and the Lockheed L-1011-200 TriStar (the first was delivered on 16 January 1976) for longer-haul services to London, Amsterdam, Paris, Karachi and Bombay.

In 1985 Gulf Air ceased operations to Dubai, which had established Emirates Airlines as its own national flag carrier, and now concentrates the bulk of its operations on the advanced aircraft of Airbus and Boeing.

Iberia Airlines

Country of origin: Spain

Generally accepted abbreviation: IB

Address: Calle Velasquez 130, Madrid E-28006, Spain

Type of operation: International, regional and domestic scheduled and charter passenger and cargo services

Shareholding: Government-owned

Subsidiaries: Viva (99.4%); Aerolineas Argentinas (83%); Aviaco (32.9%), Ladeco (37.5%), Royal Air Maroc (2%) and VIASA (45%)

Personnel: 23,575

Fleet:
4 x Airbus A300B4-200
22 x Airbus A320
4 x Airbus A340-300
23 x Boeing Model 727-200 Advanced
7 x Boeing Model 747-200B
8 x Boeing Model 757
4 x McDonnell Douglas DC-9-32
5 x McDonnell Douglas DC-10-30
24 x McDonnell Douglas MD-87

Orders:
8 x Airbus A321
4 x Airbus A340-300

Main bases and hubs: Barcelona, Madrid and Miami

Route network: A domestic element with destinations including Almeria, Arrecife, Barcelona, Bilbao, Granada, Ibiza, Jerez, La Coruña, Las Palmas, Madrid, Mahón, Málaga, Melilla, Murcia, Oviedo, Palma, Puerto del Rosario, San Sebastián, Santa Cruz de la Palma, Santa Cruz de Tenerife, Santander,

Santiago de Compostela, Seville, Valencia, Valladolid, Valverde, Vigo, Vitoria, and Zaragoza; a European element to destinations such as Amsterdam, Athens, Berlin, Brussels, Copenhagen, Dublin, Düsseldorf, Frankfurt, Geneva, Hamburg, Istanbul, Lisbon, London, Luxembourg, Lyon, Manchester, Marseille, Milan, Moscow, Munich, Nice, Oporto, Paris, Pisa, Rome, Stockholm, Vienna and Zürich; an American element with destinations such as Asunción, Bogotá, Buenos Aires, Cancún, Caracas, Guatemala, Havana, Lima, Los Angeles, Malabo, Managua, Mexico City, Miami, Montevideo, Montreal, New York, Panama, Quito, Rio de Janeiro, San José, San Juan, San Pedro Sula, San Salvador, Santiago, Santo Domingo, São Paulo, and Toronto; and an African and Asian element to destinations such as Cairo, Casablanca, Dakar, Tangier, Tel Aviv and Tokyo

Simulators: 1 x Airbus A300B4
1 x Airbus A320-200
1 x Boeing Model 727-200
2 x McDonnell Douglas DC-930
1 x McDonnell Douglas MD-87

Maintenance services: Iberia Airlines of Spain Maintenance & Engineering Division specialises in airframes and engines with 3,155 staff

History: Currently ranked 20th in the world and sixth in Europe, Iberia Airlines is the national flag carrier of Spain and is more properly known as Lineas Aereas de Espana. This operator was created in 1927 with 51% owned by the Spanish government and 49% by private interests in which the German airline Deutsche Lufthansa predominated. Deutsche Lufthansa was responsible mainly for the establishment of the airline on a sound technical basis, and consonant with the other airlines that comprised the German 'continental system' of airlines stretching as far north as Finland, as far west as Spain and south-east to the Balkans.

Iberia's network was confined initially to Spain and the Spanish territories in North Africa, and the airline's operations came to an abrupt halt with the outbreak of the Spanish Civil War in 1936. The airline was in essence refounded in 1940, one year after the end of the civil war and again with the aid of Lufthansa, and for the duration of World War II restricted its operations to domestic services. During the war, in which Spain was a non-participant, Iberia was completely nationalised.

Expansion began in 1946, with the opening of a transatlantic service to South America using the Sud-Est SE.161 Languedoc four-engined airliner. Commercial success followed, and Iberia was gradually able to develop its network into other parts of the Spanish-speaking world, notably Cuba and Mexico, and in 1954 started a scheduled service to New York. By the middle of the 1950s Iberia's fleet comprised the Bristol Type 170, Convair CV-440 and Douglas DC-3 twin-engined transports for its short-range routes, the Douglas DC-4 four-engined airliner on its medium-haul routes, and the Lockheed L-1049 Super Constellation four-engined airliner on its long-haul routes. Turbine power made its appearance in Iberia livery during 1961 in the form of the four-engined Douglas DC-8 and the two-engined Sud-Aviation Caravelle.

From this time Iberia has increased its network and fleet quite quickly and extensively, and by mid-1980 the airline had some 110 aircraft in service or awaiting delivery. The airline now operates its domestic network mainly with the McDonnell Douglas DC-9 and MD-87, its European network with the Airbus A300, Airbus 320 and Boeing Model 727-200, and its long-haul network with the Boeing Models 747 and 757 and the McDonnell Douglas DC-10-30.

Iran Air

Country of origin: Iran

Generally accepted abbreviation: IR

Address: Iran Air Building, Mehrabad Airport, Tehran 13185775, Iran

Type of operation: International, regional and domestic scheduled and charter passenger and cargo services

Shareholding: Iran Air is wholly owned by the government of Iran in the form of the Ministry of Roads

Subsidiaries: Iran Air Tours and Iran Hotels

Personnel: 11,855

Fleet: 2 x Airbus A300-600
5 x Airbus A300B2
4 x Boeing Model 707-300C
2 x Boeing Model 727-100
5 x Boeing Model 727-200
3 x Boeing Model 737-200
3 x Boeing Model 747-100/200
1 x Boeing Model 747F
4 x Boeing Model 747SP
6 x Fokker 100

Main base and hub: Tehran

Route network: A domestic element serving 23 cities, and an international element with destinations including Abu Dhabi, Almaty, Amsterdam, Ashkhabad, Athens, Bahrain, Baku, Beijing, Bombay, Damascus, Doha, Dubai, Frankfurt, Geneva, Hamburg, Istanbul, Jiddah, Karachi, Kuala Lumpur, Kuwait, Larnaca, London, Madrid, Moscow, Muscat, Paris, Rome, Sharjah, Tashkent, Tokyo, and Vienna

Continued on next page

Iran Air continued from previous page

Simulators: 1 x Boeing Model 707-300
1 x Boeing Model 727-200

Maintenance services: Iran Air specialises in airframes and engines with 410 licensed airframe engineers, 520 licensed engine engineers, and 80 licensed avionics engineers

History: Iran Air, also known as Homa (an acronym of its Persian name), was created during February 1962 by the amalgamation of two existing operators, namely Iranian Airways and Persian Air Services, to become the state-owned national flag carrier. Iranian Airways had been created as a private airline in December 1944, and began operations on 31 May 1945 with its first scheduled service launched in May 1946 to connect Tehran and Meshed. A domestic network was subsequently developed using DC-3 aircraft. The airline's route network and capacity grew steadily, allowing the establishment of regional services to Baghdad, Beirut and Cairo by the end of 1946, and long-haul services to Paris in April 1947.

Persian Air Services had been created in the course of 1954, and began operations the following year with a cargo service between Tehran and Geneva using Avro York four-engined transport aircraft operated under charter by Trans-Mediterranean Airways. Regional and international services were then introduced, and in 1960 a Douglas DC-7C and a Boeing Model 707 were leased from Sabena.

Iran Air began operations in 1962 with the pool of aircraft inherited from its two predecessors, but acquired its own jet-powered aircraft in 1965 with the first of several Boeing Model 727-86 machines, of which the first was received on 4 July. The acquisition of more and larger aircraft allowed Iran Air to expand its route network, which soon included Frankfurt, London and Moscow. In 1964 the airline reached agreement with Pan American for the provision, over a three-year period, of management and technical support. This was a considerable fillip to the airline's overall capabilities and operating viability, and in March 1976 Iran Air moved into the arena of wide-body aircraft with the introduction of Boeing Model 747SP-86 aircraft, which allowed the start of services to New York.

The severing of relations with the USA, following the fall of the Shah and the introduction of a fundamentalist Islamic regime, combined with the following 10-year 1st Gulf War against Iraq to reduce the utility of the airline's American-supplied aircraft, for which no additional spares could be obtained on the open market, so it has been only with the introduction of European aircraft, such as Airbus A300 and Fokker 100, that the airline's fortunes have started to rise once more.

Japan Airlines

Country of origin: Japan

Generally accepted abbreviation: JL

Address: 4-11 Higashi-Shinagawa Zchome, Shinagawa-KV, Tokyo 104, Japan

Type of operation: International, regional and domestic scheduled passenger and cargo services

Shareholding: Tokyo Marine & Fire Insurance, Industrial Bank of Japan, Fukoku Mutual Life Insurance, Nippon Dantai Insurance, Dowa Fire & Marine Insurance, Yasuda Fire & Marine Insurance, Dai-Ichi

Kangyo Bank, Kokusai Kogyo and Tokai Bank

Subsidiaries: Japan Asia Airways (90.5%), Japan Air Charter (82%), Japan TransOcean Air (51%) and DHL International (25%)

Marketing alliances: Joint services with Air France and American Airlines

Personnel: 20,098

Fleet:
4 x Boeing Model 737-400
2 x Boeing Model 747-100
20 x Boeing Model 747-200B
8 x Boeing Model 747-200F
9 x Boeing Model 747-300
4 x Boeing Model 747-300SR
24 x Boeing Model 747-400
8 x Boeing Model 747-400D
3 x Boeing Model 767-200
17 x Boeing Model 767-300
3 x Boeing Model 777-200
12 x McDonnell Douglas DC-10-40
9 x McDonnell Douglas MD-11

Orders:
10 x Boeing Model 777-200
5 x Boeing Model 777-300
18 x Boeing Model 747-400
2 x McDonnell Douglas MD-11

Options:
10 x Boeing Model 777-200
10 x McDonnell Douglas MD-11

Main base and hub: Tokyo (Narita)

Route network: A domestic element to destinations such as Akita, Fukuoka, Fukushima, Hakodate, Hiroshima, Kagoshima, Komatsu, Kona, Kumamoto, Matsuyama, Nagasaki, Nagoya, Niigata, Obihiro, Oita, Okinawa, Osaka, Sapporo, Sendai, and Yamagata; an American element with destinations including Anchorage, Atlanta, Chicago, Fairbanks, Honolulu, Los Angeles, Mexico City, New York, Rio de Janeiro, San Francisco, São Paulo, and Vancouver; an Australasian and Pacific element with destinations such as Auckland, Bangkok, Beijing, Brisbane, Cairns, Christchurch, Delhi, Denpasar, Guam, Hong Kong, Honolulu, Jakarta, Khabarovsk, Kuala Lumpur, Manila, Nagoya, Pusan, Saipan, Seoul, Shanghai, Singapore, and Sydney; and a European element with destinations such as Amsterdam, Frankfurt, London, Madrid, Milan, Moscow, Paris, Rome, and Zürich

Simulators:
1 x Beech King Air 90
4 x Boeing Model 747-200
1 x Boeing Model 747-300
4 x Boeing Model 747-400
1 x Boeing Model 767-200
1 x Boeing Model 777-200
1 x McDonnell Douglas DC-10-40
1 x McDonnell Douglas MD-11

Maintenance services: Japan Airlines specialises in airframes and engines with 2,695 licensed airframe engineers, 745 licensed engine engineers, and 225 licensed avionics engineers

History: Currently ranked sixth in the world and first in Asia, Japan Air Lines was created in July 1923 by Seibei Kawanishi, a Japanese aircraft designer and manufacturer, for the operation of services to the holiday resort of Beppu on Kyushu Island. On 30 October 1928 the government of Japan established the Nihon Kokuyuso Kaishiki Kaisha (Japan Air Transport Company), and in the spring of 1929 this organisation engineered the merger of Tozou Teiki Kokukwai and Japan Air Lines for the operation of services within Japan. In 1938 International Airlines merged with NKKK to form the Japan Air Lines Company, and in August 1939 this was reorganised to form Greater Japan Air Lines which began international services from Tokyo to Bangkok in June 1940. Through Japan's involvement in World War II, Greater Japan Air Lines operated

Continued on next page

Japan Airlines continued from previous page

as a transport adjunct of the Japanese armed forces, and ceased all operations with the surrender of Japan in August 1945.

Japanese Air Line was the name of an operator created on 1 August 1951 by a group of private investors, and initially restricted its operations to domestic services within the Japanese home islands using aircraft and crews leased from Northwest Airlines. The first two types operated by the revived Japanese carrier were the Martin 2-0-2 and the Douglas DC-4, the former a twin-engined type of which the first was received on 25 October 1951, and the latter a four-engined type first received on 2 November. The airline had very ambitious plans, however, and on 18 November 1952 ordered two de Havilland Comet 2 turbojet-powered airliners, neither of which was delivered. Another order was placed for five examples of the Douglas DC-6A and DC-6B, but the airline lacked adequate capital for such an expansion and financial restructuring became necessary.

On 1 October 1953 the company was reorganised as Japan Air Lines, and this marked the full renaissance of the pre-war airline as the Japanese national flag carrier, with a 50% stake in the company held by the Japanese government. Shortly before this, Japan Air Line had received three examples of the Douglas DC-6A from Flying Tigers and Slick Airlines, and the aircraft were then upgraded to DC-6B standard for the inauguration of the airline's service across the Pacific to the USA shortly after they had entered revenue-earning service on the service linking Tokyo and Sapporo on 2 October 1953.

On 19 November 1955 Japan Air Lines moved into the turbojet-powered age with an order for the Douglas DC-8-32 four-engined airliner: the first of these aircraft was received on 16 July 1960 for use on the airline's first trans-polar service on the route from Tokyo to London via Anchorage, and, from 12 August, on the route linking Tokyo and San Francisco via Wake Island and Honolulu. On 1 April 1960 Japan Air Lines started a collaborative service with Air France between Tokyo and Paris over the trans-polar route with Boeing Model 707-328 four-turbofan aircraft, and on 21 July 1962 the airline received the first of another four-engined jet type, the Convair CV-880, which was used on 4 October of the same year to launch Japan Air Lines' first service to Europe via India and the Middle East. As soon as its new turbojet-powered aircraft had become established in terms of performance and reliability, Japan Air Lines transferred all its surviving piston-engined aircraft to service on its domestic network.

On 17 April 1967 a joint venture by Japan Air Lines and Aeroflot saw the inauguration of the first direct service between Tokyo and Moscow, and although this initially used the Soviet airline's Tupolev Tu-114 and later its Ilyushin Il-62 airliners, Japan Air Lines later played its part in the service with its own aircraft. Additional services to Soviet destinations were added later.

Japan Air Lines took delivery of its first wide-body transport, a Boeing Model 747-146 four-turbofan type, on 22 April 1970, and improved its service across the Pacific from 1 July; another version of the 'jumbo jet', the Model 747SR-46, was used by Japan Air Lines on the high-density route between Tokyo and Okinawa from October 1973. From 9 April 1976 the Model 747 was partnered by another wide-body transport, the McDonnell Douglas DC-10-40 three-turbofan type, and since that time the operator has standardised on Boeing and McDonnell Douglas aircraft.

In the 1980s the government of Japan started to sell its shareholding in Japan Air Lines, which now trades as Japan Airlines and achieved full privatisation in November 1987 as the government sold its remaining 34.5% shareholding.

KLM Royal Dutch Airlines

Country of origin: The Netherlands

Generally accepted abbreviation: KL

Address: PO Box 7700, Schiphol Airport (East) 1117 ZL, The Netherlands

Type of operation: International and regional scheduled passenger and cargo services

Shareholding: KLM is a publicly quoted company

Subsidiaries: ALM Antillean (40%), Air UK (45%), KLM City Hopper (100%), Martinair (50%), Northwest Airlines (25%), and Transavia (80%)

Marketing alliances: Air UK, Garuda Indonesia, Jet Airways of India, Northwest Airlines, Eurowings, Air Excel, Cyprus Airways, Austrian Airlines, Japan Airlines, Nippon Cargo Liners, and Atlas Airways

Notes: KLM has a 45% share of Air UK, which provides feeder services to Amsterdam from nine UK regional airports, and also possesses 80% and 25% stakes in Transavia and Northwest Airlines respectively. During 1993 the level of co-operation between KLM and Northwest was increased, helped by the open-skies agreement between the USA and the Netherlands that was signed in late 1992, and KLM now has access to Northwest's domestic US network in return for Northwest access to KLM's routes in Europe via codesharing agreements

Personnel: 26,030

Fleet:
- 6 x Airbus A310-200
- 15 x Boeing Model 737-300
- 12 x Boeing Model 737-400
- 3 x Boeing Model 747-300
- 10 x Boeing Model 747-300 Combi
- 5 x Boeing Model 747-400
- 11 x Boeing Model 747-400 Combi
- 5 x Boeing Model 767-300ER
- 6 x Fokker 70
- 9 x McDonnell Douglas MD-11

Orders:
- 4 x Boeing Model 737-300
- 4 x Boeing Model 747-400
- 5 x Boeing Model 767-300ER
- 1 x McDonnell Douglas MD-11

Main base and hub: Amsterdam

Route network: An African element with destinations such as Cape Town, Casablanca, Dar es Salaam, Lagos, Lusaka, Johannesburg, and Nairobi; an 11-point American element with destinations such as Detroit, Guatemala, Lima, Memphis, Mexico City, Minneapolis/St Paul, Panama City, and San José; an Asian and Pacific element with destinations including

Beijing, Bombay, Delhi, Dhaka, Hong Kong, Jakarta, Kuala Lumpur, Osaka, Seoul, Singapore, Sydney, and Tokyo; a 65-point European element with destinations in 25 countries; and a Middle Eastern element to destinations such as Dubai, Tel Aviv and Tehran

Simulators: 1 x Airbus A310-300
1 x Boeing Model 737-300
1 x Boeing Model 737-400
2 x Boeing Model 747-300
2 x Boeing Model 747-400
1 x Boeing Model 767-300ER
1 x McDonnell Douglas DC-10-30
1 x McDonnell Douglas MD-11

Maintenance services: KLM Engineering & Maintenance specialises in airframes and engines with 1,600 licensed airframe engineers, 425 licensed engine engineers, and 250 licensed avionics engineers

History: Currently ranked 11th in the world and fourth in Europe, the Koninklijke Luchtvaart Maatschappij is the national flag carrier of the Netherlands and the oldest operating airline in the world. Generally known as KLM, this organisation can trace its origins to 7 October 1919, when a group of banking and business interests established the airline, which started operations on 17 May 1920 with a service from Amsterdam to London with a de Havilland D.H.16 transport. In the following years a route network was built up with destinations in Belgium, Denmark, France, Germany and Switzerland, generally with Fokker F.III, F.VII and F.VIIb-3m aircraft.

On 1 October 1931 KLM inaugurated a very far-sighted and adventurous route from Amsterdam to Djakarta in the Netherlands East Indies. Here KLM had already established the first of two colonial subsidiaries when it created KNILM (predecessor of Garuda) in October 1928, while the second came into existence at Curaçao in the Netherlands Antilles and started operations on 19 January 1935 with routes through the Caribbean to Barbados, Colombia, the Guianas, Trinidad and Venezuela. These routes, later supplemented by services to Cuba and Miami, operated throughout World War II at a time when all the airline's other operations had ceased.

KLM resumed European operations on 17 January 1945, and a rapid build-up of its capabilities allowed the start of services to New York, Curaçao and Brazil during 1946. Between 1946 and 1953 KLM's route network grew in size quite dramatically, and to cope with the greater demand for its service the airline invested in the latest types of airliner, including the Douglas DC-6 and Lockheed Constellation four-engined types and the Convair CV-240 and -340 twin-engined types. In April 1957 an important milestone in the airline's fleet modernisation was the introduction of the Douglas DC-7C, which was flown on the trans-polar route linking Amsterdam and Tokyo. On 6 June of the same year KLM advanced into the era of turbine propulsion with the receipt of its first turboprop-powered airliner, the Vickers Viscount 803, for use on the airline's regional network in Europe. Greater capacity was provided from 15 December 1959 with the revenue-earning debut of the larger Lockheed L-188 Electra, which was flown mainly on the airline's Middle and Far Eastern services.

KLM's first pure-jet airliner was the Douglas DC-8, of which the first example was delivered on 19 March 1960 for use from 16 April on the route linking Amsterdam and New York. As was the general practice with long-haul operators, KLM moved into the wide-body era with the Boeing Model 747, in this instance a Model 747-206B, the first of which reached the airline on 16 January 1971. The four-turbofan Model 747 and three-turbofan McDonnell Douglas DC-10-30 (later supplemented by the upgraded MD-11 derivative) came to comprise the bulk of KLM's longer-haul fleet through the 1970s and 1980s, although a newer type now in service is the Boeing Model 767-300ER.

KLM's fleet of shorter-haul jet aircraft was initially based on the McDonnell Douglas DC-9 twin-turbofan type, which replaced the Viscount and Electra in 1966, but this type gradually gave way to another twin-turbofan type, the Boeing Model 737 that is now flown in two variants and has been supplemented by the larger Airbus A310-200 that is also powered by two turbofans. Feeder and domestic services are undertaken by Fokker 70 aircraft.

Airbus Industrie A300

During the 1960s the aerospace companies of Europe became increasingly concerned about the virtual monopolisation of the world's airline fleets by aircraft from American companies, most especially Boeing but to a lesser extent Douglas (from 1967 McDonnell Douglas) and Lockheed. As a consequence, Airbus Industrie was created as a grouping primarily of British, French, Spanish and West German interests to undertake an international collaborative programme for the design, development, manufacture and marketing of a family of wide-body transport aircraft.

The concept originated in 1965 as an Anglo-French effort to develop a high-capacity airliner for British European Airways and Air France; West Germany entered the programme in 1967 with the signature on 26 September 1967 of a memorandum of understanding by the three relevant governments.

The initial tri-national plan was for a 330,000lb (149,688kg) airliner with a powerplant of two Rolls-Royce RB.207 turbofan engines, but this concept was then reduced with the withdrawal of official British involvement after the government had decided that an adequate market was in no way guaranteed, which left Hawker Siddeley to maintain a British share on a company basis rather than a national basis. The design of a smaller A300B emerged in December 1968 with a maximum weight of 275,575lb (125,000kg), a powerplant of two British or American turbofan engines each rated at some 45,000lb st (200.17kN), and accommodation for 252 passengers.

Two A300B1 prototypes were built, and the first of these made its maiden flight on 28 October 1972 with a powerplant of two General Electric CF6-50A turbofan engines. These two aircraft had a fuselage 8ft 8in (2.64m) shorter than that of the production model, which had an overall length of 177ft 5in (54.08m), but retained the same span of 147ft 1in (44.84m).

Production of the A300 family is shared among the Airbus partners, who comprise Aérospatiale in France, MBB (now DASA) in Germany, British Aerospace in the UK, and CASA in Spain, with Fokker in the Netherlands as an associate. The aircraft are assembled in Toulouse, to which major components are ferried from the various national manufacturing sites.

Production of the Airbus family of airliners began with the A300B2 (later A300B2-100) with CF6-50C or -50C2 engines, and first flown on 28 June 1973. The A300B2K (later A300B2-200), first flown on 30 July 1976, introduced Krüger flaps on the roots of the wing's leading edges for better field performance, while the A300B2-220 (together with the higher-weight A300B2-320) introduced Pratt & Whitney JT9D-59A engines when first flown on 28 April 1979. The A300B4 (later A300B4-100 with CF6 engines and A300B4-120 with JT9D engines) was a longer-range development with enlarged fuel capacity and higher

The family relationship between the Airbus airliners of the wide-body type, with two powerful turbofan engines pod-mounted below and ahead of the wing leading edges, is readily apparent from these illustrations of an Airbus A340 operated by Virgin Airways (left) and an Airbus A300-600 of Thai Airways International (above).

weights, and was first flown on 26 December 1974. A structurally strengthened, higher-weight, development is the A300B4-200 with provision for additional fuel in the rear cargo hold. The A300B4-200FF, first flown on 6 October 1981, has a more advanced cockpit manned by a two- rather than three-man crew. The A300C4 is a convertible freighter version derived from the A300B4, with a reinforced floor and side-loading door ahead of the wing, and first flew in mid-1979. The A300-600 was launched in 1980 as an advanced version of the A300B4 with a number of major improvements that include a rear fuselage revised to the profile of the A310 to permit the incorporation of two more seat rows, the use of composites and simplified systems for lower structure weight, and a powerplant based on the engines mentioned above or alternatively advanced units such as the 56,000lb st (249.10kN) Pratt & Whitney PW4156, the 58,000lb st (258.00kN) PW4158, or the 53,000lb st (235.76kN) Rolls-Royce RB.211-524D4A. The first A300-600 flew on 8 July 1983 with JT9D-7R4H1 engines.

The A300-600R was introduced in 1986 with improved features such as small wingtip fences, a trimming fuel tank in the tailplane, and a number of new internal features: this model has accommodation varying from a maximum of 375 in one class to 267 in two classes.

French and West German certification of the A300B2 was obtained on 15 March 1974, and this initial variant entered service on 30 May 1974 with Air France. The debuts of later models took place on 23 November 1976 (A300B2K with South African Airways), 1 June 1975 (A300B4 with Germanair), and 8 January 1982 (A300B4-200FF with Garuda). The first A300C4 convertible type entered service with Hapag-Lloyd at the end of 1979, the first A300-600 was handed over to Saudi Arabian Airlines on 26 March 1984, and the first updated A300-600 reached Thai Airways International during October 1985.

Soon after launching the A300, Airbus started to consider a number of future derivatives of this baseline type with designations from A300B5, and by 1974 had decided that the types which offered the greatest potential were the A300B9 with a lengthened fuselage, the A300B10 with a shortened fuselage, and the A300B11 with a larger wing and a four-engined powerplant. Of these three types, the A300B9 and A300B11 were further developed in conceptual terms as the TA9 and TA11 respectively as the precursors of the current A330 and A340, while the A300B10 became the A310.

Interest in a short/medium-range airliner of this medium-capacity type increased during the mid-1970s as several European airlines indicated their requirement for such an airliner for service from 1983. The A310 was finally defined at the end of 1978, when the fuselage was fixed at 13 frames shorter than that of the A300, but with some reprofiling of the rear fuselage to allow the passenger seating to be extended farther to the rear.

The wing was structurally similar to that of the A300 but incorporated new aerodynamics that took advantage of extensive development work by British Aerospace (BAe), successor to Hawker Siddeley. With government approval, BAe became a full partner in the Airbus organisation on 1 January 1979, its 20% share being reflected in the work-share on the A310, in which Aérospatiale, MBB, CASA and Fokker were committed on a basis similar to that for the A300.

The first A310 flew at Toulouse on 3 April 1983 with a powerplant of two JT9D-7R4 turbofan engines, while the third aeroplane, which made its first flight on 5 August 1982, had CF6-80A3 turbofan engines.

The short- and medium-range versions of the A310 were initially designated as the A310-100 and A310-200 with maximum take-off weights of 266,755lb (121,000kg) and 291,005lb (132,000kg). The A310-100 was then dropped, and the A310-200 was evolved with optional higher weights of 305,556lb (138,600kg) and 313,051lb (142,000kg) although the fuel capacity remained constant at 12,077 Imp gal (54,900 litres).

The A310-300 was developed as a longer-range derivative with additional fuel capacity in a tailplane trim tank and optional underfloor tanks. The A310-300 is available at two weights as listed above, and also has small wingtip fences, which were then applied retrospectively to the A310-200. The first A310-300 made its maiden flight on 8 July 1985 with a powerplant of two JT9D-7R4E turbofan engines, while the second example first flew on 6 September of the same year with a powerplant of two CF6-80C2 turbofan engines. Powerplant options for the A310-200 include the JT9D-7R4D1 rated at 48,000lb st (213.51kN), the JT9D-7R4E1 is rated at 50,000lb st (222,41 kN), the CF6-80C2-A2 or -80A3 rated at 50,000lb st (222.41kN), and the PW4150 rated at 50,000lb st (222.41kN). Any of the 50,000lb st (222.41kN) engines can be fitted on the A310-300, and convertible passenger/freight and all-freight variants are available as the A310C and A310F respectively.

The A310-200 received certification in France and West Germany on 11 March 1983, in the UK during January 1984, and in the USA early in 1985. The first deliveries were made on 29 March 1983 to Swissair and Lufthansa, which flew their first revenue-earning services with the new type on 12 and 21 April 1983 respectively.

The A310-300 with JT9D engines received certification in France and West Germany on 5 December 1985 and entered service with Swissair later in the same month.

Airbus took the decision in favour of creating a short/medium-range airliner with seating for 150 passengers during the course of June 1981, at the end of a 10-year period of design involving all major European aircraft manufacturers either directly or indirectly as separate companies or as part of collaborative teams. The most immediate ancestor for the resulting A320 was the Aérospatiale AS.200, which was a designation that covered a family of related designs and projects in the mid-1970s. In 1977 Aérospatiale joined BAe, MBB and VFW-Fokker in the Joint European Transport (JET) study group, the objective of which was to create a short/medium-range airliner of notable quietness and operating economy.

The JET effort was taken under Airbus's wing when BAe became an Airbus partner in January 1979, and the studies continued under the SA (Single-Aisle) designation to create the SA-1, SA-2 and SA-3 concepts with differing fuselage lengths. As the concepts were further refined the revised designation A320 was adopted in 1981, but even at this stage the best size for the new airliner had still not been finalised even though the aeroplane was generally listed as a 150-seat type as this was the typical mixed-class accommodation thought likely to be the airlines' requirement in the 1990s.

Even as the type was initially marketed, however, there was still interest in a version with larger passenger capacities, so A320-100 and A320-200 variants were offered with single-class accommodation at 32in (0.81m) seat pitch for a capacity of 154 or 172 passengers depending on the fuselage length. Air France announced its intention to purchase both these variants, but before it was able to reveal the formal launch of the new airliner in March 1984, Airbus had decided to produce only a single version with its fuselage sized for 162 passengers: this variant was offered at two weights with different fuel capacities, and it was to these options that the A320-100 and A320-200 designations were now applied.

The A320 was a fresh design although its structure was nonetheless based on the concepts already embodied in the A300 and A310. Much use was made of the latest materials such as composites, and also incorporated were advanced-technology systems and equipment including a quadruplex fly-by-wire control system, sidestick controllers for the two pilots, computerised control functions, an EFIS (Electronic Flight Instrument System) and an ECAM (Electronic Centralised Aircraft Monitor).

Development and construction of the A320 were allocated to the Airbus partners in the same way as those of the A300 and A310, with BAe (24%)

responsible for the wing, Aérospatiale (34%) for the forward fuselage and nose, Deutsche Airbus (35%) for the centre and rear fuselage, CASA (5%) for rear fuselage panels and tailplane, and Belairbus (2%) for the wing leading edge.

The first two variants of the A320 were the A320-100 and A320-200, which have the same overall dimensions, including a span of 111ft 3in (33.91m) and a length of 123ft 3in (37.58m), but different fuel capacities and therefore different maximum weights. The initial choice of engines was between the CFM International (General Electric/SNECMA) CFM56-5 and the International Aero-Engines (IAE) V2500 turbofans.

The A320 prototype made its maiden flight on 22 February 1987 with a powerplant of two CFM56-5 engines, and the type received European certification just over one year later on 26 February 1988, and the first aircraft were delivered to Air France and British Airways at the end of March 1988.

Developments of the basic A320, as the A320-200 was renamed after production of the A320-100 ceased after the completion of 21 aircraft, include the A319 with a shortened fuselage for the accommodation of 124 passengers in a two-class layout, and the A321 with a lengthened fuselage for the accommodation of 195 passengers in a two-class layout. The A321 is marketed in two forms, as the basic A321 and as the extended-range A321-200 with a more robust structure, greater fuel capacity and a higher-rated powerplant.

By the middle of the 1980s Airbus had undertaken considerable research into the technical possibility and commercial feasibility of A300 developments with a lengthened fuselage and/or other modifications, and concluded that it had two options identified as the TA9 high-capacity medium-range type with a two-engined powerplant and as the TA11 long-range development of the TA9 with a four-engined powerplant. As indicated by the 'TA' designation, these options were based on a two-aisle cabin layout and retained the fuselage cross-section of the A300. Early in 1986 Airbus had decided that it should add both types to its product list to ensure the maintenance of a marketing credibility in relation to the offerings of the American aerospace industry.

As Airbus reached the stage of marketing the two types, their designations were changed from TA9 and TA11 to A330 and A340 respectively. These types are unusual in that they are based on a common airframe (with essentially the same fuselage, wing and tail unit) for both the two- and four-engined models. The fuselage uses the same cross-section as those of the A300 and A310 although in combination with a new

Although based on the aerodynamic design of its predecessors and using the same essential structural methods, the A320 (seen here in prototype form) is a wholly new type with a more advanced wing, a fly-by-wire control system with sidestick controllers, and a state-of-the-art 'glass' two-crew cockpit with an electronic flight instrument system and an electronic centralised aircraft monitor.

and longer central section to carry the wing and provide some 17ft (5.2m) more length for increased passenger accommodation. The wing, which is again common to both models, is entirely new and of advanced design with the highest aspect ratio of any large airliner planned to date: the wing's most notable feature is its variable-camber facility, with a computer to tailor the camber (by small movements of the trailing-edge flaps) to suit the weight, speed and altitude at which the aeroplane is flying. Only minor aerodynamic differences are required to allow for the difference in the number of the engines in the A330 and A340, and the structure is also identical except for some differences in skin thickness and engine pylon mountings. The cockpit and systems are based on those of the A320, with fly-by-wire controls, sidestick controllers and digital integrated displays.

Until early in 1987, thought was given to the use of the 28,660lb st (127.49kN) CFM56-5-S2 and the 29,980lb st (133.36kN) IAE SuperFan derivative of the V2500, but Airbus opted for a powerplant of two CF6-80E1A2 turbofans each rated at 67,500lb st (300.25kN) for the A330 and of four CFM56-C2 turbofans each rated at 31,200lb st (138.78kN) for the A340.

The first A330 flew on 5 November 1992 and the type entered service in January 1994 with Air Inter, while the first A340 flew on 25 October 1991 and the type entered service in March 1993 with Air France and Lufthansa. Both types are still under development in versions optimised for the increasing number of niches into which the world airline operation market is splitting.

Korean Air

Country of origin: South Korea

Generally accepted abbreviation: KE

Address: 41-3 Seosomun-Dong, Chung-Gu, Seoul, South Korea

Type of operation: Scheduled passenger and cargo services

Shareholding: Korean Air's parent company is the Han Jin Group

Subsidiaries: None

Notes: Korean Air signed an August 1995 agreement with Airmax, an American cargo management organisation, to establish a cargo hub in the mid-western USA

Personnel: 15,000

Fleet:
8 x Airbus A300B4
2 x Airbus A300F4-200
25 x Airbus A300-600R
2 x Boeing Model 747SP
4 x Boeing Model 747-200B/C
12 x Boeing Model 747-200F
3 x Boeing Model 747-300
23 x Boeing Model 747-400
12 x Fokker 100
5 x McDonnell Douglas MD-11
11 x McDonnell Douglas MD-82
1 x McDonnell Douglas MD-83

Orders:
9 x Airbus A330
9 x Boeing Model 747-400
4 x Boeing Model 777-200
8 x Boeing Model 777-300

Options:
10 x Airbus A330
5 x Boeing Model 747-400
8 x Boeing Model 777

Main base and hub: Seoul

Route network: A domestic element to destinations such as Cheju, Chinju, Kunsan, Mokp'o, P'ohang, Pusan, Sokch'o, Taegu, Ulsan, and Yosu; a European elements to destinations including Amsterdam, Frankfurt, London, Milan, Moscow, Paris, Rome, and Zürich; an African element to destinations such as Cairo; an American element to destinations such as Anchorage, Chicago, Guam, Honolulu, Los Angeles, Mexico City, New York, São Paulo, Toronto, and Vancouver; an Asian and Pacific element to destinations including Bangkok, Beijing, Bombay, Brisbane, Fukuoka, Hong Kong, Jakarta, Kagoshima, Kuala Lumpur, Kumamoto, Manila, Nagasaki, Nagoya, Niigata, Oita, Okayama, Osaka, Pinang, Sapporo, Shanghai, Singapore, Sydney, Taipei, Tokyo, and Zhengzhou; and a Middle Eastern element to destinations such as Bahrain, Jiddah and Tel Aviv

Simulators:
1 x Airbus A300-600
1 x Boeing Model 727-200
1 x Boeing Model 747-200
1 x Boeing Model 747-400
1 x Cessna Citation II
1 x Fokker 100
1 x McDonnell Douglas MD-82
1 x Piper Cheyenne V

History: Currently ranked 18th in the world and sixth in Asia, the operator now known as Korean Air began operations in May 1947 with the name Korean National Airlines to fly domestic services using small Stinson Voyager single-engined aircraft that were soon replaced by Douglas DC-3 twin-engined machines. The airline ceased all operations during the Korean War (1950-53), but soon after its revival the airline flew an inaugural international service to Iwakuni and Tokyo with a Douglas DC-4 leased from Civil Air Transport. The airline bought its first DC-4 in October 1953.

In August 1959 Korean National Airlines purchased one Lockheed L-749A Constellation four-engined airliner, and in June 1962 the government of South Korea reorganised the airline, which thereupon became Korean Air Lines. During the second half of the 1960s the airline enhanced its longer-haul capability by purchasing two examples of the Lockheed L-1049H Super Constellation, and these machines

were used for both charter work in South-East Asia and for a three- but later five-times-per-week service between Seoul and Osaka. During 1967 the Super Constellations were supplemented and then supplanted on this route by the Douglas DC-9-32, of which the airline received its first example on 19 July 1967.

Korean Air Lines was operating a steadily growing domestic network during this period, moreover, and this received a considerable fillip in late 1963 by the introduction of the airline's first turboprop-powered type, the Fokker F.27 Friendship Mk 200, of which the first was delivered on 20 December.

In March 1969 the government of South Korea sold its controlling interest to the Han Jin Transportation Group, and the airline has been privately owned since that time. Regional and international capability was enhanced in 1969 by the airline's receipt of its first Boeing Model 720-025 on 29 September, and in 1971 by the receipt of its first Boeing Model 707-3B5C in August.

On 13 July 1972 Korean Air Lines leased its first Boeing Model 727-100 three-turbofan airliner for medium-haul services, and later obtained four more aircraft of the same type before it introduced the improved Model 727-200 in 1980. The first wide-body airliner to serve with Korean Air Lines was the Boeing Model 747-2B5B, a four-turbofan type of which the first was accepted on 1 May 1973, and this pioneering transport was later followed by two other wide-body airliners, namely the McDonnell Douglas DC-10-30 three-turbofan type of which the first was delivered on 9 February 1975 and the Airbus A300B4-2C two-turbofan type of which the first was delivered on 1 August.

The growing numbers of these three types available to Korean Air Lines from the early 1970s allowed the airline to develop the extent and capacity of its route network, and it now operates to numerous points in the Far East, Asia, the Middle East, Europe and the USA in addition to its domestic network.

The airline has also continued to upgrade its fleet, with local and feeder services flown by the Fokker 100, domestic services by the McDonnell Douglas MD-80 series of aircraft updated from the DC-9 series, and longer-haul services by the latest variants of the Model 747 family augmented by the MD-11 development of the DC-10 and, in the near future, by the Airbus A330 and Boeing Model 777.

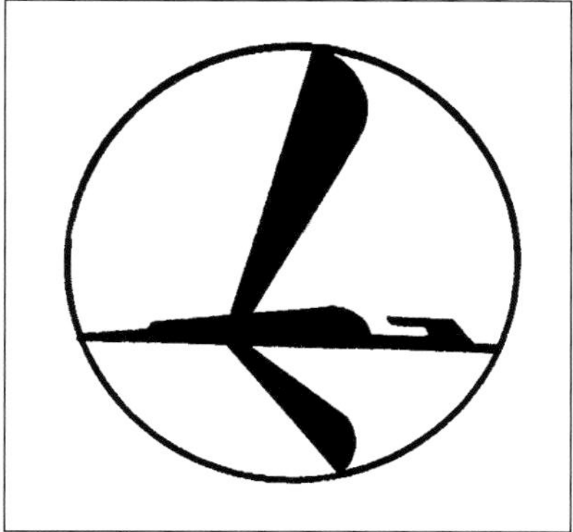

LOT-Polish Airlines

Country of origin: Poland

Generally accepted abbreviation: LO

Address: 39, 17 Stycznia Street, Warsaw PL-00-908, Poland

Type of operation: International, regional and domestic scheduled and charter passenger services

Shareholding: The Polish government and private investors

Subsidiaries: LOT Ground Services, LOT Catering Ltd, and LIM

Marketing alliances: None

Personnel: 3,945

Fleet:
- 8 x ATR 72-200
- 2 x Boeing Model 737-300
- 4 x Boeing Model 737-400
- 6 x Boeing Model 737-500
- 2 x Boeing Model 767-200
- 2 x Boeing Model 767-300

Orders:
- 2 x Boeing Model 737-300
- 2 x Boeing Model 737-400
- 2 x Boeing Model 737-800
- 1 x Boeing Model 767-300ER

Main base and hub: Warsaw

Route network: A domestic element to destinations such as Gdansk, Kraków, Poznan, Szczecin, and Wroclaw; and regional and international elements to destinations such as Bangkok, Chicago, Cologne, Damascus, Dubai, Düsseldorf, Frankfurt,

Continued on next page

LOT-Polish Airlines continued from previous page

Hamburg, Larnaca, London, New York, Oslo, Paris, Rome, Split, and Stockholm; a service between Zagreb and Warsaw is shared between LOT and Croatian Airlines

Simulators: Details not available

Maintenance services: Baza Techniczna PLL LOT with 670 staff

History: The Polish national flag carrier, Polskie Linje Lotnicze (LOT) can trace its history to the creation of two privately owned companies, namely Aero Lloyd Warschau and Aero TZ, that were established in 1922. Initially, each carrier had the Junkers F 13 single-engined machine that was the world's first all-metal transport aeroplane: Aero Lloyd started services on the routes linking Warsaw with Danzig and Lwów on 5 September 1922, while Aero TZ began operations with services from Warsaw to Posen via Lodz, and to Brno in Czechoslovakia. In 1925 Polish interests bought out the German holding in Aero Lloyd, which was then renamed Aerolet.

On 1 January 1929 the government of Poland took over all civil airline activities in Poland to create the nationalised carrier Polskie Linje Lotnicze (LOT), whose main equipment at the time of its formation was still the F 13, complemented by the Fokker F.VIIa single-engined transport and, later in the same year, the Fokker F.VIIb-3m three-engined development of the F.VIIa. LOT grew steadily during the early 1930s, and by 1934 was able to start a service between Warsaw and Beirut via Lwów, Cernauti, Bucharest, Sofia, Salonika (now Thessaloniki), Athens and Tel Aviv. By mid-1939 the airline's capabilities had improved considerably as a result of the introduction of equipment such as the Douglas DC-2, of which the first two had been delivered on 3 August 1935. These medium-capacity aircraft were followed in the first two months of 1936 by four examples of the Lockheed L-10A Electra small-capacity transport, which was used to launch services north-west to Copenhagen via Gdynia and also north to Helsinki via the capitals of the Baltic states. LOT also operated a fleet of German-built Ju 52/3m three-engined transports which, like the DC-2s, were powered by Polish-built Bristol Pegasus radial engines.

On 1 September 1939 Germany invaded Poland to begin World War II, and all Polish civil air operations immediately ceased: LOT's strength at that time was two DC-2 and 15 Electra and Super Electra aircraft, and of these only one Electra did not manage to escape to the neutrality of neighbouring countries. Poland was overrun in only one month, and no civil air operations were possible.

On 6 March 1945 (two months before the end of the war in Europe), however, Polish communists with the advancing Soviet forces were able to re-form LOT with a fleet strength that soon rose to 20 examples of the Lisunov Li-2 (the Soviet licence-built version of the Douglas DC-3). By the end of 1945 LOT was operating services to points as distant as London. The operator bought nine examples of the DC-3 during 1946, and during 1947 received the first three of an eventual five examples of the Sud-Est SE.161 Languedoc four-engined transport, the first of them arriving on 5 July.

More new equipment was introduced on 24 April 1949, when LOT received its first Ilyushin Il-12 two-engined transport, and three of these wholly inefficient machines remained on strength to November 1959. In 1955 LOT began scheduled services to Moscow, and on 20 June took delivery of its first Ilyushin Il-14 improved twin-engined transport, which finally supplanted the Il-12. LOT also operated a more advanced Western type in the form of five Convair CV-240 twin-engined transports, of which the first was received on 2 October 1957.

LOT's first turboprop-powered airliner was the Ilyushin Il-18B, of which the first entered revenue-earning service on the route between Warsaw and Moscow on 25 April 1961. The growing availability of this four-engined type enabled LOT to expand and improve its network to the Middle East, and even to begin services into Africa. LOT also bought three examples of the Vickers Viscount 804 to complement the Il-18B on lower-density routes, and received the first of these aircraft on 11 November 1962.

In 1966 LOT received 10 examples of the twin-turboprop Antonov An-24V to take over from the Il-14 on its domestic network and some regional routes, and the first of these machines reached Warsaw on 22 March for its operational debut on the route linking Warsaw and Wroclaw on 20 April. This Soviet type rapidly became the backbone of LOT's domestic and short-haul regional network.

LOT's first jet-powered transport was the Tupolev Tu-134, of which the first two entered service during November 1968, and this short/medium-haul type was complemented from the spring of 1972 by the larger and longer-ranged Ilyushin Il-62 that entered services on routes to destinations such as London, Milan, Moscow and Paris.

By the mid-1980s LOT was operating international services to points in Europe, North America, North Africa, the Middle East and Asia with aircraft such as the An-24, Il-18, Il-62, Tu-134 and Tu-154. With the disintegration of the Soviet-dominated Eastern bloc in the late 1980s, Poland was able to exercise a greater degree of autonomy in the sources it selected for its aircraft, and has since turned increasingly to Western manufacturers for aircraft that are more expensive in capital terms but also considerably more economical to run than their Russian counterparts. With the exception of the Tu-134 and Tu-154, therefore, LOT has been able to retire its Soviet-supplied airliners in favour of the ATR 72 for its local and feeder services, the Boeing Model 737 for its short- and medium-haul services, and the Boeing Model 767 for its long-haul services.

Lufthansa German Airlines

Country of origin: Germany

Generally accepted abbreviation: LH

Address: Von Gablenz Strasse 2-6, Köln D50679, Germany

Type of operation: International and regional scheduled and charter passenger and cargo services

Shareholding: Government of Germany and private investors

Subsidiaries: Lufthansa CityLine (100%), Condor (100%), DHL International (25%), Lauda Air (39.7%), Luxair (130%), Sun Express (40%), Lufthansa Cargo Airline

Marketing alliances: Mutual partnerships with Ansett, Canadian Airlines International, South African Airways, Thai Airways International; major agreements with SAS and VARIG; codesharing with United Airlines on Scandinavian routes, Adria Airways and Air Dolmiti; and pacts with Finnair, Lauda Air and Luxair

Notes: In 1993 Lufthansa established Lufthansa Express to operate its European regional routes. In October 1994 the majority of Lufthansa was sold to private investors as a result of a share issue in which the government of Germany did not participate. Other elements of the airline's restructuring effort include the establishment of separate subsidiaries for its cargo, technical and systems operations, and on 1 January 1996 Lufthansa separated its technical and freight operations into new autonomous companies known as Lufthansa Technik and Lufthansa Cargo. In May 1994 Lufthansa came to an agreement with Air India to operate German flights to Madras and Calcutta in exchange for an extra Indian flight to Berlin and one other city. Lufthansa has a codesharing agreement with United Airlines allowing Lufthansa flight numbers to Wichita, San José, Santa Ana, Ontario (California), Charlotte, Raleigh, and Tucson. In May 1995 Lufthansa signed a preliminary agreement about co-operation with South African Airways, and in the autumn of 1995 ended its thrice-weekly service between Frankfurt and Sydney, replacing this with connections operated by marketing partners Lauda Air, Thai Airways International and United Airlines. Early in 1996 Lufthansa started a co-operative agreement with SAS to pool flights between Scandinavia and Germany, co-ordinate other routes, and co-operate on other services, and in another agreement implemented on 1 January 1996 it co-ordinated its route planning with the Slovenian operator Adria Airways to improve connections between the two countries

Personnel: 57,740

Fleet:
11 x Airbus A300-600
11 x Airbus A310-300
6 x Airbus A319-100
33 x Airbus A320-200
20 x Airbus A321-100
6 x Airbus A340-200
8 x Airbus A340-300
19 x Boeing Model 737-200
39 x Boeing Model 737-300
7 x Boeing Model 737-300QC
6 x Boeing Model 737-400
30 x Boeing Model 737-500
6 x Boeing Model 747-200
4 x Boeing Model 747-200 Combi
17 x Boeing Model 747-400
1 x McDonnell Douglas DC-10

Orders:
20 x Airbus A319
11 x Airbus A321-100
1 x Airbus A340-300
3 x Boeing Model 737-300
2 x Boeing Model 747-400

Main bases and hubs: Berlin (Tempelhof), Bremen, Cologne/Bonn, Düsseldorf, Frankfurt, Hamburg, Hannover, Munich and Stuttgart

Route network: A European element to destinations including Amsterdam, Ankara, Antalya, Antwerp, Athens, Baku, Barcelona, Bari, Basle, Bastia, Bergamo, Bergen, Berlin, Bilbao, Billund, Birmingham, Bologna, Bonn, Bremen, Brussels, Bucharest, Budapest, Cagliari, Catania, Cologne, Copenhagen, Dresden, Dublin, Düsseldorf, East Midlands, Eindhoven, Ekaterinburg, Faro, Florence, Frankfurt, Friedrichshafen, Genoa, Glasgow, Gothenburg, Graz, Guernsey, Hamburg, Hannover, Helsinki, Innsbruck, Iráklion, Istanbul, Izmir, Jersey, Jönköping, Katowice, Kiel, Kiev, Larnaca, Las Palmas, Leipzig, Lille, Linz, Lisbon, Ljubljana, London, Lyon, Maastricht, Madrid, Málaga, Malmö, Malta, Manchester, Mannheim, Marseille, Milan, Minsk, Moscow, Munich, Munster, Naples, Nice, Novosibirsk, Nuremberg, Odessa, Olbia, Oporto, Oslo, Palma de Mallorca, Paris, Pisa, Prague, Rennes, Reykjavík, Riga, Rome, Rostock-Laage, Rotterdam, Saarbrücken, St Petersburg, Salzburg, Sofia, Stavanger, Stockholm, Strasbourg, Stuttgart, Tallinn, Tenerife, Thessaloniki, Toulouse, Trieste, Turin, Turku, Valencia, Venice, Verona, Vienna, Vilnius, Visby, Warsaw, Westerland, Zagreb, and Zürich; a North American element with destinations such as Atlanta, Boston, Chicago, Dallas, Los Angeles, Mexico City, Miami, Montreal, New York, and San Francisco; a South American element with destinations such as Bogotá, Buenos Aires, Lima, Rio de Janeiro, São Paulo, and Santiago (Chile); an Asian and Pacific element to destinations including Bangalore, Bangkok, Beijing, Bombay, Delhi, Hong Kong, Jakarta, Karachi, Kuala Lumpur, Madras, Manila, Nagoya, Osaka, Seoul, Shanghai, Singapore, Sydney, and Tokyo; an African element to destinations such as Cairo, Harare, Johannesburg, Nairobi, Tripoli, and Tunis; and a Middle Eastern element with destinations such as Tel Aviv

Simulators:
2 x Airbus A300-600
2 x Airbus A310-300
2 x Airbus A320-200
2 x Airbus A340-200/300
4 x Beech Bonanza A36/B38
1 x Boeing Model 707-300C
2 x Boeing Model 737-200
5 x Boeing Model 737-300/400/500
1 x Boeing Model 737-300EFIS
1 x Boeing Model 747-200
2 x Boeing Model 747-400
1 x Boeing Model 757-200
1 x Boeing Model 767-300
5 x Piper Cheyenne IIIA

Maintenance services: Lufthansa Technik specialises in airframes and engines with 1,500 licensed airframe engineers, 1,500 licensed engine engineers, and 750 licensed avionics engineers

History: Currently ranked third in the world and second in Europe, Lufthansa is Germany's

Continued on next page

Lufthansa continued from previous page

national flag carrier and can trace its lineage to 1919 and the establishment of a pioneering airline named Deutsche Luftreederei that operated a primitive service between Berlin and Weimar. A more immediate ancestor was Deutsche Luft Hansa, which came into existence on 6 January 1926 as a nationalised amalgamation of two other early German private operators, namely Deutsche Aero Lloyd and Junkers Luftverkehr. By 1939 and the outbreak of World War II, the company had become Deutsche Lufthansa and was the largest and most successful European airline operating an extensive network within Europe as well as services to South America, the Middle East and the Far East. Moreover, in addition to its own network of routes, Lufthansa also had access to services in China and through South America by means of a group of associated airlines established with a modest measure of German funding coupled with German impetus and technical expertise.

During the early 1930s the airline was involved in the clandestine training of pilots for the Luftwaffe, and by 1939 these crews had become the backbone of the German air force bomber squadrons. Deutsche Lufthansa continued to operate on a limited basis during World War II, but ceased flights in April 1945 and was banned by the victorious Allies in May 1945.

On 6 January 1953 a provisional holding company was formed as Luftag with support from the German federal railways and the state of Nordrhein-Westphalia. Soon after this the new airline was able to draw on private as well as government financing for the ordering of four examples each of the Lockheed L-1049G Super Constellation four-engined airliner and the Convair CV-340 twin-engined airliner.

On 16 August 1954 Luftag changed its name to Deutsche Lufthansa, and on 1 April 1955 the airline flew its first domestic service with a CV-340. From this time onward, expansion was fairly rapid, and Deutsche Lufthansa soon expanded its network over most parts of the European continent, beginning with services to London, Madrid and Paris. It was on 8 June 1955 that the operator flew its first intercontinental service when a Super Constellation reached New York from Hamburg via Düsseldorf and Shannon.

In December 1958 Deutsche Lufthansa placed in service its first turboprop-powered airliner, namely a Vickers Viscount 814 that had been received on 5 October. Deutsche Lufthansa, or Lufthansa as it was now commonly known, moved still further into the era of advanced-technology airliners on 3 February 1960, when it took delivery of its first Boeing Model 707-430 four-turbofan transport, and flew its first service non-stop from Frankfurt to New York on 17 March. The Model 707 was followed into Lufthansa service by another Boeing jetliner, namely the Model 727-230 three-turbofan type: the first of this important medium-haul model was received on 22 February 1964, and the type was operated mainly on the airline's steadily growing network of European routes.

Lufthansa became the first airline to order the Boeing Model 737 twin-turbofan short-haul airliner early in 1965, and the first two of an eventual 21 Model 737-100 aircraft were delivered to Lufthansa on 27 December 1967. This type was also used almost without variation on the European network.

The first wide-body aircraft ordered by Lufthansa was the Boeing Model 747-130, of which the first was delivered on 10 March 1970, and with the Douglas DC-10-30 this type constituted the core of Lufthansa's long-haul fleet during the 1970s and 1980s, shorter-haul routes being entrusted to the Airbus A300 as well as to the Boeing aircraft.

Lufthansa is a major operator of turbofan-powered Boeing aircraft, and also of a number of Airbus types. The airline now operates a very large route network, and its main subsidiaries are Condor Flugdienst formed in 1961 to carry out charter and inclusive tour flights for the parent company, Lufthansa Cargo Airline formed in 1977 for international and domestic scheduled and charter freight services, and Lufthansa CityLine (so named in March 1992 after creation in 1958 as Ostfriesische Lufttaxi for regional and domestic feeder services and then renamed Ostfriesische Lufttransport in 1970 and Deutsche Luftttransport in 1974).

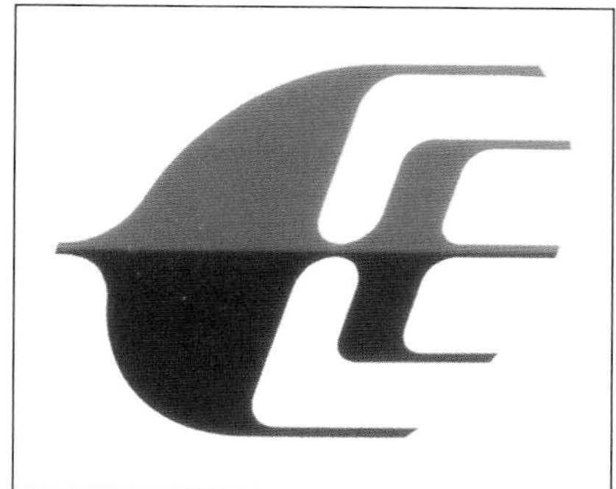

Malaysia Airlines

Country of origin: Malaysia

Generally accepted abbreviation: MH

Address: 33rd Floor, Bangunan MAS, Jalan Sultan Ismail, Kuala Lumpur, Federal Territory 50250, Malaysia

Type of operation: International, regional and domestic scheduled and charter passenger and cargo services

Shareholding: Bank Negara Malaysia (32%), Brunei Investment Agency (10%), Royal Brunei Airlines (10%), Kumpulan Wang Amanah Pencen (11.6%), Pemengang Amanah Raya Malaysia (9.7%), and Employees Provident Fund Board

Subsidiaries: Royal Air Cambodge (40%), Syarikat Pengangkutan Senai, Pengang Kargo Udara, Abacus Distribution Systems, MAS Hotels & Boutiques, Airfoil Service, Aircraft Engine Repair & Overhaul, MAS Academy, MAS Catering, MAS Engineering Services, MASKARGO, MAS Golden Boutiques, MAS Golden Holidays, and Tiara Malaysia Airlines

Marketing alliances: Codesharing with Ansett Australia, Ansett New Zealand, British Midland, frequent-flyer service with Singapore Airlines and Cathay Pacific, and alliance with Virgin Atlantic

Notes: Malaysia Airlines' shares were offered for sale in 1985 by the government of Malaysia, which retained a 'Special Share' to ensure control of major policies. In November 1992 the company doubled its capital, and now operates services to 57 international destinations (except the CIS) and 36 domestic destinations

Personnel: 19,615

Fleet:
1 x Airbus A300B4
12 x Airbus A330
2 x Boeing Model 737-300F
41 x Boeing Model 737-400
9 x Boeing Model 737-500
2 x Boeing Model 747-200F
1 x Boeing Model 747-300
13 x Boeing Model 747-400P
6 x de Havilland Canada DHC-6 Twin Otter
10 x Fokker 50
4 x McDonnell Douglas DC-10
5 x McDonnell Douglas MD-11

Orders:
10 x Boeing Model 747-400
11 x Boeing Model 777

Options:
10 x Boeing Model 747-400P
11 x Boeing Model 777-200
4 x Boeing Model 777-300

Main base and hub: Kuala Lumpur

Route network: A domestic element to destinations including Alor Setar, Bakalalan, Bario, Belaga, Bintulu, Ipoh, Johor Baharu, Kapit, Kota Baharu, Kota Kinabalu, Kuala Lumpur, Kuala Terengganu, Kuching, Kudat, Labuan, Lahad Datu, Langkawi, Lawas, Layang-Layang, Limbang, Long Lellang, Long Pasia, Long Semado, Long Seridan, Marudi, Miri, Mukah, Mulu, Pinang, Sahabat, Sandakan, Semporna, Sibu, Tawau, and Tomanggong; an African element to destinations such as Cape Town and Johannesburg; an American element to destinations such as Buenos Aires, Los Angeles and Mexico City; an Asian element to destinations including Bandar Seri Begawan, Bangkok, Cebu, Chiang Mai, Delhi, Denpasar, Hanoi, Hat Yai, Ho Chi Minh City, Jakarta, Karachi, Madras, Manila, Medan, Phnom Penh, Phuket, Pontianak, Singapore, Surabaya, Tarakan, and Ujung Padang; an Australasian element to destinations such as Adelaide, Auckland, Brisbane, Cairns, Darwin, Melbourne, Perth, and Sydney; a European element to destinations such as Amsterdam, Brussels, Frankfurt, Istanbul, London, Madrid, Munich, Paris, Rome, Vienna, and Zürich; a Middle Eastern element to destinations such as Dubai and Jiddah; and a Pacific Rim element to destinations such as Beijing, Fukuoka, Guangzhou, Hong Kong, Kaosiung, Nagoya, Osaka, Seoul, Taipei, and Tokyo

Simulators:
1 x Airbus A330-300
1 x Boeing Model 737-200
1 x Boeing Model 737-300/400/500
3 x Boeing Model 737-400
1 x Fokker 50
1 x McDonnell Douglas DC-10-30

Maintenance services: Malaysia Airlines specialises in airframes and engines with a staff of 2,635

History: The national flag carrier of Malaysia and currently enjoying rankings of 30th in the world and eighth in Asia, Malaysia Airlines was incorporated with the name Malaysian Airlines System on 1 October 1972 although it is a descendant of Malayan Airways, itself a descendant of Wearne's Air Services. Created in 1937 by Straits Steamship, Ocean Steamship and Imperial Airways, Wearne's Air Services flew its first service on 28 June 1937 between Singapore and Penang via Kuala Lumpur and Ipoh using a de Havilland D.H.89A Dragon Rapide. Wearne's Air Services continued in operation up to 7 December 1941, when the Japanese attacked Pearl Harbor and the American and British possessions in the Far East to precipitate the Pacific War of World War II.

It was not until 1947 that Mansfield & Co. Ltd. made plans to form Malayan Airways and to resume the Malayan routes that Wearne's Air Services had pioneered. The new airline's first revenue-earning service was a charter flight on 2 April 1947 using the new operator's first equipment, an Airspeed Consul, and its first scheduled service followed on 1 May. The airline had ambitious plans for longer services with greater passenger loads, so in the period from August 1947 to March 1948 it bought five Douglas DC-3 twin-engined aircraft from British Aviation Services. The airline ended its link with British Aviation Services late in 1947, and early in 1948 BOAC acquired a 10% shareholding in Malayan Airways. In the same year a bilateral agreement with Siam Airways made it possible for Malayan Airways to start a weekly service to Bangkok from April, and over the next three years the airline began to expand fairly quickly. By the end of 1951 Malayan Airways had a fleet of 11 DC-3 transports and, after the completion of further airports in Borneo, two D.H.89A Dragon Rapide aircraft were acquired from BEA for services to destinations in the remoter parts of this large island.

With the emergence of the Federation of Malaya on 31 August 1957, the decision was taken to spur the growth of Malayan Airways from an essentially domestic operator into an international airline that would be the flag carrier of the new nation. To further this objective BOAC and Qantas each took a 32%

Continued on next page

Malaysia Airlines continued from previous page

shareholding in the airline, and moves to rationalise the domestic network and fleet resulted in the incorporation into the airline's fleet of three de Havilland Canada DHC-3 Beaver single-engined bush transports previously operated by Federation Air Services, and the transfer of the two D.H.89A aircraft to newly created Borneo Airways. More important, however, was the leasing from Qantas of a Douglas DC-4 four-engined transport during 1958 for use on the airline's first long-haul service to Hong Kong.

On 1 August 1959 Malayan Airways received its first turbine-powered aircraft in the form of two Vickers Viscount 760 transports, and these airliners soon entered revenue-earning service on the routes linking Singapore with Kuala Lumpur, Jakarta and Borneo. In March 1960 the airline leased Lockheed Super Constellation aircraft from Qantas for the service to Hong Kong, but this service ended in October for lack of adequate traffic. Malayan Airways then leased Bristol Britannia four-turboprop aircraft from BOAC, with which to operate the route from September 1961 in conjunction with Cathay Pacific Airways.

In 1961 Malayan Airways decided that the time was ripe for replacement of its DC-3 aircraft, and the type selected was the Fokker F.27 Friendship Mk 200, of which five were ordered in February 1962 for delivery from May 1963. Malayan Airways' first pure-jet airliner was a de Havilland Comet 4, leased in December 1962 from BOAC for the service linking Singapore with Jakarta and Hong Kong.

During November 1963 the creation of Malaysia out of the Federation of Malaya resulted in a change of name, Malayan Airways thus becoming Malaysian Airways. During the later part of 1965 Malaysian Airways bought five examples of the Comet 4 from BOAC for the first stage of a planned expansion of the airline's international route network. In 1966 the governments of Malaysia and Singapore acquired a joint controlling interest in the airline, and further change followed on 1 November 1967 when Malaysian Airways became Malaysia-Singapore Airlines. Soon after this the airline decided to re-equip the fleet with five Boeing Model 737-112 twin-turbofan and three Boeing Model 707-312B four-turbofan airliners for its short- and long-haul services respectively: the first Model 707 was received on 28 May 1968, and the first Model 737 on 16 July 1969. On 15 December 1968 Malaysia-Singapore Airlines took delivery of two Britten-Norman BN-2A Islander twin-engined light transports for the operation of rural services in the eastern part of Malaysia. In October 1970 Malaysia-Singapore Airlines finally secured the right to operate flights to London (Heathrow).

The contract between Malaysia and Singapore for the operation of a joint airline ended in the course of December 1972 in line with the two countries' earlier decision to establish their own national flag carriers, and the Malaysian Airline System was established on 1 October 1972 with a fleet of Model 737, F.27 and Islander aircraft for services in the Malaysian peninsula as well as to Sabah and Sarawak, and in 1974 the operator inaugurated a service to London with Model 707 aircraft.

By the middle of the 1970s, the growth of the Malaysian Airline System's network and traffic made it sensible to start the acquisition of wide-body aircraft, of which the first was a McDonnell Douglas DC-10-30 three-turbofan type accepted on 2 August 1976, with two additional aircraft following in 1977 and 1981. Further expansion required still more capacity, and in 1982 the Malaysian Airline System received the first of an initial two examples of the Boeing Model 747-236B four-turbofan transports, and this type soon replaced the DC-10 on the airline's European services. The Malaysian Airline System then placed an order for five examples of the twin-turbofan Airbus A300B4, of which the first was accepted on 3 November 1979, and this type was used mainly on the airline's Asian route network in conjunction with three DC-10 aircraft, with the Model 737 aircraft plying the shorter-haul regional and domestic networks, and the F.27, BN-2A and Twin Otter machines servicing feeder and local services.

In October 1987 the name of the operator was changed from Malaysian Airline System to Malaysia Airlines, and this carrier now operates a large network with a fleet based on a growing number of advanced transport aircraft.

Northwest Airlines

Country of origin: USA

Generally accepted abbreviation: NW

Address: 5101 Northwest Drive, St Paul, Minnesota 55111-3034, USA

Type of operation: International, regional and domestic scheduled and charter passenger and cargo services

Shareholding: Employees (27%), KLM Royal Dutch Airlines (18.8%), Alfred Checchi (11%), and Gary Wilson (11%)

Subsidiaries: Northwest Aerospace Training, Northwest PARS Holding, Northwest Aircraft, MLT and NWA Leasing

Marketing alliances: KLM Royal Dutch Airlines, Asiana, Northwest Air Link, Aloha Air, Aloha Airlines, Eurowings and Pacific Island Aviation, and lesser alliances with Alaska Airlines and Asiana, and a feeder alliance with Express Airlines I, Horizon Air Industries, Mesaba Airlines, Trans States Airlines and Business Express operating as Northwest Airlink

Notes: Northwest Airlines is the world's fourth largest airline and serves more than 240 destinations in 22 countries, and its alliance with KLM is considered one of the most advanced in the airline business anywhere in the world

Personnel: 47,000

Fleet:
- 50 x Airbus A320-200
- 47 x Boeing Model 727-200
- 3 x Boeing Model 747-100
- 28 x Boeing Model 747-200/200F
- 10 x Boeing Model 747-400
- 48 x Boeing Model 757-200
- 22 x McDonnell Douglas DC-9-10
- 106 x McDonnell Douglas DC-9-30
- 12 x McDonnell Douglas DC-9-40
- 35 x McDonnell Douglas DC-9-50
- 11 x McDonnell Douglas DC-10-30
- 21 x McDonnell Douglas DC-10-40
- 8 x McDonnell Douglas MD-80

Orders:
- 20 x Airbus A330
- 4 x Boeing Model 747-400
- 29 x Boeing Model 757-200

Main bases and hubs: Detroit, Minneapolis/St Paul, Memphis and Tokyo (Narita)

Route network: A domestic element to more than 104 cities in 45 states of the USA; an Asian and Pacific element to destinations including Bangkok, Beijing, Bombay, Delhi, Fukuoka, Guam, Hong Kong, Manila, Nagoya, Osaka, Saipan, Seoul, Shanghai, Singapore, Taipei, and Tokyo; a European element to destinations such as Amsterdam, Frankfurt, London, and Paris; a Canadian element to destinations such as Calgary, Edmonton, Halifax, Montreal, Ottawa, Regina, Saskatoon, Toronto, Vancouver, and Winnipeg; a Caribbean element to destinations including Bermuda, Grand Cayman, Montego Bay, St Maarten, and San Juan; and a Mexican element to destinations such as Cancún, Cozumel, Zihuatanejo and Puerta Vallarta

Maintenance services: Details not available

History: Currently ranked seventh in the world and fourth in North America, the operator now known as Northwest Airlines was created on 1 August 1926 as Northwest Airways by a group of businessmen from Detroit and the twin cities of Minneapolis and St Paul. The new airline flew its first service on 1 October using a Curtiss Oriole to deliver a load of mail from St Paul to Chicago. The airline flew its first passenger service over the same route in July 1927 with a fleet of three Stinson Detroiter aircraft. Adverse weather led to a suspension of services between the late autumn of 1927 and June 1928, and in September of that year the airline acquired better-equipped Hamilton H.47 aircraft to provide a greater likelihood of being able to maintain services during the winter months.

In 1931 Northwest Airways inaugurated its first international route, in this instance to Winnipeg in Canada, and in the same year bought two examples of the Sikorsky S-38 amphibian flying boats for services to Duluth. During 1932 the airline gained greater independence when the 45% shareholding in the company held in equal portions by Transcontinental Air Transport and the Aviation Corporation of America was bought out, and in the following year the airline was able to buy Lockheed Model 10A Electra modern twin-engined airliners to replace the ageing Ford Tri-Motors three-engined transports that were currently its operational mainstay. The Electra remained in service for eight years and proved very successful.

In 1934 the operator was renamed Northwest Airlines, and in 1937 adopted the more capable Lockheed Model 14 Super Electra, but as this lacked the capacity of the Douglas DC-3 operated by rival operators it was replaced during 1939 by an initial seven DC-3 aircraft ordered in 1938 and delivered from 22 April 1939. Northwest Airlines flew its first revenue-earning service with the DC-3 in the same month on the route linking the Twin Cities and Chicago, and by the middle of the following month this route had been extended west to Seattle. The DC-3, of which the airline eventually operated 36 examples, remained in service up to 1958.

During World War II, in which the United States was involved from 1941 to 1945, Northwest Airlines flew transport services from Minneapolis to Fairbanks in Alaska, undertook pilot training for the US Army Air Forces on the Curtiss C-46 Commando twin-engined transport, and at its St Paul base modified more than 3,000 examples of the Consolidated B-24 Liberator and North American B-25 Mitchell bombers.

Conventional airline operations returned in the middle of 1945 as the defeat of Japan became imminent, and in June the airline was granted an extension of its service from Milwaukee via Detroit to New York. This longer service required more-capable equipment, and Northwest Airlines placed an order for the Douglas DC-4 four-engined airliner that entered service on the airline's most important American routes from March 1946. The DC-4 was soon supplemented from 1947 by the Martin 2-0-2, a twin-engined type that entered service first with Northwest Airlines.

Northwest Airlines had now extended its horizons across the Pacific Ocean to Tokyo and Manila via Anchorage, and flew its first service on this route on 15 July 1947. On 29 July 1948 Northwest Airlines operated its first service to the Hawaiian Islands from Seattle and Portland, and the increasing importance of this area were reflected in a change of name to Northwest Orient Airlines during 1947.

Continued on next page

Northwest continued from previous page

Soon after the end of World War II the airline had decided to buy the Lockheed Constellation four-engined airliner, but in 1948 Northwest Orient Airlines actually ordered 10 examples of the rival Boeing Model 377 Stratocruiser as this offered the type of economical high-altitude performance needed for flights across the Pacific. The first of the Stratocruiser airliners was delivered on 22 June 1949, and these aircraft were initially put into service on the Honolulu route and remained in service until 12 September 1960 when they were delivered to Lockheed as part of a trade-in deal when Northwest Orient bought the Lockheed L-188 Electra four-turboprop airliner.

Soon after this the United States became involved in the Korean War (1950-53), and during this conflict Northwest Orient flew more than 1,400 two-way services across the Pacific on behalf of the military. The establishment of Japan Air Lines in August 1951 was made possible by Northwest Orient Airlines' provision of technical support and aircraft, the latter comprising DC-4 and Martin 2-0-2 machines, but in October 1952 Transocean Air Lines succeeded Northwest Orient Airlines in this role.

In the early 1950s Northwest Orient Airlines decided that its growth was being hampered by the limited capacity of its DC-4 aircraft, and from September 1953 leased from Flying Tigers four examples of the Douglas DC-6A freighter that were then revised to an all-passenger configuration. The airline later took additional DC-6 aircraft, and the type served Northwest Orient with considerable success for 12 years, the last of its DC-6B airliners being sold to United Arab Airlines on 10 June 1965. In April 1953 the airline placed an order for six (later reduced to four) examples of the Lockheed L-1049G Super Constellation, and became the first operator of this type on 15 February 1955, when it supplanted the DC-4 on the operator's Far Eastern services. Northwest Orient Airlines flew the Super Constellation for only two years, however, for on 28 February 1957 it took delivery of its first Douglas DC-7C, the type it had selected to replace both the Stratocruiser and the Super Constellation on its Pacific routes and longer domestic services.

Northwest Orient Airlines only operated one turboprop-powered airliner, namely the Electra mentioned above: the airline ordered the type in November 1958, received it on 19 July 1959, and flew its first service with the type on 1 September 1959 on the route linking Minneapolis and New York via Milwaukee. Only one year later, on 18 May

1960, Northwest Orient received its first pure-jet type in the form of the Douglas DC-8-32, which was flown on the operator's Pacific routes from 8 July 1960. Three years later Northwest Orient Airlines replaced its DC-8 aircraft with Boeing Model 720-051B four-engined machines, of which the first two were received on 22 June 1961. The airline soon added the closely related Boeing Model 707-351 to its fleet, and for the remainder of the 1960s this long-haul type was the mainstay of Northwest Orient's fleet together with the Boeing Model 727 three-turbofan type (first delivered on 12 November 1964) that provided a medium-haul capability.

Like other major operators, Northwest Orient Airlines adopted the Boeing Model 747 wide-body transport soon after its introduction, and took delivery of its first Model 747-151 on 30 April 1970 for use on the airline's domestic and international services on 22 June and 1 July 1970 respectively on the route linking the Twin Cities and New York, and that between Chicago and Tokyo via Seattle. The next wide-body type to enter service with Northwest Orient was the Douglas DC-10-30 ordered in 1968 and delivered from 10 November 1972.

Northwest Orient Airlines continued to grow during the 1970s, and in April 1979 reached another milestone with the start of services from Seattle to Europe, where the first destinations were Copenhagen and Prestwick. In the 1980s the operator became an American pioneer of the products of the first European manufacturer of wide-body aircraft when it ordered the Airbus A320. Although it considered a merger with National Airlines in 1971, Northwest Orient neither merged with nor took over another operator until 12 August 1986, when it took over Republic Airlines. The airline is also the second oldest American airline to have retained its basic identity since creation, but was reorganised in 1985 to create NWA as the holding company for the core airline (now renamed as Northwest Airlines) and several subsidiaries.

Northwest Airlines currently operates the McDonnell Douglas DC-9 family (five variants including the updated MD-80) as its standard short-haul type for low-density routes, the Airbus A320 as its standard short/medium-haul type for medium-density routes, the Model 727 as its standard medium-haul type for medium-density routes, and the DC-10 and Model 747 as its standard long-haul type for high- and medium-density routes respectively. More advanced types are currently on order and option to keep this major airline fully abreast of the latest developments in airliner technology.

Olympic Airways

Country of origin: Greece

Generally accepted abbreviation: OA

Address: 99-100 Syngrou Avenue, Athens, Greece

Type of operation: International, regional and domestic scheduled passenger and cargo services

Shareholding: Government-owned

Subsidiaries: Olympic Aviation, Olympic Catering, Olympic Airtours, Macedonian Airlines, and Galileo Hellas

Marketing alliances: Swissair, VASP

Personnel: 9,825

Fleet:
2 x Airbus A300-600R
6 x Airbus A300-B4
3 x Boeing Model 727-200
11 x Boeing Model 737-200
7 x Boeing Model 737-400
4 x Boeing Model 747-200B

Main base and hub: Athens

Route network: A domestic element with services from Athens to some 34 Greek Island and mainland destinations; a European element with destinations including Amsterdam, Barcelona, Belgrade, Berlin, Brussels, Bucharest, Copenhagen, Düsseldorf, Frankfurt, Geneva, Istanbul, Larnaca, London, Madrid, Marseille, Milan, Munich, Paris, Rome, Stuttgart, Tirana, Vienna, and Zürich; an African element to destinations such as Alexandria, Benghazi, Cairo, Johannesburg, and Nairobi; an American element to destinations such as Montreal, New York and Toronto; an Asian and Australasian element to destinations such as Bangkok, Melbourne and Sydney; and a Middle Eastern element to destinations including Beirut, Dubai, Jiddah, Kuwait, Riyadh, and Tel Aviv

Simulators:
1 x Airbus A300B4
1 x Boeing Model 737-200
1 x Boeing Model 737-400
1 x Boeing Model 747-200

Maintenance services: Olympic Airways specialises in airframes and engines with 375 licensed airframe engineers, 375 licensed engine engineers, and 206 licensed avionics engineers

History: The origins of Olympic Airways, the national flag carrier of Greece, can be traced to 1951 and the establishment of Technical and Aeronautical Exploitations Co. by the amalgamation of the Aeroporike Metaphore Ellados, Hellas and TAE companies. The operator's services were mainly local, but the new airline did not fare well as a result of the twin problems of obsolete aircraft and the lack of capital. The Greek government nationalised the airline in 1955, but this failed to improve matters.

It was at this stage that Aristotle Onassis, the shipping magnate, offered to take over the airline, providing additional capital and management capability, to create a successful national flag carrier. The government of Greece accepted the offer, and Onassis was awarded a 50-year concession as the national flag carrier and sole operator of domestic routes. Onassis renamed Technical and Aeronautical Exploitations as Olympic Airways, and one of the first changes was the retirement of the airline's obsolete Douglas DC-4 four-engined airliners in favour of more-advanced Douglas DC-6B four-engined machines leased from the French airline Union Aeromaritime de Transport. After careful assessment of its route network, Olympic Airways opted to concentrate on its European and Mediterranean operations before developing longer-haul services.

By 1961 the airliner fleet operated by Olympic Airways had been extensively overhauled to include 4 examples of the jet-powered de Havilland Comet 4B leased from BEA, 4 Douglas DC-6B and 2 DC-4 aircraft, as well as 13 DC-3 machines for local services, with 2 four-jet Douglas DC-8s about to be delivered.

Continued on next page

Olympic continued from previous page

Growth and profitability followed before rising fuel prices and a declining market reversed the trend, and as losses mounted Onassis sold Olympic Airways back to the Greek government in August 1975, at which time the airline's network connected Greece to some 25 points in Africa, Asia, Australia, Europe and North America.

By 1978 however, the airline was again in difficultie and in December an agreement with Swissair provided assistance with the management and further reorganisation of the airline, which now operates the Airbus A300 and Boeing Model 727 respectively on its short-haul routes of the high- and medium-density types respectively, the A300-600R on its medium-haul routes, and the Boeing Model 747 on its long-haul routes.

A wholly-owned subsidiary, Olympic Aviation, has complete operational autonomy but is in effect the domestic partner of Olympic Airways with a route network spanning some 34 destinations in the Greek mainland and islands from bases at Athens, Thessaloniki, Chios, Ioánnina, Kárpathos, Kásos, Límnos, Mykonos, Mytilene, Ródhos, and Santoríni. Olympic Aviation's fleet comprises four ATR 42, six ATR 72, seven Dornier Do 228, and five Shorts SD-330 aircraft.

Pakistan International Airlines

Country of origin: Pakistan

Generally accepted abbreviation: PK

Address: PIA Building, Quaide Azam International Airport, Karachi 75200, Pakistan

Type of operation: International and regional scheduled and charter passenger and cargo services

Shareholding: Government of Pakistan (56%)

Subsidiaries: None

Personnel: 20,400

Fleet:
- 9 x Airbus A300B4
- 6 x Airbus A310-300
- 2 x Boeing Model 707-300C
- 6 x Boeing 737-300
- 6 x Boeing Model 747-200B
- 2 x Boeing Model 747-200B Combi
- 2 x de Havilland Canada DHC-6 Twin Otter
- 13 x Fokker F.27 Friendship Mk 200/400

Main bases and hubs: Islamabad, Lahore, Karachi and Peshawar

Route network: An African element to destinations such as Cairo, Nairobi and Tripoli;

an Asian and Pacific Rim element to destinations including Bangkok, Beijing, Bombay, Colombo, Delhi, Dhaka, Jakarta, Kathmandu, Kuala Lumpur, Malé, Manila, Singapore, Tashkent, and Tokyo; a European element to destinations such as Amsterdam, Athens, Copenhagen, Frankfurt, Istanbul, London, Manchester, Moscow, Paris, Rome, and Zürich; a Middle Eastern element to destinations such as Abu Dhabi, Al Ain, Amman, Baghdad, Bahrain, Damascus, Dhahran, Doha, Dubai, Fujairah, Jiddah, Kuwait, Muscat, Ras al-Khaimah, Sharjah, Tehran, and Riyadh; and a North American element with destinations such as New York and Toronto

Simulators: 1 x Airbus A300B4
1 x Boeing Model 707-320B
1 x Boeing Model 747-200

Maintenance services: Pakistan International Airlines specialises in airframes and engines with 325 licensed airframe engineers, 75 licensed engine engineers, and 305 licensed avionics engineers

History: After a short period of independence, Pakistan decided in 1951 that it needed a national flag carrier airline; the government of the country accordingly established Pakistan International Airlines in this role, and on 25 May ordered three examples of the Lockheed L-1049C Super Constellation four-engined airliner as the new operator's initial equipment. Pakistan International Airlines flew its first service with the Super Constellation on 7 June 1954 on the route linking Karachi and Dacca (now Dhaka), which were the main cities of the country's western and eastern halves, of which the latter is now Bangladesh. On 1 February 1955 the airline flew its first international service, between Karachi and London via Cairo.

On 11 March 1955 Pakistan International Airlines formally took over the assets and routes of another Pakistani operator, Orient Airways, which had in effect been part of Pakistan International Airlines since October 1953. The consolidation of the two airlines meant that Pakistan International Airlines could enlarge its domestic network with 11 Douglas DC-3 and two Convair CV-240 aircraft, which left the Super Constellation machines wholly free for international services.

Modernisation of the fleet used for domestic and regional operations was now a matter of high priority, and in May 1956 the airline placed an order for three examples of the Vickers Viscount 815 four-turboprop airliner, the first of which was accepted in the UK on 2 January 1959 for a debut in revenue-earning service on the service linking Karachi and Delhi on 31 January. Further enhancement came in 1961 with the debut of the Fokker F.27 Friendship twin-turboprop type, of which the first was received on 3 January 1961. The availability of the F.27 for operation on the routes linking the major Pakistani cities freed the DC-3 fleet for use on new services to the remoter parts of East Pakistan.

Pakistan International Airlines was the first Asian airline with pure-jet aircraft, in the form of Boeing Model 707-121 machines leased from Pan American World Airways for use from 7 March 1960 on the London service that was extended to New York on 5 May 1961. On 21 December 1961 Pakistan International Airlines began to receive its own jet aircraft when it took delivery of the first of three Boeing Model 720-040B aircraft, whose availability permitted the operator to enlarge its international route network.

In 1963 Pakistan International Airlines called off its New York service, but on 29 April 1964 became the first non-communist airline to operate a service to the Chinese city of Shanghai. In 1971 East Pakistan secured its independence as Bangladesh, and Pakistan International Airlines ceased operations to that country. The airline's fleet and network were both reduced, but the service to New York was resumed in 1972. Regional capability was now poor, and as a result Pakistan International Airlines ordered four examples of the Hawker Siddeley HS.121 Trident, of which the first was accepted on 1 March 1966. The aircraft were later sold to the Civil Aviation Administration of China in 1970.

The first wide-body airliner used by Pakistan Intrnational Airlines was the McDonnell Douglas DC-10-30 three-turbofan type, which the airline first received on 1 March 1974. A pair of Boeing Model 747-282B four-turbofan aircraft (initially leased from TAP Air Portugal) followed in April 1976, and on 3 March 1980 the airline accepted its first Airbus A300B4-203 two-turbofan type subsequently complemented by the A310-300.

The A300, A310 and Model 747 are currently the mainstays of Pakistan International Airlines' medium- and long-haul operations, with feeder and local services provided by the Boeing Model 737-300 and F.27 Friendship.

Boeing 747

It was in the early 1960s that Boeing started to develop its fourth type of jet-powered airliner, and the largest yet to be built anywhere in the world. The programme was a by-product, in the shorter term, of the work the company had undertaken for a large military transport for the US Air Force's CHX requirement. When Lockheed won the military order with its C-5A Galaxy, Boeing soon started to consider civil alternatives of its military project with a 'double-bubble' fuselage and a mid-set wing, but eventually adopted a more conventional airliner configuration similar to that of its pioneering Model 707 although on a much larger scale. The design that then emerged as the Model 747 was based on a fuselage with a single main deck, wide enough over most of its length for 10-abreast seating with two aisles; the flight deck was at a higher level, with a small passenger cabin to its rear and accessed by a spiral stairway from the main deck.

By 1965 the basic concept of this huge airliner, with seating for up to 500 passengers, had been settled and the powerplant had been confirmed as a quartet of the all-new Pratt & Whitney JT9D turbofan. The launch order for the new airliner was planned by Pan American and was delivered on 14 April 1966.

The first Model 747 made its maiden flight on 9 February 1969 at Everett, Washington, where Boeing had established a wholly new production facility for the massive airliner, which as a result of its huge size soon became known as the 'jumbo jet'.

Later development of the basic design has yielded a growing number of variants and subvariants, most of which have retained the overall dimensions and configuration of the first Model, although it is worth noting that the Model 747-300 introduced a longer upper deck, while the Model 747-400 retained this extended upper deck in combination with a longer-span wing fitted with distinctive drag-reducing 'winglets' on its tips.

The original Model 747 was powered by four JT9D-1 or -3 turbofans each rated at 43,500lb st (193.50kN) dry, and had a maximum take-off weight of 710,000lb (322,056kg). Other engines that were introduced on this variant as the maximum take-off weight was steadily increased included the JT9D-3A, -3W, -7 and -7W, and after the introduction of the next major variant the original Model 747 was redesignated as the Model 747-100.

This next variant, first flown on 11 October 1970 as the Model 747B, was the Model 747-200 with increased weights, more fuel and more-powerful engines. A variant introduced in 1973 for operation at reduced weights was the Model 747SR (Short-Range) that was later redesignated as the Model 747-100B, and is operated mainly in Japan for high-capacity services over short ranges. Alternative variants of the Model 747-200 were then introduced to service for the freighter or convertible passenger/freighter roles as the Model 747F and Model 747C respectively with an upward-hinging nose for straight-in freight loading: the first examples of the Model 747F and Model 747C made their maiden flights on 30 November 1971 and 23 March 1973 respectively, and 1974 saw the appearance of the Model 747M Combi with a large side-loading freight door to the rear of the wing and, in some examples, a nose-loading door. All these Model 747 variants are dimensionally similar with a span of 195ft 8in (59.64m) and length of 231ft 10in (70.66m), but the Model 747SP (Special Performance) that made its initial flight on 4 July 1975 has a fuselage shortened by 48ft 0in (14.63m) for typical mixed-class accommodation for 288 passengers, a taller vertical tail surface, and other less obvious changes.

The Model 747 was certificated on 30 December 1969 and entered revenue-earning service on 21 January 1970 when Pan American started a transatlantic service with the type. The Model 747-200 was certificated on 23 December 1970 and entered revenue-earning service with KLM early in 1971. Certification of the Model 747F arrived on 7 March 1972 and the type entered service with Lufthansa on 19 April 1972; the Model 747C convertible variant with nose-loading door was certificated on 24 April 1973 for service with World Airways; and the Model 747M Combi entered service in 1974 with Sabena. Of the two other variants listed above, the Model 747SR entered service with Japan Air Lines on 9 October 1973 and the Model 747SP with Pan American in May 1976.

After launching the Model 747 in 1966, Boeing started to consider a 'stretched' version of the basic airliner with any or all of several features, such as more-powerful engines, greater fuel capacity and higher maximum take-off weights, to improve the aeroplane's operating economics and to widen its operational capabilities. However, plans to enlarge the passenger capacity came to fruition only slowly: the two possible 'stretches' studied in the 1970s were the lengthening of the fuselage by 'plugs' fore and aft of the wing for a maximum capacity of 600, and the introduction of an upper deck along most of the length of the fuselage behind the current bulge to provide a capacity for 1,000 or more passengers.

The decline in the market for air travel that occurred from the early 1980s, as a result of the Arab nations' increase in oil prices, rendered both of these changes redundant, and a more modest 'stretch' was developed in 1980, when Boeing suggested an upper deck extended to the rear by 23ft 4in (7.11m) to double this deck's seating area. The new variant was initially known as the Model 747SUD (Stretched Upper Deck), then as the Model 747EUD (Extended Upper Deck), and finally as the Model 747-300.

The value of the upper-deck seating for airlines is suggested by this area's steady development: the original Model 747 certification allowed only eight passengers in the upper cabin; then the introduction of a smoke barrier increased the limit to 16; the later replacement of the original spiral stairway by a straight unit permitted an increase to 24; the addition of a second emergency exit boosted seating to 32 or 45 passengers with a spiral or straight stairway respectively; and the introduction of an upper-deck fairing lengthened to the rear allowed the carriage of 69 passengers in the Model 747-300 and later developments.

Boeing committed itself to production of the Model 747-300 on the basis of a Swissair order for both passenger and Model 747-300M Combi versions. The first Model 747-300 made its maiden flight on 5 October 1982 with JT9D-7R4G2 engines, and the second example flew on 10 December 1982 with CF6-50E2 engines.

The Model 747-300 is available with powerplant and maximum take-off weight options similar to those of the Model 747-200. The Model 747-300M Combi has a side-loading freight door in the fuselage to the rear of the wing to provide capability for mixed passenger and freight loads, while the Model 747-300SR is a short-range variant that operates at lower weights for a higher flight/flight hour ratio. A further development of the stretched upper deck concept is embodied in the Model 747-400 that Boeing launched in October 1985 on the basis of a 10-aircraft order placed by Northwest Airlines and followed in March 1986 by a 14-aircraft order from Singapore Airlines. The Model 747-400 differs from the Model 747-300 in the extensive nature of the changes effected in its structure and systems, an advanced 'glass' flightdeck for operation by a two-man crew, extended wingtips fitted with winglets that increase the span to 212ft 2in (64.67m), and a choice of advanced-technology engines of the 'lean burn' type such as the 56,000lb st (249.10kN) Pratt & Whitney PW4056, the 59,000lb st (262.45kN) General Electric CF6-80C2, and the 56,000lb st (249.10kN) Rolls-Royce RB.211-524D4D.

The Model 747-300 was certificated on 7 March 1983 and entered service with Swissair on 28 March with JT9D engines, while the first operator to fly the Model 747-300 with CF6-50E2 engines was UTA from 1 April 1983; the first airline to operate the Model 747-300 with RB.211-524D4 engines was Qantas from 25 November 1984.

The Model 747-400 was certificated on 10 January 1989 with the PW4056 engine, and the variants with the CF6-80C and RB.211-524G engines followed on 8 May and 8 June 1989 respectively. In May 1990 Boeing decided to cease marketing of all variants except the Model 747-400, and the 1,000th 'jumbo jet' delivered was a Model 747-400 handed over to Singapore Airlines on 12 October 1993. The subvariants of the Model 747-400 basic passenger transport include the Model 747-400 Combi, Model 747-400F, Model 747-400 Domestic with special two-class accommodation for 568 passengers, and the Model 747-400 Performance Improvement Package announced in 1993 with a number of enhanced features to reduce structure weight, provide a higher take-off weight, and reduce drag.

Boeing is actively considering a number of other developments offering greater payload/range performance for such time as the market will justify the cost of such a development.

Philippine Airlines

Country of origin: The Philippines

Generally accepted abbreviation: PR

Address: PAL Building, 1 Legaspi Street, Legaspi Village, Makati Metro Manila 1059, Philippines

Type of operation: International, regional and domestic scheduled passenger and cargo services

Shareholding: PR Holdings (67%) and the government of the Philippines (33%)

Notes: During 1992 a 67% controlling share in the carrier was sold to PR Holdings, a consortium of local banking investors, by the government of the Philippines, which retains the balance of the equity. The airline flies services to 43 domestic destinations and 34 overseas destinations. Since May 1995, when it revealed crippling losses, Philippine Airlines has started to renew its fleet and restructure its route network

Personnel: 14,125

Fleet:
12 x Airbus A300B4
4 x Airbus A340-200
2 x Airbus A340-300
12 x Boeing Model 737-300
9 x Boeing Model 747-200
3 x Boeing Model 747-400
10 x Fokker 50
3 x McDonnell Douglas DC-10-30
1 x McDonnell Douglas MD-11ER

Orders:
12 x Airbus A320
8 x Airbus A330-300
8 x Airbus A340-300
8 x Boeing Model 747-400

Main base and hub: Manila

Route network: A domestic element to destinations including Bacolod, Baguio, Basco, Bislig, Busuanga, Butuan, Cagayan de Oro, Calbayog, Camiguin, Catarman, Cebu, Cotabato, Daet, Davao, Dipolog, Dumaguete, General Santos, Iligan, Iloilo, Jolo, Kilibo, Laoag, Legaspi, Marinduque, Masbate, Naga, Ormoc, Ozamis, Pagadian, Puerto Princesa, Roxas, San Jose, Surigao, Tablas, Tacloban, Tagbilaran, Tandag, Tawi-Tawi, Tuguegarao, Virac, and Zamboanga; an American element to destinations such as Los Angeles, New York and San Francisco; a European element to destinations such as Frankfurt, London, Paris and Rome; an Asian and Pacific Rim element to destinations including Bandar Seri Begawan, Bangkok, Brisbane, Fukuoka, Ho Chi Minh City, Hong Kong, Honolulu, Jakarta, Kaohsiung, Kota Kinabalu, Kuala Lumpur, Labuan, Melbourne, Menado, Seoul, Singapore, Sydney, Taipei, Tokyo, and Xiamen; and an African and Middle Eastern element to destinations such as Abu Dhabi, Cairo, Dhahran, Dubai, Jiddah, Kuwait, and Riyadh

Simulators:
1 x BAC One-Eleven 500
1 x Boeing Model 737-300EFIS
1 x Fokker F.27 Friendship Mk 100

Maintenance services: Philippine Airlines specialises in airframes with 80 licensed airframe engineers and 80 licensed avionics engineers

History: The national flag carrier of the Republic of the Philippines, Philippine Airlines can trace its origins to 1931, when a Filipino named Andres Soriano and a number of Americans established the Philippine Aerial Taxi Co. (PATCO) for the operation initially of private and charter flights. In 1936, however, PATCO moved into the field of scheduled services and changed its name to the Philippine Air Transport Co. By 1938 PATCO was flying two scheduled services from Manila to Baguio and Legaspi. PATCO went bankrupt in July 1940, but was re-formed on 25 February 1941 as Philippine Air Lines with backing from American and Filipino interests, the former including Trans World Airlines with a 25% shareholding. The revised operator flew its first service on 15 March 1941 with a flight from Manila to Baguio, using a Beech Model 18.

Philippine Air Lines halted operations in

Qantas Airways

Country of origin: Australia

Generally accepted abbreviation: QF

Address: Qantas Centre, QCA9, 203 Coward Street, Sydney, NSW 2020, Australia

Type of operation: International, regional and domestic scheduled passenger services

Shareholding: British Airways (25%) and private investors

Subsidiaries: Australia-Asia Airlines, Eastern Australia, Southern Australia, Qantair, QH Tours, Qantas Flight Catering Holdings, Qantas Distribution Services, Asia Pacific Distribution, Qantas Information Technology, Air Pacific (10%), Travel, Southern Insurances (Singapore), QHF Insurance, Qantas Investments (US), Qantas Superannuation, Qantas Airline Systems and Research, and Air New Zealand (19.9%)

Marketing alliances: British Airways, Canadian Airlines International, American Airlines, USAir, Deutsche BA, TAT and Air Pacific

Notes: After reviewing its worldwide schedules in 1995, Qantas ended its London (Heathrow) to Manchester extension launched in August 1994 and expanded the Asian route network with a resumption of flights to China. The airline has been listed on the Australian stock exchange since the end of July 1995 after raising a substantial sum for the government of Australia when the latter's 75% shareholding was sold

Personnel: 28,950

Fleet:
4 x Airbus A300B4
16 x Boeing Model 737-300

December 1941 after Japanese forces invaded the islands, but continued after the end of World War II with a fleet of five Douglas C-47 twin-engined transports. The first scheduled service was flown on 14 February 1946 from Manila to Legaspi. Over the next 20 years more than thirty examples of the C-47, military version of the DC-3, saw service with Philippine Air Lines after being converted to civil use. The development of Philippine Air Lines in the years after World War II was extraordinarily rapid. Troop-carrying charters across the Pacific to Oakland in California began on 31 July 1946 with leased Douglas DC-4 four-engined transports, and regular passenger services to the west coast of the USA started in December 1946. Further Douglas DC-4 transports for these services were available after Philippine Air Lines had acquired Far East Air Transport on 6 May 1947.

In 1948 Philippine Air Lines bought its first four examples of the Douglas DC-6, the first of these aircraft being received on 14 April for initial service on 29 May on the route from Manila to London, via Bangkok, Calcutta, Karachi, Cairo, Rome and Madrid: from London the route crossed the Atlantic and the United States to San Francisco, and thence back to Manila. In a mere two years Philippine Air Lines had developed from a domestic operator to an airline that had a route that encircled the globe. In September 1948 the airline bought the financially failing Commercial Airlines, and late in 1950 acquired another Philippine airline, Trans Asiatic Airlines.

Further enlargement of the airline's route network to Italy and Switzerland was agreed shortly after this, and during 1953 Philippine Air Lines received authorisation to launch a service across the Pacific to Mexico. With the exception of the Hong Kong service, however, Philippine Air Lines suspended all long-haul routes in April 1954 after the loss of a DC-6 at Rome on 14 January 1954 and decreasing passenger demand for its service to San Francisco. During the mid-1950s the Hong Kong service was operated by Convair CV-340 twin-engined aircraft, of which the first had been delivered on 27 March 1953. The CV-340 was supplanted later in the decade by the Vickers Viscount 784, received on 10 May 1955 for a first service on 1 June. From the start the Viscount also operated the key domestic services to Cebu, Davao and Zamboanga.

Additional capability was provided on Philippine Air Lines' domestic routes from 1960 by the partial replacement of the C-47 by the Fokker F.27 Friendship twin-turboprop transport, of which the first was received on 23 February, and from 1967 the F.27 was itself replaced by a larger twin-turboprop type, the Hawker Siddeley HS.748 which was first received on 20 February of that year. Throughout this period, services to remote areas were undertaken by a number of de Havilland Canada DHC-3 Otter single-engined and Scottish Aviation Twin Pioneer Mk 2 twin-engined STOL transports.

Philippine Air Lines entered the era of jet-powered aircraft early in 1962 with the lease of Boeing Model 707 machines from Pan American World Airways, but these were replaced from 20 June by Douglas DC-8-53 machines leased from KLM. The availability of these four-jet aircraft permitted the resurrection of services across the Pacific to San Francisco. Further jet equipment began to enter service in May 1966 when the Viscount was replaced on domestic and regional services by the BAC One-Eleven twin-turbofan type, of which the first example was received on 19 April. For some of its domestic services Philippine Air Lines also operated the NAMC YS-11 twin-turboprop transport, of which the first four were acquired from the bankrupt Filipinas Orient Airways in January 1974.

Wide-body equipment entered service to provide additional capability on long-haul services to Europe, the USA and the Middle East. The first of these types was the McDonnell Douglas DC-10-30, of which an initial example was leased from KLM on 11 July 1974, and the second was the Boeing Model 747-2F6B that was delivered on 21 December 1979. These two types still constitute the main long-haul capability of the airline, which is now known as Philippine Airlines. On the short- and medium-haul routes to China, Japan and Singapore the Airbus A300 is the operator's mainstay, the first of these aircraft having been received on 29 November 1979.

In the late 1970s the airline decided to upgrade its medium-haul capability on lower-density routes with the three-turbofan Boeing Model 727, of which the first were Model 727-2M7 machines leased from Hughes Airwest in July and August 1979 but later replaced by a pair of Model 727-134 aircraft bought from Transair Sweden in September and October 1981. The Model 727 aircraft were later sold, and Philippine Airlines' current capability on the short- and medium-haul routes is vested in the Fokker 50 for feeder and low-density domestic services, and the Boeing Model 737-300 for high-density domestic and regional services. The airline underwent a period of acute financial difficulty during the 1980s and early 1990s, and is now seeking to re-establish itself with a larger and more capable fleet based on Model 747 aircraft and three types of Airbus transports.

22 x Boeing Model 737-400
5 x Boeing Model 747-200B/C
6 x Boeing Model 747-300
18 x Boeing Model 747-400
2 x Boeing Model 747SP
7 x Boeing Model 767-200ER
17 x Boeing Model 767-300ER

Orders: 2 x Boeing Model 767-300ER

Route network: A domestic element to destinations such as Adelaide, Alice Springs, Brisbane, Cairns, Canberra, Coolangatta, Darwin, Hobart, Launceston, Mackay, Maroochydore, Melbourne, Nhulunbuy (Gove), Perth, Proserpine, Rockhampton, Sydney, Townsville, and Yulara (Ayers Rock); an African element to destinations such as Harare and Johannesburg; an American element to destinations including Boston, Chicago, Los Angeles, New York, San Francisco, Toronto, Vancouver, and Washington DC; an Asian and Pacific element to destinations such as Auckland, Bangkok, Beijing, Christchurch, Denpasar, Fukuoka, Hong Kong, Honiara, Honolulu, Jakarta, Kuala Lumpur, Manila, Mount Hagen, Nadi, Nagoya, Nouméa, Osaka, Papeete, Port Hedland, Port Moresby, Sapporo, Seoul, Singapore, Taipei, Tokyo, and Wellington; and a European element to destinations such as Frankfurt, London and Rome

Simulators: 1 x Airbus A300B4
1 x Boeing Model 707-320
1 x Boeing Model 727-200
2 x Boeing Model 737-300EFIS
1 x Boeing Model 737-400EFIS
1 x Boeing Model 747-200
1 x Boeing Model 747-300
3 x Boeing Model 747-400
1 x Boeing Model 767-200ER
1 x Boeing Model 767-300ER

Maintenance services: Qantas Airways Engineering & Maintenance specialises in airframes and engines with 1,060 licensed airframe engineers, 1,315 licensed engine engineers, and 770 licensed avionics engineers

History: The national flag carrier of Australia and currently enjoying rankings of 14th in the world and second in Asia, Qantas Airways can trace its origins to 16 November 1920 and the establishment of the Queensland and Northern Territory Aerial Services (QANTAS). For

Continued on next page

Qantas continued from previous page

the first two years of its existence the company concentrated on air taxi and joyriding flights with two biplane types, namely an Avro Type 504K and a Royal Aircraft Factory B.E.2e, and it was only on 1 November 1922 that QANTAS flew its first scheduled service, using an Armstrong Whitworth F.K.8 for the route linking Charleville and Cloncurry. Until the mid-1930s QANTAS concentrated on the development of a 1,475-mile (2,375-km) route network in Queensland, where it was also involved in the provision of flying doctor services. In 1931, however, QANTAS had sufficient strength and capability to co-operate with Imperial Airways in the launch of the air service between the UK and Australia, and this partnership was further enhanced on 18 January 1934, when the two companies formed QANTAS Empire Airways to fly the sector between Singapore and Brisbane, initially with de Havilland D.H.86 four-engined biplanes. Further long-haul capability arrived in 1938, when QANTAS took delivery of the first of an eventual six examples of the Short 'C' or 'Empire' class flying boat that was designed for passenger and mail services within the context of the Empire Air Mail Service.

QANTAS cut back its activities during World War II, and in this period the airline's most important contribution to the Allied war effort was the implementation and operation of the eastern sector of the 'Horseshoe Route' (connecting the UK with Australasia via Durban in South Africa), using mainly two types of consolidated aircraft, namely the Catalina amphibian flying boat and the Liberator long-range landplane.

With the end of World War II in 1945 QANTAS was able to resume conventional airline services. By this time the airline was more interested in long-haul services than domestic operations, and the latter were gradually transferred to Trans-Australian Airlines from 1946. The emphasis on longer-haul routes was signalled emphatically by the nature of the aircraft ordered by QANTAS, of which the most important was the Lockheed Constellation four-engined type for which the airline contracted in October 1946.

On 3 July 1947 the government of Australia bought out QANTAS, having earlier purchased the shareholding in the company owned by BOAC as successor to Imperial Airways, and at this time the airline became the Australian national flag carrier. On 15 May 1947 QANTAS started a service across the Pacific to San Francisco, and in 1958 this formed the basis of a round-the-globe operation as the route was extended across the United States to New York, then across the Atlantic to London, and finally back to Australia via the Middle East and the Far East. On 1 December 1947 QANTAS also inaugurated its Kangaroo Service between Sydney and London using the Constellation. Continued growth was the norm for QANTAS after this, with a link to New Zealand created across the Tasman Sea in association with Tasman Empire Air Lines, in which QANTAS was a shareholder. During 1954 the service across the Pacific was extended when QANTAS took over from British Commonwealth Pacific Airlines the route from Sydney to Vancouver via Fiji, Honolulu and San Francisco.

QANTAS entered the era of turbine-powered aircraft in 1958 with the acquisition of Boeing Model 707 four-turbojet and Lockheed L-188 Electra four-turboprop airliners, of which the former was initially operated on the route across the Pacific to North America, and the latter was used to launch QANTAS's own service to New Zealand. Growth continued through the 1960s, and in August 1967 the airline changed its name to Qantas Airways. The airline now flies a very substantial route network within Australia, on which the Boeing Model 737 twin-turbofan airliner is the workhorse of the fleet after Qantas's 1992 purchase of Australian Airlines, and throughout the Pacific and Far East together with other services to North America, the Middle East and Europe; it uses a small number of Airbus A300 twin-turbofan wide-body aircraft for its regional services and a substantial fleet of Boeing Model 747 four-turbofan wide-body aircraft in four variants, in conjunction with the Model 767 twin-turbofan wide-body airliner, for its longer-haul services.

Royal Jordanian Airlines

Country of origin: Jordan

Generally accepted abbreviation: RJ

Address: PO Box 302, Amman, Jordan

Type of operation: International and regional scheduled passenger and cargo services

Shareholding: Royal Jordanian Airlines is wholly owned by the government of Jordan, but is scheduled for privatisation

Subsidiaries: Arab Wings Co., Royal Tours, Alia Hospitality Services, Royal Falcons, Alia Gateway Hotel, Royal Jordanian Boutique, Jordan Express Tourist, Jordan TV Cinema & Radio Co., Training Centre (Simulator), and Royal Jordanian Academy

Personnel: 4,970

Fleet:
4 x Airbus A310-300
3 x Airbus A320-200
3 x Boeing Model 707-320C
2 x Boeing Model 727-200
5 x Lockheed L-1011-500 TriStar

Orders: 3 x Airbus A320-200

Main base and hub: Amman

Route network: An African element to destinations such as Cairo, Casablanca and Tunis; an Asian element to destinations such as Bangkok, Calcutta, Colombo, Delhi, Jakarta, Karachi, Kuala Lumpur, and Singapore; a European element to destinations including Amsterdam, Ankara, Athens, Belgrade, Berlin, Brussels, Frankfurt, Geneva, Istanbul, Larnaca, London, Madrid, Paris, Rome, and Vienna; a Middle Eastern element to destinations including Abu Dhabi, Aden, Aqaba, Baghdad, Bahrain, Beirut, Damascus, Dhahran, Doha, Dubai, Jiddah, Muscat, Riyadh, and Sana'a; and a North American element to destinations such as Montreal, Toronto and New York

Simulators:
1 x Airbus A310-300
1 x Airbus A320-200
1 x Boeing Model 707-200
1 x Boeing Model 727-200
1 x Lockheed L-1011-500

Maintenance services: Royal Jordanian specialises in airframes and engines with 25 licensed airframe engineers, 40 licensed engine engineers, and 165 licensed avionics engineers

History: Royal Jordanian Airlines is the national flag carrier of the Hashemite Kingdom of Jordan, and although its current incarnation dates back to 1963, the background of the company can be traced to 1950, when Ismail Bilbeisi formed Air Jordan as a short-haul operator with a small fleet of Airspeed Consul aircraft operating from a base at Amman, until it was re-equipped by an American operator, Transocean Airlines, with Douglas DC-3 twin-engined and Douglas DC-

Continued on next page

Royal Jordanian continued from previous page

4 four-engined airliners at the start of a far-sighted but over-ambitious expansion effort. Air Jordan took over the failed Arab Airways, another Jordanian operator, and reconstituted this as Air Jordan of the Holy Land, but the revived airline became bankrupt in July 1960, and Air Jordan itself ran into major problems and ceased operations on 7 September of the same year.

On the same date, Jordan Airways was created as a subsidiary of Middle East Airlines, and this survived with a fleet of two Douglas DC-7C four-engined airliners until the establishment of Alia – The Royal Jordanian Airline – in December 1963. The new operator soon added a domestic and regional capability in the form of two Handley Page Herald twin-turboprop airliners that remained in service until 1965. Alia's first pure-jet equipment was the Sud-Aviation Caravelle 10R, of which the first was received on 28 July 1965, and the availability of this machine allowed the airline to extend its services to Rome and Paris, while for its domestic and regional services the airline operated leased examples of the Vickers Viscount four-turboprop airliner from late in 1966 until 31 March 1967. The Viscounts were replaced by Fokker F.27 twin-turboprop aircraft, of which the first was leased in 1967 but soon replaced by the operator's own aircraft delivered from February 1968.

Alia was now growing moderately rapidly and, to supplement and then supplant the Caravelle on its international services, Alia bought an initial two examples of the Boeing Model 707 four-jet airliner, of which the first was received on 26 January 1971, and these were followed by the airline's first Boeing Model 720-030B on 30 November 1972. Another Boeing type, the Model 727-2D3, was added to the fleet from 8 July 1974 for improved capability on medium-haul routes.

Wide-body aircraft were now available, and on 13 April 1977 Alia took delivery of its first of three such transports, a Boeing Model 747-2D3B, for services to Western Europe and the USA. Also used on the airline's lower-density long-haul routes is the Lockheed L-1011-500 TriStar, the first of which was received on 11 September 1981.

In December 1986 the name of the airline was changed to Royal Jordanian Airlines, and this now operates three of its earlier American types (the Model 707, Model 727 and the L-1011) as well as an increasing number of Airbus wide-body types such as the A310 and A320.

Sabena Belgian World Airlines

Country of origin: Belgium

Generally accepted abbreviation: SN

Address: 2 Avenue E. Mounierlaan, Brussels B-1200, Belgium

Type of operation: International and regional scheduled passenger and cargo services

Shareholding: Government of Belgium (13%), Swissair (49.5%) and Air France (33.3%)

Subsidiaries: Sobelair (100%)

Marketing alliances: Delta Air Lines and TAP Air Portugal

Notes: Swissair gained a 49% shareholding in Sabena through an agreement signed on 6 March 1995

Personnel: 9,500

Fleet:
2 x Airbus A310-200
1 x Airbus A310-300
4 x Airbus A340-200
13 x Boeing Model 737-200/200C
6 x Boeing Model 737-300
3 x Boeing Model 737-400
6 x Boeing Model 737-500
1 x Boeing Model 747-100
2 x Boeing Model 747-300
3 x McDonnell Douglas DC-10-30CF

Orders:
4 x Airbus A330-200
3 x Airbus A330-300

Main base and hub: Brussels

Route network: An African element to destinations such as Abidjan, Bamako, Banjul, Brazzaville, Bujumbura, Casablanca, Conakry, Cotonou, Dakar, Douala, Entebbe, Freetown, Kano, Kigali, Kinshasa, Lagos, Libreville, Lomé, Luanda, Nairobi, Niamey, Ouagadougou, and Tunis; an Asian element to destinations such as Bangkok and Tokyo; a European element to destinations including Amsterdam, Ankara, Antwerp, Athens, Barcelona, Basel, Berlin, Bilbao, Billund, Birmingham, Bologna, Bordeaux, Bristol, Brussels, Budapest, Copenhagen, Düsseldorf, Edinburgh, Florence, Frankfurt, Geneva, Genoa, Glasgow, Gothenburg, Hamburg, Hannover, Helsinki, Istanbul, Leeds Bradford, Lisbon, London, Luxembourg, Lyon, Madrid, Málaga, Manchester, Marseille, Milan, Munich, Naples, Newcastle, Nice, Oporto, Oslo, Paris, Prague, Rome, Sofia, Stockholm, Stuttgart, Turin, Venice, Vienna, Warsaw, and Zürich; a Middle Eastern element to destinations such as Tel Aviv; and a North American element to destinations such as Atlanta, Boston, Chicago, Montreal and New York

Simulators:
1 x Boeing Model 737-200
1 x Boeing Model 737-300/400/500
1 x McDonnell Douglas DC-10-30

Maintenance services: Sabena Technics specialises in airframes and engines with 460 licensed airframe engineers, 200 licensed engine engineers, and 190 licensed avionics engineers

History: The Belgian national flag carrier, and currently enjoying the rankings of 41st in the world and 10th in Europe, the Société Anonyme Belge d'Exploitation de la Navigation Aérienne (SABENA) was created on 23 May 1923 by business interests in Belgium and the Belgian Congo, and by the end of 1924 SABENA was operating a European route network to Amsterdam and Basel, the latter via Strasbourg, using a mix of de Havilland types as well as Breguet Bre.14 and Farman F.60 Goliath machines.

As a significant portion of the airline's capital had been provided by elements in the Belgian Congo, SABENA soon started operations in this African territory in succession to the Ligne Aerienne de Roi Albert (LARA). Although initial consideration was given to the use of waterplanes in this extensively rivered region, SABENA finally opted for landplanes and, after the clearance of the necessary airfields, services began in 1926 and 1927. The longest of the services in the Belgian Congo was that covering some 1,425 miles (2,295km) between

Boma and Elisabethville, and this was initially operated by a de Havilland D.H.50 that was supplanted later by a Handley Page W.8f.

During the early 1930s SABENA flew services on a network extending from Brussels to Copenhagen, Malmö and Berlin, using Handley Page W.8f and W.8b as well as Westland Wessex airliners and no fewer than 16 Fokker F.VIIb-3m three-engined airliners. On the pioneering service to Léopoldville in the Belgian Congo, the airline used the Savoia-Marchetti S.73 three-engined airliner. Later in the decade SABENA adopted more-modern aircraft such as the three-engined Junkers Ju 52/3m, the Savoia-Marchetti S.83 development of the S.73, and the Douglas DC-3 twin-engined transport.

As the Germans surged west in May 1940 in the course of their invasion of the Low Countries and France, SABENA managed to evacuate most of its DC-3 and Savoia-Marchetti aircraft to Britain but, after two of them had been shot down, opted to move its fleet to North Africa where most of the aircraft were captured by the Germans.

By this time the part of the airline operating in the Belgian Congo with F.VII and Ju 52/3m aircraft had effectively become independent, and expanded with a number of Lockheed aircraft (the Model 14 Super Electra and Model 18 Lodestar) during the course of World War II so that by 1945 its route network covered 20,000 miles (32,200km).

SABENA was revived in Europe after the war, and on 4 June 1947 launched its first transatlantic service to New York, via Shannon and Gander, with Douglas DC-4 four-engined transports. For service on its growing European network the airline introduced the Convair CV-240 (first received on 27 February 1949); the CV-240 was itself replaced by the improved Convair CV-340 after 13 June 1956.

SABENA inaugurated an experimental helicopter air mail service in August 1950 with Bell Model 47D light helicopters, later supplemented by larger Sikorsky S-55 machines that allowed an extension of the service to Maastricht in the Netherlands as the world's first international air mail route for helicopters. On 1 September 1953 the airline inaugurated a helicopter passenger service, and this lasted until 1966, by which time the network linked 12 Belgian cities.

SABENA had moved into the jet age on 18 February 1961 when the CV-440 was replaced by the Sud-Aviation Caravelle that entered service on the route linking Brussels and Nice, after an initial delivery on 20 January of the same year. SABENA's first jet-powered airliner was in fact the Boeing Model 707-329, which made its first revenue-earning service on 23 January 1960 between Brussels and New York, and the same type also launched a jet service to the Belgian Congo on 26 January 1960. The latter service lasted only until 28 January 1961, when SABENA ceased services to the Congo after that country's independence from Belgium and the creation of Air Congo.

While the Caravelle and Model 707 provided adequate capability for SABENA's low-density short-haul service and long-haul service respectively, the requirements of higher-density medium-haul routes necessitated new equipment that arrived in the form of the Boeing Model 727-29 three-turbofan airliner, first delivered on 25 April 1967 for a service debut on 15 June. Growing traffic on the long-haul routes also demanded more capacity and the airline, now generally known as Sabena, became an operator of the new type of wide-body transport on 19 November 1970 with the Boeing Model 747-129 four-turbofan type for its high-density services, followed on 18 September 1973 by the McDonnell Douglas DC-10-30CF three-turbofan convertible passenger and freight transport for its medium-density services. Sabena completed the first stage of the transition into its current form with the replacement of the Model 727 by the Boeing Model 737-229 that flew its first service for the airline on 15 April 1974.

Sabena then standardised on the Model 737 (now in four variants), the Model 747 (three variants) and the DC-10, later augmented by a smaller number of two Airbus types, the A310 (in two variants) and the A340.

Scandinavian Airlines System

Countries of origin: Denmark, Norway and Sweden

Generally accepted abbreviation: SK

Address: Frosundaviks Aile 1, Stockholm S-16187, Sweden

Type of operation: International and regional scheduled passenger and cargo services

Shareholding: SAS comprises three national limited companies each owned half by its government and half by private investors

Subsidiaries: Radisson SAS Hotels Worldwide, British Midland (40%) and Spanair (49%)

Marketing alliances: Continental Airlines, Lufthansa, United Airlines

Notes: In the ratio of 2:2:3 the owners of SAS are Det Danske Luftfartselskap (Danish Airlines), Det Norske Luftfartselskap (Norwegian Airlines) and Aerotransport (Swedish Airlines). SAS took control of Linjeflyg in 1992, and on 1 January 1993 integrated Linjeflyg's services with its own. The airline is notable for its development of a global network of marketing and traffic alliances: together with Swissair and Austrian Airlines, for example, it forms the European Quality Alliance collaborative grouping. Early in 1996 it started an arrangement with Lufthansa under which the two airlines pool flights between Scandinavia and Germany, co-ordinate other routes and co-operate in other services; and on 1 January 1996 SAS implemented a co-operation (including codesharing) agreement with United Airlines

Personnel: 20,900

Fleet:
14 x Boeing Model 767-300
4 x McDonnell Douglas DC-9-21
25 x McDonnell Douglas DC-9-41
38 x McDonnell Douglas MD-81
12 x McDonnell Douglas MD-82
20 x McDonnell Douglas MD-83
18 x McDonnell Douglas MD-87
6 x McDonnell Douglas MD-90

Orders:
41 x Boeing Model 737-600
2 x McDonnell Douglas MD-90

Options: 35 x Boeing Model 767-300

Main bases and hubs: Copenhagen, Oslo and Stockholm

Route network: A 'domestic' element to destinations such as Århus, Bergen, Copenhagen, Gothenburg, Oslo, Stavanger, Stockholm, and Tromsøan African, Middle Eastern and American element to destinations such as Houston, New York, San Francisco and Washington DC; an Asian and Pacific Rim element to destinations such as Bangkok, Beijing, Delhi, Hong Kong, Osaka, and Singapore; a British Isles element to destinations such as Aberdeen, Dublin, Edinburgh, Glasgow, London, and Manchester; and a European element to destinations including Gdansk, Helsinki, Kaliningrad, Kiev, Moscow, Pori, Riga, St Petersburg, Tallinn, Tampere, Turku, Vaasa, Vilnius, and Warsaw

Simulators:
1 x Airbus A320-200
1 x Boeing Model 737-300/500
1 x Boeing Model 767-300ER
2 x Fokker F.28 Fellowship Series 1000/4000
1 x Fokker 50
1 x McDonnell Douglas DC-8-63/73
2 x McDonnell Douglas DC-9-41
1 x McDonnell Douglas DC-10-10/30
3 x McDonnell Douglas MD-82/87EFIS
1 x Saab 340A

Maintenance services: SAS Sweden specialises in airframes and engines

History: The 'national' flag carrier of the three Scandinavian countries of Denmark, Norway and Sweden and currently enjoying rankings of 15th in the world and eighth in Europe, the Scandinavian Airlines System was created on 31 July 1946 as a consortium of the leading pre-World War II airlines of Denmark, Norway and Sweden, namely Det Danske Luftfart-selskap (DDL), Det Norske Luftfartselskap (DNL) and AB Aerotransport (ABA) respectively. The Danish and Norwegians were specialists in European services, but the Swedish operator had greater vision and after the war had inaugurated a service to Tehran. DDL started services on 7 August 1920 with the Junkers F 13 floatplane on the route linking Copenhagen and Berlin; ABA flew its first service on 2 June 1924 with an F 13 on the route linking Stockholm and Helsinki; and DNL made its first revenue-earning flight in April 1928.

The new consortium was divided into seven parts that were allocated in the ratio 2:2:3 to Denmark, Norway and Sweden, and its primary objective was the operation of economical services across the North

Atlantic and on other long-haul routes: in this capacity its first flight was a Douglas DC-4 service from Stockholm and Copenhagen to New York on 16 September 1946. In 1948 the three SAS partners created an SAS European Division to co-ordinate their previously separate European services, and in July of that year the consortium was enlarged by the merger of another Swedish airline, Svensk Inter-kontinental Lufttrafik, with Aerotransport. It was not until 8 February 1951, however, that the three constituent airlines agreed the establishment of a single centralised management organisation with the three airlines becoming non-operating holding companies. As late as 1954, however, the three basic elements of the airline were still flying under their own names.

During the later 1940s and early 1950s SAS launched a number of new services such as those to Buenos Aires in December 1946, Bangkok in October 1949 and Johannesburg in January 1953. By this time SAS's most important long-haul airliner was the Douglas DC-6 four-engined type, with the Douglas DC-3 and Saab 90A twin-engined types dominating on the operator's European services. SAS inaugurated the first trans-polar service between Copenhagen and Los Angeles on 15 November 1954 with DC-6B aircraft, and on 24 February 1957 added a service between Copenhagen and Tokyo with Douglas DC-7 aircraft. Two years later, SAS moved into the pure-jet age with the Sud-Aviation Caravelle, of which it received its first example on 10 April 1959.

SAS introduced the Douglas DC-8-32 four-jet airliner on its long-haul services on 1 May 1960 with a flight between Copenhagen and New York, and then pioneered the Douglas DC-9-30 and DC-9-40 twin-turbofan airliners, both developed to meet the airline's particular req-uirements, on its short-haul services in Europe from 1968.

In common with many other airlines concerned to increase market share by the adoption of the latest and most economical equipment, SAS was an early customer for the wide-body airliner with a turbofan powerplant, and received its first Boeing Model 747 on 22 February 1971. Since that time the airline has added substantial numbers of additional short- and medium-haul twin-turbofan airliners to its fleet and now operates both the DC-9 (eight variants including five of the upgraded MD-80/90 development) and the Boeing Model 737 (one variant), and for its longer-haul services has standardised on the Boeing Model 767 (one variant).

Saudia

Country of origin: Saudi Arabia

Generally accepted abbreviation: SV

Address: PO Box 620, Jiddah 21231, Saudi Arabia

Type of operation: International, regional and domestic scheduled passenger and cargo services

Shareholding: Government-owned

Subsidiaries: None

Personnel: 24,825

Fleet:
11 x Airbus A300-600
6 x Beech Bonanza A36
2 x Beech King Air A100
2 x Boeing Model 707-300C
20 x Boeing Model 737-200
7 x Boeing Model 747-100
2 x Boeing Model 747-200F
11 x Boeing Model 747-300
3 x Boeing Model 747SP
1 x Boeing Model 757
2 x Cessna Citation II
2 x Dassault Falcon 900
1 x de Havilland Canada DHC-6 Twin Otter
4 x Gulfstream Aerospace Gulfstream II
5 x Gulfstream Aerospace Gulfstream III
6 x Gulfstream Aerospace Gulfstream IV
17 x Lockheed L-1011-200 TriStar
2 x Lockheed L-1011-500 TriStar
2 x McDonnell Douglas DC-8-72
2 x McDonnell Douglas MD-11
8 x Piper PA-28 Archer

Orders:
5 x Boeing Model 747-400
23 x Boeing Model 777-200
4 x McDonnell Douglas MD-11
29 x McDonnell Douglas MD-90

Main bases and hubs: Dhahran, Jiddah and Riyadh

Route network: Domestic services between 25 points as well as routes to 52 destinations in Africa, Asia, Europe, the Middle East, the Far East, and the USA

Simulators:
1 x Airbus A300-600
1 x Boeing Model 737-200
1 x Boeing Model 747-100
1 x Lockheed L-1011-200 TriStar

Maintenance services: Details not available

History: The national flag carrier of Saudi Arabia, Saudia is currently ranked 27th in the world and was established as Saudi Arabian Airlines in May 1945, when a small fleet of Douglas C-47 twin-engined military transports was bought and converted for civil use. These aircraft began operations on air mail and charter services between Riyadh, Jiddah and Dhahran, and flew the airline's first scheduled service on 14 March 1947. The early services were designed in part to explore the commercial viability of airline operations in Saudi Arabia, and were sufficiently encouraging for the airline to place an order in 1948 for five examples of the Bristol Type 170 Wayfarer twin-engined transport, a high-wing type with fixed landing gear admirably suited to operations to and from semi-prepared airstrips. In 1951 Saudi Arabian Airlines moved toward standard airline operations with an order for five examples of the Douglas C-54 Skymaster four-engined military transport, revised to DC-4 civil standard. The airline received its first examples of the Wayfarer on 28 June 1949 and the first two examples of the C-54 in June 1952.

In 1952 Saudi Arabian Airlines ordered the first three of an eventual 10 examples of the Convair CV-340 twin-engined airliner, and accepted the first two of these on 3 June 1954. The airline gradually enlarged its domestic network, and late in 1961 launched its first international services to neighbouring countries in the Middle East as well as to Bombay, Cairo and Karachi using its first pure-jet type, the Boeing Model 720-068B, of which the initial pair were received on 20 December 1961.

Continued on next page

Saudia continued from previous page

On 8 February 1967 Saudi Arabian Airlines took delivery of its first Douglas DC-9-15 twin-jet airliner as the first stage in the modernisation of its high-density domestic services, on which it initially complemented and then supplanted the CV-340 on the routes linking Riyadh, Jiddah and Dhahran. Another major step in the airline's development was the inauguration of services to London in May 1967. In the same year, Saudi Arabian Airlines contracted for two examples of the Boeing Model 707 four-turbofan airliner, and took delivery of the first of these machines on 8 January 1968. These advanced aircraft were initially operated on a non-stop service between Riyadh and London, supplemented late in 1969 by a link with Algiers.

In 1972 Saudi Arabian Airlines changed its name to Saudia, and on 14 March of that year took delivery of its first Boeing Model 737 twin-turbofan airliner for a further boost to its domestic route network. The delivery of additional aircraft of the same type finally permitted the retirement of the CV-340 piston-engined aircraft and the sale of the DC-9 turbine-engined machines. By the end of the decade Saudia was becoming well established as the operator of high-density services on long-haul routes, following the adoption of its first wide-body airliner, the Lockheed L-1011-100 TriStar three-turbofan type of which the first was received on 25 June 1975. The continued growth of traffic on long-haul routes demanded still more capacity, however, and on 1 June 1977 the airline received two Boeing Model 747-2B4B four-turbofan airliners on lease from Middle East Airlines: the aircraft were later returned as Saudia started a programme to buy the Model 747 in moderately large numbers, and the first of the airline's own Model 747 aircraft was received on 24 April 1981.

Saudia is now the largest airline in the Middle East with its domestic services operated mainly by the Model 737, its medium-haul services by the Airbus A300-600, and its long-haul passenger and freight services by a combination of TriStar and Model 747 aircraft, with significant upgrading and expansion in view with the delivery of the McDonnell Douglas MD-90 for short/-medium-haul services, more Model 747 aircraft for long-haul services, and the new Boeing Model 777 twin-turbofan type also for long-haul services. Saudia also operates a significant number of two- and three-engined 'bizjets' for the movement of VIP passengers, including members of the Saudi royal family.

Singapore Airlines

Country of origin: Singapore

Generally accepted abbreviation: SQ

Address: Airline House, 25 Airline Road 1781, Singapore

Type of operation: International and regional scheduled passenger and cargo services

Shareholding: Singapore Airlines has 20 major shareholders including Delta Air Lines Holdings (2.7%), Swissair (0.6%), and the government of Singapore (54%)

Subsidiaries: Singapore Airlines has 21 subsidiary companies including Silk Air (100%) and Singapore Airlines (Mauritius)

Marketing alliances: Swissair and Delta Air Lines

Notes: Established as the wholly government-owned national airline of Singapore, Singapore Airlines has gradually undergone a measure of privatisation with the government now holding only 54% of the stock

Personnel: 25,750

Fleet:
6 x Airbus A310-200
17 x Airbus A310-300
1 x Boeing Model 747-200F
4 x Boeing Model 747-300
3 x Boeing Model 747-300 Combi
36 x Boeing Model 747-400
5 x Boeing Model 747-400F
1 x McDonnell Douglas DC-8-73F

Orders:
17 x Airbus A340-300
9 x Boeing Model 747-400
28 x Boeing Model 777

Main base and hub: Singapore

Route network: An African element to destinations such as Cairo, Cape Town, Durban, Johannesburg, and Mauritius; an American element to destinations such as Dallas/Fort Worth, Los Angeles, New York, San Francisco, and Vancouver; an Asian and Pacific element to destinations including Bandar Seri Begawan, Bangkok, Beijing, Bombay, Calcutta, Colombo, Delhi, Denpasar, Dhaka, Fukuoka, Guangzhou, Hangzhou, Hanoi, Hiroshima, Ho Chi Minh City, Hong Kong, Jakarta, Kaohsiung, Karachi, Kathmandu, Kota Kinabalu, Kuala Lumpur, Kuching, Macau, Madras, Malé, Manila, Nagoya, Osaka, Pinang, Sendai, Seoul, Shanghai, Surabaya, Taipei, and Tokyo; an Australasian element to

destinations such as Adelaide, Auckland, Brisbane, Cairns, Christchurch, Darwin, Melbourne, Perth, Port Moresby, and Sydney; a European element to destinations including Amsterdam, Athens, Berlin, Brussels, Copenhagen, Frankfurt, Istanbul, London, Madrid, Manchester, Paris, Rome, Vienna, and Zürich; and a Middle Eastern element to destinations such as Abu Dhabi, Dubai and Dhahran

Simulators: 1 x Airbus A310-200
1 x Airbus A310-300
1 x Airbus A340-300
2 x Boeing Model 747-300
2 x Boeing Model 747-400
1 x Boeing Model 757-200
1 x Learjet 31A

Maintenance services: SIA Engineering specialises in airframes and engines with 310 licensed airframe engineers, 310 licensed engine engineers, and 205 licensed avionics engineers

History: The national flag carrier of Singapore and currently enjoying rankings of 16th in the world and third in Asia, Singapore Airlines came into existence on 28 January 1972 following the emergence of Singapore as a state independent of the Federation of Malaysia. This resulted in the division of the previous Malaysia-Singapore Airlines into two individual portions that became the national flag carriers of Malaysia and Singapore, and Singapore Airlines began operations on 1 October 1972, serving the same international routes that had been the preserve of Malaysia-Singapore Airlines, and with the same fleet of Boeing Model 707 and Boeing Model 737 four- and two-turbofan airliners.

On 2 April 1973 Singapore Airlines began a daily service to London, and on 31 July of the same year began a major expansion in capability with the receipt of its first wide-body type, in this instance the four-turbofan Boeing Model 747-212B, that was soon com-plemented by another wide-body transport, the three-turbofan McDonnell Douglas DC-10-30, to provide the core of the airline's long-haul fleet for high- and medium-density services. The two-turbofan Airbus A300B4-203, first delivered on 20 December 1980, comp-lemented these two long-haul types on Singapore Airlines' medium- and short-haul services as a high-capacity type, in concert with small numbers of the three-turbofan Boeing Model 727-212, which entered service in September 1977, as its medium-capacity counterpart.

Singapore Airlines currently flies scheduled passenger and cargo services to destinations mainly in Australia, Asia, Europe and North America with a fleet now based on the Airbus A310 twin-turbofan type (two variants) for shorter-haul operations and the Model 747 (five variants) for longer-haul operations. Considerable expansion is planned as new aircraft are introduced to complement the existing fleet; if all the airline's options are exercised, Singapore Airlines will become an even greater force in regional and world airline services.

South African Airways

Country of origin: South Africa

Generally accepted abbreviation: SA

Address: Airways Towers, PO Box 7778, Johannesburg 2000, South Africa

Type of operation: International, regional and domestic scheduled and charter passenger and cargo services

Shareholding: South African Airways is a subsidiary of Transnet, which is wholly owned by the government of South Africa

Subsidiaries: Alliance (40%)

Marketing alliances: American Airlines, Lufthansa, British Midland, Thai Airways International, Ansett Australia, Alliance, SA Express, and Airlink

Notes: South African Airways became a division of Transnet, a nationalised company, on 1 April 1990. In May 1995 the airline started negotiations to extend its codesharing agreement with American Airlines, and on 9 July 1995 inaugurated a non-stop service from Cape Town to Frankfurt. In May 1995 the airline signed a preliminary co-operative agreement with Lufthansa, and in August 1995 contracted with Air New Zealand on the co-operative development of business opportunities in South Africa, New Zealand and Australia, as well as investigation of possible joint ventures at common gateways in Asia and Australia

Personnel: 11,100

Fleet:
8 x Airbus A300B/C
7 x Airbus A320-200
13 x Boeing Model 737-200
5 x Boeing Model 747-200B
1 x Boeing Model 747-200F
4 x Boeing Model 747-300
4 x Boeing Model 747-400
1 x Boeing Model 747SP
1 x Boeing Model 767-200ER
2 x Douglas DC-3
2 x Douglas DC-4

Orders:
2 x Boeing Model 747-400
7 x Boeing Model 777-200

Main bases and hubs: Cape Town, Durban and Johannesburg

Route network: An African element to destinations such as Blantyre, Bulawayo, Harare, Kinshasa, Lilongwe, Luanda, Lusaka, Maputo, Mauritius, Nairobi, Victoria Falls, and Windhoek; and an overseas element to destinations including Amsterdam, Bangkok, Bombay, Buenos Aires, Dubai, Düsseldorf, Frankfurt, Hong Kong, Ilha do Sal, London, Miami, Munich, New York, Paris, Perth, Rio de Janeiro, São Paulo, Singapore, Taipei, Tel Aviv, Sydney, and Zürich

Simulators:
1 x Airbus A300B2K
1 x Airbus A320-200
1 x Boeing Model 707-320C
2 x Boeing Model 737-200
2 x Boeing Model 747-200/200B

1 x Boeing Model 747-400

Maintenance services: South African Airways Technical specialises in airframes and engines with 3,100 engineers and 295 licensed avionics engineers

History: The national flag carrier of South Africa and currently ranked 44th in the world, South African Airways can trace its origins to August 1929 and the creation of Union Airways that operated de Havilland D.H.60 Gipsy Moth lightplanes on charter flights and mail services from Port Elizabeth to Cape Town. Durban and Johannesburg. On 1 February 1934 the nationalised South African Railways and Harbours Administration acquired Union Airways and its five single-engined aircraft, which by now included types such as the Junkers F 13 and W 34. One year later, South African Airways took over South West Africa Airways, which had been operating an air mail service between Kimberley and Windhoek since 1932, and with this acquisition South African Airways began to grow as a significant domestic and African operator with the three-engined Junkers Ju 52/3m and twin-engined Junkers Ju 86 types as its most important aircraft in the later part of the 1930s. In 1938 the airline also bought four examples of the Airspeed Envoy light transport, and these were flown on services to Durban, where passengers could board the flying boats that operated long-haul services to overseas destinations.

During World War II South African Airways received more-modern equipment in the form of the Lockheed Model 18 Lodestar, but this type was soon transferred to military service until 1944, when it was used for a resumption of South African Airways' civil operations. A major step in the airline's revival was the introduction of the 'Springbok Service' in co-operation with BOAC: this route between Johannesburg and London was inaugurated on 10 November 1945 using an Avro York four-engined transport. The airline later used another seven of this interim type, all of these leased from BOAC, until services could be undertaken with the Douglas DC-4, of which the airline received its first example on 26 April 1946.

Another type that entered service with South African Airways in 1946 was the Douglas C-47 Dakota, an ex-military type derived from the pre-war DC-3 and converted for civil use. The Dakota was used by South African Airways in large numbers and remained in fruitful service until 1970. On 15 December 1946 South African Airways received its first de Havilland D.H.104 Dove Series 1 twin-engined transport, a second example being delivered late in 1947: these two machines were flown on the services linking Johannesburg with Lourenço Marques and Durban with Bloemfontein. Another British airliner that entered service with South African Airways in 1947 was the Vickers Viking 1B, a larger twin-engined type that was first received on 31 July as replacement for the Lodestar on the service linking Johannesburg and Bulawayo. By the end of 1947, therefore, South African Airways had a mixed fleet of 41 aircraft.

The first pressurised airliner used by South African Airways was the Lockheed L-749A Constellation: the first of this type was delivered on 24 April 1950 and entered revenue-earning service on the route between South Africa and Europe as a replacement for the DC-4.

In was late in 1952 and during 1953 that South African Airways flew its first pure-jet aircraft, in the form of a de Havilland D.H.106 Comet 1 leased from BOAC, but this was withdrawn after only a short time as a result of technical problems. The airline therefore had to rely once more on piston-engined aircraft, of which one of the most successful was the Douglas DC-7B that started on the service to London on 21 April 1956 as successor to the Constellation.

South African Airways' domestic and regional services were upgraded considerably by the advent of the Vickers Viscount 813 four-turboprop airliner, of which the first two of an eventual eight were received on 26 October 1958. The Viscount remained in service until 1972, when the seven surviving aircraft were sold to British Midland Airways as the Viscount was replaced by the Boeing Model 727 three-turbofan airliner.

On 1 October 1960 the Boeing Model 707-355 four-turbofan transport replaced the DC-7B on the route to London, and although the type was initially operated on passenger services it was later relegated to freight operations as more-advanced equipment was taken into service. The most important of these types was the Boeing Model 747 wide-body airliner, of which the two most important early variants were the Model 747-244B and Model 747SP-44, first received on 22 October 1971 and 19 March 1976 respectively.

South African Airways currently operates a large fleet of Model 747 aircraft on its longer-haul routes, while shorter-haul services are provided by the Airbus A300, Airbus A320 and Boeing Model 737 aircraft that have supplanted the Boeing Model 727 and Hawker Siddeley HS.748 aircraft operated in the 1980s and early 1990s.

Swissair

Country of origin: Switzerland

Generally accepted abbreviation: SR

Address: PO Box 8058, Zürich-Flughafen CH-8058, Switzerland

Type of operation: International, regional and domestic scheduled and charter passenger and cargo services

Shareholding: Singapore Airlines (0.6%), Delta Air Lines (4.5%), government bodies in Switzerland (20.5%)

Subsidiaries: Crossair (56.1%), Balair/CTA (93.4%), Delta Air Lines (4.6%), Sabena (49.5%), SBAG Singapore (0.6%), and Gate Gourmets

Marketing alliances: Delta Air Lines

Personnel: 17,365

Fleet:
8 x Airbus A310-300
5 x Airbus A319-100
14 x Airbus A320-200
6 x Airbus A321-100
5 x Boeing Model 747-300
13 x McDonnell Douglas MD-11
10 x McDonnell Douglas MD-81

Orders:
3 x Airbus A319-100
4 x Airbus A320-200
2 x Airbus A321-100
9 x Airbus A330-200
3 x McDonnell Douglas MD-11

Options: 8 x Airbus A321-111

Main bases and hubs: Basel and Zürich

Continued on next page

Route network: This includes 125 destinations in 67 countries, and comprises an African element to destinations such as Abidjan, Accra, Algiers, Banjul, Brazzaville, Cairo, Cape Town, Casablanca, Dakar, Dar es Salaam, Douala, Harare, Johannesburg, Kinshasa, Lagos, Libreville, Nairobi, Tunis, and Yaounde; an American element to destinations including Atlanta, Boston, Buenos Aires, Chicago, Cincinnati, Montreal, New York, Philadelphia, Rio de Janeiro, Santiago (Chile), São Paulo, Toronto, and Washington; an Asian and Pacific Rim element to destinations such as Bangkok, Beijing, Bombay, Delhi, Hong Kong, Karachi, Manila, Seoul, Singapore, and Tokyo; a European element to destinations including Amsterdam, Ankara, Athens, Barcelona, Basel/Mulhouse, Berlin, Bern, Bilbao, Birmingham, Bordeaux, Brussels, Bucharest, Budapest, Copenhagen, Düsseldorf, Frankfurt, Geneva, Genoa, Gothenburg, Graz, Hamburg, Hannover, Helsinki, Istanbul, Izmir, Kiev, Klagenfurt, Larnaca, Linz, Lisbon, Ljubljana, London, Los Angeles, Luxembourg, Lyon, Madrid, Málaga, Malta, Manchester, Marseille, Milan, Minsk, Moscow, Munich, Nice, Oporto, Oslo, Palma de Mallorca, Paris, Prague, Rome, St Petersburg, Salzburg, Sofia, Stockholm, Strasbourg, Stuttgart, Thessaloniki, Tirana, Toulouse, Tunn, Valencia, Vienna, Warsaw, Zagreb, and Zürich; and a Middle Eastern element to destinations such as Abu Dhabi, Beirut, Damascus, Dubai, Jiddah, Riyadh, Tehran, and Tel Aviv

Simulators: 1 x Airbus A310
2 x Airbus A321-100
1 x Boeing Model 747-300
1 x Fokker 100
1 x McDonnell Douglas MD-11
1 x McDonnell Douglas MD-81
1 x McDonnell Douglas MD-82

Maintenance services: Swissair Engineering & Maintenance specialises in airframes and engines with 1,500 licensed airframe engineers, 400 licensed engine engineers, and 300 licensed avionics engineers

History: The national flag carrier of Switzerland and currently enjoying ranking of 12th in the world and seventh in Europe, Swissair can trace its origins to March 1931 and its creation by the amalgamation of Balair and Ad Astra, two pioneering Swiss air transport companies. From the outset the new airline decided to set a fast pace in its growth by the adoption of the latest equipment. In 1932 Swissair was the first European airline to operate the four-passenger Lockheed Orion, a single-engined low-wing monoplane with retractable landing gear, and the fastest small air transport of its day. Also in 1932, Swissair introduced the Curtiss Condor twin-engined biplane to European service, and although this machine was slow it was also very comfortable and carried a stewardess (for the first time in European service) to look after the 16 passengers.

By the time the outbreak of World War II in 1939 interrupted the development of air transportation throughout most of Europe, Swissair was operating a fleet of five Douglas DC-3, three Douglas DC-2, one de Havilland D.H.89 Dragon Rapide, one Fokker F.VIIa and one Compte AC.4 aircraft. Scheduled services were suspended during the war, but were resumed in July 1945, some two months after Germany's defeat.

By 1949 Swissair was able to inaugurate a service to New York with the Douglas DC-4 four-engined airliner that was soon replaced by the Douglas DC-6B that offered full cabin pressurisation, amongst other improvements. The availability of this longer-range type improved safety margins on the North Atlantic route, and also made it possible for Swissair to introduce new services to South America, as well as to Tokyo via South-East Asia, in the early 1950s. The DC-6B was superseded on the airline's long-haul routes by the Douglas DC-7.

Even as this improvement of its long-haul network was being implemented, Swissair was also developing its capability in Europe and to the Middle East. Destinations in all parts of Africa were added in the 1960s, and Swissair's network now extends to all continents except Australasia.

In the course of 1960 Swissair introduced to service its first jet-powered airliner in the form of the Sud-Aviation Caravelle III, eight examples of which were leased from SAS. The airline operated these French aircraft for European regional services, but kept faith with Douglas in its long-haul aircraft when it contracted for the four-engined Douglas DC-8. Early experience with the Caravelle and the DC-8 confirmed that the future lay with turbine propulsion, and Swissair switched rapidly to the latest airliners to create a fleet (in service or on order) that, by 1981, comprised 3 Boeing Model 747-200B, 11 Airbus A310, 5 McDonnell Douglas DC-8-62, 12 DC-9-32, 1 DC-9-33F, 12 DC-9-51, 15 DC-9-81 and 11 DC-10-30 aircraft for the full range of short-, medium- and long-haul services.

Since that time Swissair has standardised on the Fokker 100 for use on its domestic services, the McDonnell Douglas MD-81 for low-density short-haul services, the Airbus A310 and A320 for high-density short/-medium-haul services, and the McDonnell Douglas MD-11 and Model 747-300 for use on medium- and high-density long-haul services respectively.

KLM, SAS and Swissair collaborate on the technical maintenance of their Model 747 and DC-9 aircraft as a means of reducing costs, and there was another collaborative arrangement covering the DC-10 and MD-11 aircraft operated by KLM, SAS, Swissair and UTA.

TAP Air Portugal

Country of origin: Portugal

Generally accepted abbreviation: TP

Address: Aeroporto de Lisboa, Apartado 50194, Lisboa Codex 1704, Portugal

Type of operation: International and domestic scheduled passenger and cargo services

Shareholding: TAP Air Portugal is a public limited company, the majority of its capitol being held by the State (100%)

Subsidiaries: ESTA-Hotel and Restaurant Management, AP Tours, Cateringpor, Megasis, Lojas Francas de Portugal SA, Air Portugal Tours, Air Macau (25%), Caravela Tours, AIA Catering and Air São Tomé

Marketing alliances: Codesharing with British Midland, Delta Air Lines, Haburg Airlines, Portugalia, Taag Angola Airlines

Personnel: 7,448

Fleet:
5 x Airbus A310-300
6 x Airbus A320-200
4 x Airbus A340-300
6 x Boeing Model 737-200
10 x Boeing Model 737-300
3 x Lockheed L-1011-500 TriStar

Orders: 18 x Airbus A319-100

Main base and hub: Lisbon

Route network: A domestic element to destinations such as the Azores, Faro, Madeira and Oporto; an African element to destinations including Abidjan, Bissau, Brazzaville, Dakar, Johannesburg, Kinshasa, Luanda, Maputo, Sal, and São Tomé; an American element to destinations such as Boston, Caracas, Curaçao, New York, Newark, Recife, Rio de Janeiro, Salvador da Bada Bahia, Santo Domingo, and São Paulo; a European element to destinations including Amsterdam, Athens, Barcelona, Berlin, Bologna, Brussels, Copenhagen, Frankfurt, Geneva, Hamburg, London, Luxembourg, Lyon, Madrid, Milan, Munich, Nice, Oslo, Paris, Rome, Stockholm, Vienna, and Zürich; a Far Eastern element to destinations including Bangkok, Macau; and a Middle Eastern element to destinations including Brazzaville and Tel Aviv

Simulators:
1 x Airbus A300-600
1 x Airbus A300B4
1 x Boeing Model 737-400
1 x Boeing Model 747-200
1 x Boeing Model 747-400

Maintenance services: TAP Air Portugal specialises in airframes and engines with 700 licensed airframe engineers, 185 licensed engine engineers, and 165 licensed avionics engineers

History: The national flag carrier of Portugal, Transportes Aereos Portugueses (TAP) was created on March 14, 1944 by the civil aeronautics secretariat of the Portuguese government as a route-proving organisation, but the original plan of passing on the fruits of TAP's endeavours to commercial airlines (once these had been established) was abandoned, and TAP was itself turned into a scheduled airline on 14 March 1945. The new operator made its first flight on 19 September 1946 with a service from Lisbon to Madrid using a Douglas DC-3 twin-engined airliner. Scheduled services deeper into the continent of Europe began in 1947, in which year the airline also began flights to Lourenço Marques via Luanda, the capital cities of Portugal's African colonies of Mozambique and Angola, initially with the DC-3 but later with the Douglas DC-4 four-engined airliner. In 1950 the service was curtailed to end at Luanda.

By 1953 the airline's costs had risen to the point at which the government of Portugal decided it was sensible to sell off TAP to the private sector.

On 15 July 1955 TAP received its first example of the Lockheed L-1049G Super Constellation four-engined airliner, and this type entered service on the route to Luanda and Lourenço Marques as well as on some longer-range European routes. In 1960 the airline leased two Douglas DC-6B four-engined

Continued on next page

TAP Air Portugal continued from previous page

airliners from the French airline UAT and, having realised the necessity for turbine-powered aircraft, secured a pooling agreement with British European Airways to operate de Havilland Comet 4B turbojet- and Vickers Viscount turboprop-powered aircraft. These agreements soon lapsed, however, as TAP started to receive its own turbine-powered aircraft, starting on 13 July 1962 with its first Sud-Aviation Caravelle VIR.

These arrangements provided mainly for short- and medium-haul routes, but in 1960 the airline had gained an important long-haul capability with the lease from Sabena of two examples of the Boeing Model 707-329 pending the delivery of its own Model 707 aircraft, of which the first was a Model 707-3H2B received on 18 December 1965. The availability of this advanced type allowed TAP to expand its turbine-powered operation from June 1966, to include destinations such as Rio de Janeiro, which had previously been served in association with Panair do Brasil (now VARIG) with Douglas DC-7C aircraft via Ilha do Sol and Recife. In 1969 TAP started a service linking Lisbon with New York, and two years later added a service to Montreal.

Further short- and medium-haul capability arrived early in 1967 with delivery of the airline's first Boeing Model 727-82 three-turbofan airliner, and this type was soon the mainstay of the operator's European routes. A superior long-haul capability was achieved on 20 December 1971 with the delivery of the airline's first wide-body transports, in the form of two Boeing Model 747-282B four-turbofan airliners that entered service in February 1972, and in 1982 a further fillip was provided by the delivery of the first of five Lockheed L-1011-500 TriStar three-turbofan transports to replace the airline's Model 707 aircraft.

In 1975 TAP was nationalised, in March 1979 it changed its name to TAP Air Portugal, and in 1991 the airline became a public limited company with most of the shareholding retained by the government of Portugal.

TAP Air Portugal has now standardised on the Boeing Model 737 (two variants) for its short-haul services, and a combination of the Airbus A310, A320 and A340 for its medium- and long-haul services, and is currently disposing of its surviving TriStar aircraft.

Thai Airways International

Country of origin: Thailand

Generally accepted abbreviation: TG

Address: 89 Vibhavadi Rangsit Road, Bangkok 9 10900, Thailand

Type of operation: International, regional and domestic scheduled passenger services

Shareholding: Government of Thailand (92.86%)

Subsidiaries: None

Marketing alliances: Joint services with Air New Zealand, Ansett, Japan Airlines, Lufthansa, SAS, and United Airlines

Notes: In 1992 the airline's shares were listed on the Thai stock exchange, changing Thai Airways International from a wholly government-owned operator into a partially privatised company

Personnel: 21,540

Fleet:
4 x Airbus A300B4
16 x Airbus A300-600/600R
2 x Airbus A310-200
8 x Airbus A330-300
2 x ATR 42

2 x ATR 72
7 x Boeing Model 737-400
6 x Boeing Model 747-200
2 x Boeing Model 747-300
12 x Boeing Model 747-400
3 x McDonnell Douglas DC-10
4 x McDonnell Douglas MD-11

Orders: 4 x Boeing Model 777-200

Main base and hub: Bangkok

Route network: A large number of domestic destinations as well as 51 destinations in 36 other countries, and comprises an American element to destinations including Los Angeles; an Asian element to destinations such as Bandar Seri Begawan, Beijing, Calcutta, Chiang Mai, Colombo, Delhi, Denpasar, Dhaka, Fukuoka, Guangzhou, Hanoi, Ho Chi Minh City, Jakarta, Kaohsiung, Karachi, Kathmandu, Kuala Lumpur, Kunming, Lahore, Manila, Nagoya, Osaka, Pinang, Phnom Penh, Seoul, Singapore, Taipei, Tokyo, Vientiane, and Yangon; an Australasian element to destinations such as Auckland, Brisbane, Melbourne, Perth and Sydney; a European element to destinations including Amsterdam, Athens, Brussels, Copenhagen, Frankfurt, Istanbul, London, Madrid, Paris, Rome, Stockholm, and Zürich; and a Middle Eastern element to destinations such as Dubai and Muscat

Simulators: 1 x Airbus A300-600
1 x Airbus A300B4
1 x Boeing Model 737-400
1 x Boeing Model 747-200
1 x Boeing Model 747-400

Maintenance services: Thai Airways International specialises in airframes and engines

History: The national flag carrier of the kingdom of Thailand and currently ranked 25th in the world and seventh in Asia, Thai Airways International resulted from an agreement signed on 14 December 1959 between the government of Thailand and Scandinavian Airlines System: 70% of the shareholding was held by the government of Thailand and the remaining 30% by SAS, which provided the necessary aircraft and management capability. The new airline's first two aircraft, leased from SAS on 2 April 1960, were Douglas DC-6B four-engined transports, and these entered revenue-earning service on 1 May. Thai Airways International later leased another six DC-6B aircraft, the last of which was returned on 3 April 1964.

Thai Airways International's primary route was that linking Bangkok with Tokyo, and to ensure the maximum possible load factors on this strongly competitive route, the airline leased two Convair CV-990A four-jet airliners from SAS: this type arrived on 15 May 1962 and made its operational debut on 18 May: at that time the CV-990A was the fastest airliner in the world, and its operation gave Thai Airways International a decided edge over its competitors.

The DC-6B was gradually supplanted by leased Sud-Aviation Caravelle III twin-jet aircraft, first delivered on 26 December 1963 for service on the airline's shorter-haul services from 1 January 1964. By this time South-East Asia was beginning to emerge as a major destination for the burgeoning tourist trade, and to meet the demand for additional capacity on its shorter-haul services, Thai Airways International leased a pair of Douglas DC-9-41 twin-jet transports from SAS, the two aircraft reaching Thailand on 28 and 29 January 1970. In April of the same year a more advanced longer-haul capability appeared in the form of two Douglas DC-8-33 four-engined transports, and the DC-8 and DC-9 soon became the mainstay of the airline's operations, numerous DC-8 variants being added to the fleet over the following years.

The availability of these aircraft in 1970

Thai Airways continued from previous page

allowed Thai Airways International to start its own inclusive tour programme under the name Royal Orchid Holidays, and a new service to Sydney via Singapore was launched in April 1971. This great expansion in the airline's first decade of operation turned Thai Airways International into the third largest regional operator in the Far East.

The majority of the airline's tourist trade arrived from Europe, so it made sound commercial sense for Thai Airways International to extend its route network to that continent, the first such service being to Copenhagen via Moscow on 3 June 1962 with a DC-8. On 2 November 1973 a service from Bangkok to Frankfurt and London was inaugurated, and this link made it possible for the airline to offer a through service between London and Sydney.

Continuing growth in demand during the first half of the 1970s persuaded the airline to move into the market for wide-body aircraft, and Thai Airways International received its first such aircraft, a McDonnell Douglas DC-10-30 three-turbofan airliner leased from UTA, on 30 May 1975. This machine was soon complemented and then supplanted by the airline's own DC-10 aircraft, which became the mainstay of its longer-haul services in the later 1970s and 1980s, while additional capacity was provided on medium- and short-haul services by the purchase of Airbus A300 twin-turbofan aircraft that finally replaced the DC-8 after delivery of the first machine on 25 October 1977. The A300 was later complemented by the A310, another twin-turbofan type.

In November 1979 an improved capability of high-density services over long-haul routes was provided by the arrival of the first of the airline's four-turbofan wide-body aircraft, a Boeing Model 747-2D7B. Thai Airways International inaugurated a service to the USA across the Pacific with a Douglas DC-10-30 flying the route to Seattle and Los Angeles on 30 April 1980, but on 1 November 1980 the Model 747 replaced the DC-10 on the North Pacific and European routes, thereby increasing passenger capacity by a significant degree.

Thai Airways International now operates a substantial route network with a fleet standardised on the two types of ATR twin-turboprop transport for local services, the BAe 146 four-turbofan and Boeing Model 737 two-turbofan transports for short-haul services, the A300 and A310 for medium-haul services, and a combination of the Airbus A330, Model 747 (three variants), DC-10 and upgraded MD-11 for its longer-haul services.

THY Turkish Airlines

Country of origin: Turkey

Generally accepted abbreviation: TK

Address: General Administration Building, Ataturk Airport Yesilkey, Istanbul 34830, Turkey

Type of operation: International and domestic scheduled and charter passenger and cargo services

Shareholding: Government of Turkey (99.4%)

Subsidiaries: Cyprus Turkish Airlines (50%) and Sun Express (50%)

Personnel: 8,565

Fleet: 7 x Airbus A310-200
7 x Airbus A310-300
4 x Airbus A340-300
4 x Avro RJ70
10 x Avro RJ100
3 x Boeing Model 727-200
28 x Boeing Model 737-400
2 x Boeing Model 737-500

Orders: 1 x Airbus A340-300

Route network: A domestic element to 26 destinations in Turkey including Adana, Ankara, Antalya, Denizli, Istanbul, and Izmir; and an international element to destinations such as Abu Dhabi, Alma-Ata, Amman, Athens, Bahrain, Baku, Bangkok, Barcelona, Beirut, Bucharest, Cologne, New York, Nice, Osaka, Rome, Singapore, Strasbourg, Tashkent, and Tokyo

Simulators: 1 x Airbus A310

I x Airbus A340
I x Boeing Model 737-400
I x Boeing Model 737-500

Maintenance services: THY Turkish Airlines specialises in airframes and engines with 65 licensed engine engineers and 165 licensed avionics engineers

History: Turk Hava Yollari, generally known as THY Turkish Airlines, is the national flag carrier of the Turkish republic, and can trace its origins to 20 May 1933, when the Turkish defence ministry established Turkiye Devlet Hava Yollari (Turkish State Airlines) as replacement for the airline that had been operated by Curtiss, the US aircraft manufacturer. The first route operated by Turkiye Devlet Hava Yollari was that linking Istanbul and Ankara via Eskisehir. In 1935 the airline came under the aegis of the Turkish ministry of public works, and on 3 June 1938 was transferred to the ministry of transport.

In September 1937 the airline had received its first three examples of the de Havilland D.H.86B Express biplane airliner, and these were followed in December by a fourth machine of the same type to complement de Havilland D.H.89 biplanes. The availability of this fleet made it possible for Turkiye Devlet Hava Yollari to enlarge its domestic network to the point at which, in 1939, it linked Istanbul, Eskisehir, Izmir, Ankara, Adana, Kayseri and Diyarbakir.

No growth was possible during World War II (in which Turkey was neutral) as no new aircraft could be acquired, but after the end of the war in 1945 Turkiye Devlet Hava Yollari started to fly winter services using a sizeable fleet of Douglas DC-3 twin-engined airliners. The airline flew only domestic services up to 1947, when it expanded into international services, starting with the route to Athens. The other main type flown by the airline, in this instance for short-haul services, was the de Havilland D.H.114 Heron 2B four-engined airliner, the first two of which were received on 15 February 1955. There followed another five of the same type, which remained in service until 1966.

On 1 March 1956 the operations of Turkiye Devlet Hava Yollari were replaced by those of Turk Hava Yollari, which had come into existence in May 1955 as a new corporation established by the Turkish government to control national air transport. The Turkish government had a 51% holding in Turk Hava Yollari, and BOAC owned 6.5% as a result of a payment that allowed the new operator to place a July 1957 order for modern equipment in the form of five Vickers Viscount 794 four-turboprop airliners, of which the first was received on 21 January 1958 with the other four following later in the year. The Viscounts were placed in domestic service during May, and international services – initially to Brussels but soon to a number of other European destinations – started during the summer of 1964.

On 15 January 1960 Turk Hava Yollari contracted for a total of 10 Friendship twin-turboprop airliners in the form of five Fokker F.27 and five Fairchild F-27 aircraft, the first American-built F-27 being accepted on 1 July 1960, with the first three Dutch-built F.27 aircraft following on 27 October. The availability of the full Friendship fleet allowed the replacement of the DC-3 on Turk Hava Yollari's domestic network.

More-advanced turbine-powered aircraft were now clearly essential, and the first pure-jet type to be used by Turk Hava Yollari was a Douglas DC-9-14 received on lease from the manufacturer on 7 August 1967, and the airline's first DC-9-32 followed on 9 July 1968. Turk Hava Yollari leased four examples of the Boeing Model 707-321 four-turbofan airliner from Pan American in 1971, the first being delivered right at the beginning of the year. The availability of these larger aircraft with their longer range permitted the airline to enlarge its route network into the Middle East, and further expansion became possible two years later with the airline's receipt of its first wide-body airliner, a McDonnell Douglas DC-10-10 delivered on 1 December 1972; on 13 January 1973, Turk Hava Yollari accepted the first of six Fokker F.28 Fellowship twin-turbofan airliners, allowing a start on the programme to replace the F.27 on domestic services. The last of the new types to be delivered in this period of re-equipment and expansion was the Boeing Model 727-2F2 three-turbofan type, of which the first pair was received on 21 November 1974 for a considerable boost in the airline's medium-haul capability.

The next type to enter service was the de Havilland Canada DHC-7 Dash-7 four-turboprop airliner, the first of three such aircraft being accepted in June 1983.

Turk Hava Yollari has since standardised on the BAe Jetstream ATP twin-turboprop type for local services, the closely related Avro RJ100 and BAe 146 four-turbofan types for short-haul services, the Boeing Model 737 (two variants) for higher-capacity short- and medium-haul services, and a combination of the Airbus A310 and A340 for its high-capacity medium- and long-haul services.

Trans World Airlines

Country of origin: USA

Generally accepted abbreviation: TW

Address: One City Center, 515 North 6th Street, St Louis, Missouri 63101, USA

Type of operation: International, regional and domestic scheduled passenger services

Shareholding: Trans World Airlines is a publicly owned company listed on the American Stock Exchange in which the employees hold some 30% of the shares

Subsidiaries: None

Marketing alliances: Trans States Airlines, operating as trans World Express

Notes: In January 1979 the Trans World Corporation became Trans World Airlines' parent company, and in December 1982 the TWC shareholders agreed to sell the airline which, on 1 February 1984, became a separate and publicly owned company. In 1995 the airline completed the implementation of a major financial restructuring, and the reorganised airline is now owned in part by its American employees who invested wage and benefit concessions in exchange for about 30% of the shares

Personnel: 23,000

Fleet:
39 x Boeing Model 727-200
8 x Boeing Model 747-100
2 x Boeing Model 747-200B
6 x Boeing Model 757-200
12 x Boeing Model 767-200
2 x Boeing Model 767-300
10 x Lockheed L-1011 TriStar
7 x McDonnell Douglas DC-9
51 x McDonnell Douglas MD-80
30 x McDonnell Douglas MD-82
23 x McDonnell Douglas MD-83

Orders:
10 x Airbus A330
14 x Boeing Model 757-200

Options:
10 x Airbus A330
14 x Boeing Model 757-200

Main bases and hubs: New York and St Louis

Route network: This includes more than 100 destinations in the Americas, Europe and the Middle East

Simulators:
1 x Boeing Model 727-200
1 x Boeing Model 747-100
1 x Boeing Model 767-200
1 x Lockheed L-1011-200 TriStar

Maintenance services: Trans World Airlines specialises in airframes and engines with 1,000 licensed airframe engineers, 600 licensed engine engineers, and 500 licensed avionics engineers

History: Currently ranked 21st in the world and seventh in North America, Trans World Airlines can trace its origins to 1926 and the creation of Western Air Express. This operator undertook air mail services in the USA, starting with the route linking Los Angeles and Salt Lake

City, and during 1929 began a process of enlargement by taking over Standard Air Lines.

Transcontinental Air Transport was established on 16 May 1928, and in July 1929 undertook its first transcontinental service across the USA, using a Ford Tri-Motor three-engined airliner between Columbus and Los Angeles: the sector between Texas and Los Angeles was completed by the Santa Fe Railway, which had an interest in Transcontinental Air Transport. Late in 1929 the airline bought Maddux Airlines for the acquisition of its services in the San Francisco and San Diego areas.

On 16 July 1930 Western Air Express merged with Transcontinental Air Transport to create a major operator initially known as Transcontinental and Western Air, but in 1934 the original Western Air Express element was bought out and became the basis of Western Airlines. Transcontinental and Western Air was renamed Trans World Airlines in 1945, but the official name was changed to Trans World Airlines, Inc in 1950, retaining the abbreviation TWA that is generally used for this long-established operator.

During the early 1930s the airline approached Douglas to build the aeroplane that would revolutionise the air travel industry all over the world. This was the DC-1 that paved the way for the very good DC-2, which itself led to the classic DC-3 that entered service with Transcontinental and Western Air in June 1937. The importance attached by the airline to the use of the latest equipment was reflected in its adoption of the world's first pressurised airliner, the Boeing Model 307 Stratoliner four-engined machine, in July 1940, and this important type entered service on the airline's route between Chicago and Los Angeles. Further development was effectively halted during America's involvement in World War II between 1941 and 1945, and in this period the airline undertook transport, training and modification work for the US military.

After World War II, Transcontinental and Western Air operated its first international service on 5 February 1946, using a Lockheed L-049 Constellation four-engined airliner on the route between New York and Paris. On 19 October 1953, some 30 months after it had become Trans World Airlines, the airline inaugurated a non-stop coast-to-coast service across the USA with the Lockheed L-1049A Super Constellation.

The airline moved into the turbine-powered age on 20 March 1959 when it introduced the Boeing Model 707-131 four-turbojet airliner on the route between San Francisco and New York. On 31 December 1969 the airline received its first Boeing Model 747-131 four-turbofan airliner, the pioneer of the wide-body type of air transport, and on 9 May 1972 took delivery of its first Lockheed L-1011 TriStar three-turbofan airliner. The Model 747 and L-1011 became the mainstays of Trans World Airlines' long-haul operations for high- and medium-density services respectively, before being replaced by modern fuel-efficient Boeing 767-200/300 and Boeing 757-200 aircraft.

Despite a number of financial and administrative setbacks in more recent times, Trans World Airlines has emerged as a major force in American and world air transport, and currently operates a large number of modern aircraft to maintain its capability and market share.

United Airlines

Country of origin: USA

Generally accepted abbreviation: UA

Address: 1200 East Algonquin Road, Elk Grove Township, Illinois 60666, USA

Type of operation: International, regional and domestic scheduled passenger services

Shareholding: United Airlines is a publicly owned company in which the employees own some 55% of the shares

Subsidiaries: None

Marketing alliances: Codesharing with Ansett Australia, Royal Brunei Airlines, Emirates Airlines, Air Canada and, on Scandinavian routes, Lufthansa

Notes: In 1994 a majority of United Airlines' employees took a 55% stake in the company in return for labour concessions. The airline was launch customer for the Boeing Model 777, with which it started services on 7 June 1995, and now serves 104 domestic and 40 international airports

Personnel: 83,230

Fleet:
36 x Airbus A320
75 x Boeing Model 727-200
63 x Boeing Model 737-200
101 x Boeing Model 737-300
57 x Boeing Model 737-500
15 x Boeing Model 747-100
9 x Boeing Model 747-200
26 x Boeing Model 747-400
92 x Boeing Model 757-200
19 x Boeing Model 767-200
23 x Boeing Model 767-300ER
16 x Boeing Model 777-200

26 x McDonnell Douglas DC-10-10
7 x McDonnell Douglas DC-10-30

Orders: 29 x Airbus A319
15 x Airbus A320
21 x Boeing Model 747-400
6 x Boeing Model 757-200
20 x Boeing Model 777

Options: 39 x Airbus A320
135 x Boeing Model 737
40 x Boeing Model 747-400
29 x Boeing Model 757
5 x Boeing Model 767
34 x Boeing Model 777

Main bases and hubs: Chicago (O'Hare), Denver, San Francisco and Washington (Dulles)

Route network: A domestic element to 105 destinations including Honolulu, Los Angeles, Nashville, San Francisco, and Washington DC; an African element to destinations including Cairo; an Asian and North Pacific element to destinations such as Bandar Seri Begawan, Bangkok, Beijing, Brunei, Delhi, Guam, Hong Kong, Kuala Lumpur, Manila, Osaka, Phuket, Port Moresby, Saipan, Seoul, Shanghai, Singapore, Taipei, and Tokyo; an Australasian and South Pacific element to destinations such as Adelaide, Auckland, Brisbane, Cairns, Canberra, Christchurch, Gold Coast, Hobart, Melbourne, Perth, Sydney, and Wellington; a Canadian element to destinations such as Calgary, Halifax, Ottawa, Quebec, Toronto, and Vancouver; a Central American element to destinations such as Huatulco, Lazaro Cardenas, Mexico City, Monterrey, Morelia, Querétaro, Salina Cruz, and San Luis Potosí; a Caribbean element to destinations including Antigua, Curaçao, Freeport, Governors Harbour, Grand Cayman, Haiti, Kingston, Marsh Harbour, Montego Bay, Nassau, North Eleuthera, St Kitts, San Juan, Treasure Cay, and Trinidad; a European element to destinations such as Amsterdam, Belfast, Berlin, Birmingham, Bonn, Brussels, Budapest, Cologne, Copenhagen, Düsseldorf, Edinburgh, Frankfurt, Geneva, Glasgow, Gothenburg, Hamburg, Hannover, Helsinki, Kiev, Larnaca, Leeds Bradford, Leipzig, London, Madrid, Malta, Milan, Munich, Naples, Nice, Nuremberg, Oslo, Paris, Prague, Rome, Stockholm, Stuttgart, Tallinn, Tashkent, Teesside, Vienna, Vilnius, and Zürich; a Middle Eastern element to destinations such as Abu Dhabi, Amman, Dubai and Jiddah; and a South American element to destinations including Antofagasta, Arica, Belo Horizonte, Buenos Aires, Caracas, Concepción, Copiapó, Guatemala City, Guayaquil, La Serena, Lima, Montevideo, Panama City, Puerto Montt, Punta Arenas, Quito, Rio de Janeiro, San José, San Salvador, Santiago, and São Paulo

Maintenance services: Details not available

History: Currently ranked second in the world and first in North America, United Airlines can trace its origins to the formation by Henry Ford, the motor vehicle magnate, of an air mail operator that undertook its initial service on 3 April 1925 between Detroit and Chicago. On 6 April 1926, Walter T. Varney started mail services in the north-west area of the USA and, on 12 May, National Air Transport started its own mail services between Chicago and Dallas operating 10 Curtiss Carrier Pigeons. On 31 July of the same year, Bill Stout (who had worked for Henry Ford's airline) also began air mail and passenger services between Detroit and Grand Rapids. Another airline, Pacific Air Transport, operated its first service from Los Angeles to Seattle on 15 September 1926.

All these airlines became involved in the creation of United Airlines, but the operator's most direct ancestor was Boeing Air Transport, which flew its first service on 1 July 1927 between Chicago and San Francisco, a distance of some 1,920 miles (3,090km) with one of the operator's 24 Boeing Model 40A biplane transports. On 1 January 1928 Boeing Air Transport took over control of Pacific Air Transport's operations, and on 17 December the two companies effected a complete merger. During this period, Fred Rentschler of Pratt & Whitney suggested a partnership of his aero engine company and the Boeing Airplane Company, and this resulted in the formation of the United Aircraft and Transport Corporation (UATC) on 1 February 1929, and on 30 June of the same year UATC bought Stout Air Services and Ford's airline; on 7 May 1930 UATC assumed control of National Air Transport, and Varney Air Lines became a subsidiary on 30 June 1931.

On 1 July 1931, therefore, all of these pioneering airlines were part of UATC, and the new operator now possessed a route network spanning the USA between New York in the east and California in the west as well as Chicago in the north and Dallas in the south, although UATC gave up the route between Chicago and Dallas during 1934.

As it had links with one of the most far-sighted aircraft manufacturers in the country, UATC was inevitably the first customer for the Boeing Model 247, which was the first of what may be described as the 'modern airliners' as it was of all-metal construction with a cantilever low-set wing, enclosed accommodation for the crew and passengers, and retractable main landing gear units. The type made its maiden flight on 8 February 1933 and rapidly entered service with UATC, making its first revenue-earning flight on 30 March. By the end of June 1933 UATC had 30 Model 247 aircraft in service, but discovered that the aeroplane had poor performance at high-altitude airports, but this problem was solved by the introduction of a variable-pitch propeller designed by Hamilton Standard, an associate of Pratt & Whitney within UATC, and this created the more effective Model 247D. UATC eventually operated 70 of the 75 Model 247 aircraft, which was built in only modest numbers as the forthcoming Douglas DC series offered greater payload capacity.

In 1934, newly enacted anti-trust law forced the division of UATC into independent components, and on 1 May of that year the airline became United Air Lines, which absorbed Pennsylvania Central Airline. In January 1940 United Air Lines somewhat belatedly started to operate the Douglas DC-3. In July of the previous year, however, United Air Lines had ordered six examples of the conceptually advanced Douglas DC-4 (later DC-4E) four-engined airliner, and had placed the prototype in limited experimental service on 1 June 1939. The type had too many advanced features for adequate reliability, however, and therefore did not enter production.

Late in 1940 United Air Lines received a contract to train military personnel at the Oakland Training Center, and by 1943 some 5,000 mechanics had been trained. By this time America was fully embroiled in World War II, and the airline devoted most of its energies to further the US war effort. This included a service from 15 May 1942 between Fairfield in Ohio and Anchorage in Alaska, and from 27 June of the same year a service from Salt Lake City to Anchorage. On 23 September 1942 United Air Lines started to fly Douglas C-54 Skymaster four-engined transport aircraft on routes out into the Pacific theatre, a service that lasted to 31 March 1945. In January 1942 the airline was contracted to modify Boeing B-17 Flying Fortress bombers for photographic work, and some 5,500 Boeing aircraft were cycled through United Air Lines' Cheyenne facility for modification work.

On 11 September 1944 United Air Lines ordered the Douglas DC-4 four-engined civil version of the C-54, but cancelled this contract in October 1945 when the US government released a large number of the C-54 model that were surplus to military requirements, and

the type entered service in March 1946 on the service linking Chicago and Washington DC, followed by the service between California and Hawaii in May 1947. On 24 November 1946 United Air Lines took delivery of its first Douglas DC-6 four-engined transport, followed on 11 April 1951 by the improved DC-6B. Pending the delivery of adequate numbers of the DC-4 and the DC-6 series, United Air Lines operated most of its services with a civilian variant of the Douglas C-47 Skytrain/Dakota twin-engined military transport, itself a derivative of the DC-3, and in 1946 United Air Lines was operating 77 of this type including 21 leased aircraft. United Air Lines operated the C-47/DC-3 until 1949.

On 20 February 1951 United Air Lines placed an order for 30 examples of a considerably more advanced twin-engined type, the Convair CV-340, for its shorter-haul services, and took delivery of the first of these machines on 12 May of the same year. However, United Air Lines had become aware of a technology gap in its long-haul fleet and ordered the Douglas DC-7 and, as an interim measure until this advanced type could be delivered, flew the Boeing Model 377 Stratocruiser, which entered service on 1 December 1953. The airline accepted its first DC-7 on 10 April 1954 for service from 1 June, and sold its Stratocruiser fleet to BOAC only a few months later.

The DC-7 was United Air Lines' long-haul mainstay through most of the 1950s, but toward the end of the decade the airline appreciated the need for more-advanced aircraft and, retaining its recent partiality for Douglas products, ordered the DC-8-11 (later -12 and finally -22) four-jet airliner that was a slightly belated rival to the Boeing Model 707. United Air Lines received its first DC-8 on 29 May 1959 for operational service from 18 September of the same year. United Air Lines was not blind to the merits of Boeing aircraft, however, and complemented the long-haul DC-8 with the medium-haul Model 720-022 that entered service on 5 July 1960 on the route linking Chicago and Los Angeles via Denver.

In July 1960 United Air Lines revealed its intention to buy the troubled Capital Airlines, and the deal – at that time the largest merger in US airline history – was completed on 1 June 1961: the combined airlines operated to 116 cities with a fleet of 267 aircraft, many of the shorter-haul services in the eastern and central United States being operated by a total of 20 Sud-Aviation Caravelle VIR twin-jet airliners imported from France.

During the early 1960s United Air Lines needed to revive its medium-haul fleet, and opted for the Boeing Model 727-22 three-turbofan transport that entered service on 6 February 1964 on the route between San Francisco and Denver. United Air Lines eventually took very large numbers of the Model 727 in steadily improved models, and the ultimate Model 727-200 variant is still in large-scale use. United Air Lines then became the first American airline to order the Boeing Model 737, the twin-turbofan short-haul partner to the Model 727, and the first of this type was delivered on 29 December 1967. Like the Model 727, the Model 737 is still in service with United Airlines in three advanced variants. These two Boeing aircraft eventually replaced the Caravelle and the Vickers Viscount, the latter of which had entered service as a result of the merger with Capital.

The next major type bought was the Boeing Model 747-122 wide-body transport for long-haul operations, and the first of these aircraft was delivered on 30 June 1970. United Air Lines still flies the Model 747 in three variants, together with substantial numbers of another wide-body transport, the McDonnell Douglas DC-10 three-turbofan airliner (two variants), which entered service in its original DC-10-10 form on 14 August 1971 on the route linking San Francisco and Washington DC. Later wide-body types included in the airline's current fleet are the Airbus A320 twin-turbofan type for shorter-haul services, and three longer-haul Boeing types in the form of Models 757, 767 and 777.

The network of United Air Lines (now often Airlines) reached its current level with the 1985 purchase of the failing Pan American airline's Pacific division.

USAirways

Country of origin: USA

Generally accepted abbreviation: US

Address: 23245 Crystal Drive, Arlington, Virginia 222271, USA

Type of operation: International, regional and domestic scheduled and charter passenger and cargo services

Shareholding: USAirways is a publicly owned company of which British Airways is currently disposing of its 24% interest

Subsidiaries: Allegheny Commuter Airlines, Piedmont Airlines, PSA Airlines, USAir Leasing and Services, and USAir Fuel Corporation

Marketing alliances: USAir Express carriers (including Piedmont, PSA and Allegheny as well as unowned carriers), British Airways, Qantas, ANA, and Latin Pass

Notes: USAirways provides services to 130 destinations in Bermuda, the Bahamas, Canada, France, Germany, the UK, and the USA

Personnel: 42,090

Fleet:
64 x Boeing Model 737-200 Advanced
85 x Boeing Model 737-300
54 x Boeing Model 737-400
34 x Boeing Model 757-200
12 x Boeing Model 767-200ER
40 x Fokker 100
15 x Fokker F.28 Fellowship Series 4000
72 x McDonnell Douglas DC-9-30
31 x McDonnell Douglas MD-80

Orders: 40 x Boeing Model 737-300

Main bases and hubs: Charlotte, Philadelphia, Baltimore and Pittsburgh

Route network: A domestic element to destinations including Akron, Albany, Albuquerque, Allentown, Altoona, Anderson, Asheville, Atlanta, Atlantic City, Augusta, Austin, Bakersfield, Baltimore, Bangor, Beckley, Binghampton, Birmingham, Bluefield, Boston, Bradford, Bridgeport, Bristol, Buffalo, Burlington, Cedar Rapids, Champaign, Charleston, Charlottesville, Chattanooga, Chicago, Cincinnati, Clarksburg, Cleveland, Columbia, Columbus, Cumberland, Dallas/Fort Worth, Danville, Dayton, Daytona Beach, Decatur, Denver, Des Moines, Detroit, Dodge City, Dubois, Elmira, Erie, Evansville, Fayetteville, Flint, Florence, Fort Lauderdale, Fort Myers, Fort Walton Beach, Fort Wayne, Franklin, Fresno, Gainesville, Garden City, Grand Rapids, Great Bend, Greenbrier, Greensboro, Greenville, Groton/New London, Hagerstown, Hamilton, Harrisburg, Hartford, Hays, Hickory, Hilton, Houston, Huntington, Huntsville, Indianapolis, Islip, Ithaca, Jacksonville, Jamestown, Johnstown, Kalamazoo, Kansas City, Key West, Kingston (North Carolina), Knoxville, Lancaster, Lansing, Las Vegas, Latrobe, Lebanon, Lexington, Liberal, Lincoln, Little Rock, Long Island, Los Angeles, Louisville, Lynchburg, Manchester (New Hampshire), Manhattan, Marathon, Marsh Harbour, Massena, Melbourne (Florida), Memphis, Miami, Milwaukee, Minneapolis, Mobile, Monterrey, Montgomery, Morgantown, Myrtle Beach, Naples (Florida), Nashville, Newark, New Bern, Newburgh, New Haven, New Orleans, Newport News, New York, Norfolk, North Eleuthera, Ogdensburg, Omaha, Ontario (California), Orange County, Orlando, Palm Springs, Panama City (Florida), Parkersburg, Pensacola, Peoria, Phoenix, Plattsburgh, Portland, Poughkeepsie, Providence, Raleigh/Durham, Reading, Reno, Richmond, Roanoke, Rochester, Rocky Mount, Sacramento, Saginaw, St Louis, St Thomas, Salina, Salisbury, San Antonio, San Diego, San Francisco, Santa Barbara, Saranca Lake, Sarasota, Savannah, Seattle-Tacoma, Shenandoah, Shreveport, Sioux City, Sioux Falls, South Bend, Springfield, State College, Stockton, Syracuse, Tallahassee, Tampa, Toledo, Topeka, Treasure Cay, Trenton, Tri City, Tucson, Utica, Vero Beach, Washington DC, Watertown, Westchester County, West Palm Beach, White Plains, Wichita, Wilkes-Barre, Williamsport, Wilmington, Winston-Salem, Worcester, and Youngstown; and an international element to destinations such as Athens, Bermuda, Cancún, Frankfurt, Grand Cayman, London (Gatwick), London

(Ontario), Mexico City, Montego Bay, Montreal, Munich, Nassau, Ottawa (Uplands), Paris, Rome, St Maarten, San Juan, and Toronto

Simulators: 1 x BAC One-Eleven 200/400
1 x BAe 146-200
1 x Boeing Model 727-100
1 x Boeing Model 727-200
1 x Boeing Model 737-200
4 x Boeing Model 737-300
1 x Boeing Model 737-400
1 x Boeing Model 757-200
1 x de Havilland Canada DHC-8 Dash-8-100A
1 x Fairchild FH-227B
1 x Fokker F.28 Fellowship Series 4000
1 x Fokker 100
2 x McDonnell Douglas DC-9-30
1 x McDonnell Douglas MD-82

History: Currently enjoying rankings of 10th in the world and sixth in North America, US Airways (USAir up to 1977) came into existence in its present form as recently as 1979, but can trace its origins to 5 March 1937 and the creation of All American Aviation to operate a semi-experimental air mail service (using the airborne pick-up technique) to cover 58 communities in Delaware, Maryland, Ohio, Pennsylvania and West Virginia. In March 1949 All American Aviation became All American Airways when it received permission to operate passenger services with Douglas DC-3 twin-engined airliners, and on 1 January 1953 this operator was renamed Allegheny Airlines. The airline grew steadily during the 1950s, and used its first turbine-powered aircraft in 1962, when it flew the Convair CV-540 turboprop-powered conversion of the CV-340 piston-engined airliner.

In the mid-1960s, Allegheny Airlines decided on a transfer to advanced jet-powered aircraft, and the equipment it chose was the Douglas DC-9-14, of which the first leased example was received on 29 July 1966. In 1967 the relaxation of the regulations governing air transport operations in the USA allowed the airline to start a programme of considerable development and expansion, and by the end of 1967 Allegheny Airlines had extended its sphere of operation to the whole of the north-eastern part of the USA, through the creation of Allegheny Commuter Lines that brought together a number of smaller operators to provide feeder services for Allegheny Airlines.

Further growth followed the purchase of Lake Central Airlines on 14 March 1968 and of Mohawk Airlines on 14 December 1971. The additional routes and aircraft resulting from these acquisitions turned Allegheny Airlines into a major regional operator, and on 28 October 1979 the continued expansion of Allegheny Airlines was signalled by a change of name to US Airways. The capabilities of the airline had been enhanced by the continued purchase of DC-9 aircraft for its shorter-haul services as well as the larger Boeing Model 727 three-turbofan airliner for its longer-haul services, and increased capability came with US Airway's adoption of the Boeing Model 737 twin-turbofan airliner in the forms of the Model 737-2B7 (first received on 18 November 1982) and Model 737-4B7 (first delivered on 28 November 1984), and also of the BAC One-Eleven.

US Airways merged Piedmont Airlines and Pacific Southwest Airlines into its operations during 1988 and 1989 respectively, and is now a major US domestic operator with a fleet of Boeing Model 737, Fokker F.28 Fellowship, and McDonnell Douglas DC-9 and modernised MD-80 twin-turbofan aircraft. Its growing fleet of Boeing Model 757 and Model 767 twin-turbofan aircraft are used for longer-haul services that now include a growing international element.

VARIG

Country of origin: Brazil

Generally accepted abbreviation: RG

Address: Avenida Almirante Silvio de Noronha 365, Edificio Varig, Rio de Janeiro CEP 20 021-010, Brazil

Type of operation: International, regional and domestic scheduled passenger and cargo services

Shareholding: Ruben Berta Foundation

Subsidiaries: Rio-Sul Servicos Aereos Regionais (95%) and Nordeste Linhas Aereas

Marketing alliances: Delta Air Lines, Japan Airlines, SAS, Lufthansa, LACSA, Ecuatoriana, and TAP Air Portugal

Notes: VARIG flies a network of routes to 36 destinations in Brazil and to 32 international destinations in Central and South America, North America, Europe, Africa and Asia

Personnel: 19,000

Fleet: 5 x Boeing Model 727-100F
17 x Boeing Model 737-200 Advanced
25 x Boeing Model 737-300
8 x Boeing Model 737-500
5 x Boeing Model 747-300
6 x Boeing Model 767-200ER
4 x Boeing Model 767-300ER
10 x EMBRAER EMB-120 Brasilia
10 x Fokker 50
7 x McDonnell Douglas DC-10-30

Continued on next page

VARIG continued from previous page

8 x McDonnell Douglas DC-10-30F
7 x McDonnell Douglas MD-11

Main base and hub: Rio de Janeiro

Route network: A domestic element to 36 destinations including Fortaleza, Recife, Salvador, and São Paulo; and an international element to 11 destinations in South America, seven destinations in North America, 11 destinations in Europe, one destination (Johannesburg) in Africa, and two destinations (Hong Kong and Tokyo) in Asia

Simulators: 1 x Boeing Model 707-320
1 x Boeing Model 727-106
1 x Boeing Model 737-200
1 x Boeing Model 737-300EFIS
1 x Boeing Model 747-300
1 x Boeing Model 767-200
1 x McDonnell Douglas DC-10-30

Maintenance services: VARIG specialises in airframes and engines with 215 licensed airframe engineers, 425 licensed engine engineers, and 225 licensed avionics engineers

History: Currently ranked 23rd in the world and first in South America, VARIG is the national flag carrier of Brazil, and is more formally known as Viacao Aerea Rio-Grandense. This operator was established in Brazil on 7 May 1927 by an expatriate German, Dr Otto Ernst Meyer, with assistance from the German-backed Condor Syndikat, and began its first services on 15 June of the same year with a Dornier Wal flying boat, initially on the route linking Rio de Janeiro with Pôrto Alegre. There followed a period of modest growth as many services were added to the route network, but in 1931 the airline temporarily ceased operations because of the unsuitability of its Dornier Merkur and Wal seaplanes within the Rio Grande do Sul region that was VARIG's primary operating area.

In April 1932 the airline resumed operations with two Junkers F 13 landplanes, the availability of this type allowing daily flights to some of the most popular destinations in Brazil, and further expansion of the route network became possible in 1938 with the delivery of two Junkers Ju 52/3m three-engined transports. On 5 August 1942 a de Havilland D.H.89A Rapide was used on the airline's first international service on the route linking Pôrto Alegre and Montevideo in neighbouring Uruguay. World War II was now occupying the attentions of most of the world's aircraft-manufacturing nations, and even though the airline took delivery of seven Lockheed Model 10A Electra twin-engined light transports, continued expansion of service was generally made impossible by lack of adequate aircraft. A freight service between Pôrto Alegre and Petotas was started in 1943 with F 13 and Model 10A aircraft.

The first five of an eventual large fleet of Douglas DC-3 twin-engined airliners were delivered in 1946, and were followed in the late 1940s and early 1950s by a number of the civilian version of the larger Curtiss C-46 Commando twin-engined military transport, the first of which was received on 10 May 1948.

In 1953 VARIG was granted authorisation to fly the route to New York, and for this service the airline ordered three examples of the Lockheed L-1049G Super Constellation, of which the first was received on 3 May 1955 for an initial service on 2 August. VARIG concurrently reached agreement with Pan American World Airways for the purchase of five Convair CV-240 twin-engined airliners, the first of which was accepted on 23 September 1954 for use on the Brazilian airline's domestic services. By the middle of the 1950s, VARIG appreciated that jet-powered equipment was required in order to maintain its position on the New York service, and ordered two examples of the Sud-Aviation Caravelle I from France in October 1957, the first of which was received on 16 September 1959 for an operational debut on 19 December on the route between Buenos Aires and New York via Montevideo, São Paulo, Rio de Janeiro, Belém, Port of Spain and Nassau. The Caravelle had too short a range for effective use on this service, however, and was soon superseded by the Boeing Model 707-441 four-turbofan airliner, of which the first two were received in June 1960 for first service on 2 July.

In August 1961 the government of Brazil asked VARIG to assume control of the very large network of REAL Aerovias, which had been established in February 1946 and soon become the largest airline in South America as a result of a series of mergers and purchases that gave it international capability in addition to a substantial domestic network. VARIG agreed to take over REAL and its large fleet of Douglas DC-3 and DC-6B, Curtiss C-46, Convair CV-440, and Lockheed L-188 Electra and Constellation aircraft: as a result, and in a single day, VARIG became both the largest airline in South America and one of the top 20 in the world. On 9 February 1965 VARIG took over Panair do Brasil with its fleet of two Douglas DC-8 aircraft.

At much the same time, VARIG was also concerned to improve the calibre of its domestic services by the introduction of more-advanced aircraft including the Hawker Siddeley HS.748 twin-turboprop airliner. VARIG took delivery of the first of these aircraft on 14 November 1967 and, once it had received all 10 of the aircraft it had ordered, was able to dispose of its elderly DC-3 and CV-240 machines. During the later 1960s the airline also received additional Model 707 long-haul transports, and this allowed the inauguration of new routes including those to Tokyo (26 June 1968) and to Johannesburg via Luanda (21 June 1970).

In the first half of the 1970s VARIG introduced three new types into its fleet in the form of the Boeing Model 727 three-turbofan type for its medium-haul services, and the Boeing Model 737 and McDonnell Douglas DC-9 twin-turbofan types for its short-haul services: the first examples of the Model 727-41, Model 737-341 and DC-9-30 were received on 10 October 1970, 21 October 1974 and 29 May 1974 respectively.

VARIG bought Cruzeiro do Sul, together with its routes and Model 727 and Model 737 aircraft, in June 1975: the two operators initially retained their separate identities, but a rationalisation of the two networks was inevitable and finally led to full integration. VARIG received its first wide-body aircraft in 1981, with the delivery of initial examples of the Airbus A300B4 twin-turbofan and Boeing Model 747-2L5B four-turbofan types on 3 June and 30 January 1981 respectively.

VARIG later sold its A300 aircraft, and its current fleet is based on the EMBRAER EMB-120 and Fokker 50 for local and feeder services, the Model 737 for short-haul services, and a combination of the Model 747, Model 767 and McDonnell Douglas DC-10 and updated MD-11 for long-haul services.

Virgin Atlantic Airways

Country of origin: UK

Generally accepted abbreviation: VS

Address: Ashdown House, High Street, Crawley, West Sussex RH10 1DQ, UK

Type of operation: International, regional and domestic scheduled passenger services

Shareholding: The parent company of Virgin Atlantic Airways is the Virgin Travel Group

Subsidiaries: None

Marketing alliances: Codesharing with Delta Air Lines, Malaysia Airlines, British Midland, and Midwest Express; franchising with CityJet, and marketing with Ansett Australian Airlines

Personnel: 4,000

Fleet:
5 x Airbus A340-300
1 x Boeing Model 747-100
5 x Boeing Model 747-200
4 x Boeing Model 747-400

Orders:
3 x Airbus A340-300
2 x Boeing Model 747-400

Options: Boeing Model 777

Main bases and hubs: London (Gatwick) and London (Heathrow)

Route network: Destinations include Adelaide, Athens, Boston, Dublin, Hong Kong, Johannesburg, Kuala Lumpur, Los Angeles, Manchester, Melbourne, Miami, New York, Orlando, San Francisco, Sydney, Tokyo, and Washington DC

History: Virgin Atlantic Airways was established in 1984 for the provision of low-cost scheduled air services across the North Atlantic, and has since developed its route network with an increasing number of aircraft.